W9-CCX-621

School-Based Management

Susan Albers Mohrman,
Priscilla Wohlstetter,
and Associates

Foreword by Allan Odden

School-Based Management

Organizing for High Performance

YORK COLLEGE

PENNSYLVANIA

LIBRARY

Jossey-Bass Publishers • San Francisco

Copyright © 1994 by Jossey-Bass Inc., Publishers, 350 Sansome Street, San Francisco, California 94104. Copyright under International, Pan American, and Universal Copyright Conventions. All rights reserved. No part of this book may be reproduced in any form—except for brief quotation (not to exceed 1,000 words) in a review or professional work—without permission in writing from the publishers.

Substantial discounts on bulk quantities of Jossey-Bass books are available to corporations, professional associations, and other organizations. For details and discount information, contact the special sales department at Jossey-Bass Inc., Publishers. (415) 433-1740; Fax (415) 433-0499.

For sales outside the United States, please contact your local Paramount Publishing International Office.

Manufactured in the United States of America. Nearly all Jossey-Bass books and jackets are printed on recycled paper that contains at least 50 percent recycled waste, including 10 percent postconsumer waste. Many of our materials are printed with either soy- or vegetable-based ink; during the printing process these inks emit fewer volatile organic compounds (VOCs) than petroleum-based inks. VOCs contribute to the formation of smog.

Library of Congress Cataloging-in-Publication Data

Mohrman, Susan Albers.
    School-based management : organizing for high performance / Susan Albers Mohrman, Priscilla Wohlstetter, and associates. — 1st ed.
        p.   cm. — (The Jossey-Bass education series)
    Includes bibliographical references and index.
    ISBN 0-7879-0035-4
    1. School-based management—United States.
2. Achievement motivation—United States.
3. Performance. I. Wohlstetter, Priscilla, date. II. Title. III. Series
LB2806.35.M64 1994
371.2'0093—dc20   94-17756
                                      CIP

FIRST EDITION
HB Printing 10 9 8 7 6 5 4 3 2 1   *Code 94116*

Contents

Foreword

Improving the performance of our education system is a national imperative. A higher level of student learning is the objective of the education reform strategy embodied in the Goals 2000 program approved by Congress in 1994.

Improving school performances also is a key objective of our efforts to enhance the effectiveness of how education dollars are used. When the Finance Center of the Consortium for Policy Research in Education (CPRE) began to design a research agenda on the question of how to improve educational productivity, it defined the issue as one of creating high-performance school organizations. At the beginning of that process, CPRE felt the most fruitful strategy might be through new and improved educational productivity research and indeed carved out a small research program in that area. But as alternative strategies were explored, a consensus began to develop that organizational restructuring was the most promising route.

At about the same time, I became exposed to the research and work of the Center for Effective Organizations (CEO) at the University of Southern California. Indeed my first exposure to its excellent work was Edward Lawler's *High Involvement Management*

(1986), which synthesized twenty-five years of research on efforts to improve the performance and productivity of organizations (primarily but not exclusively private-sector organizations, all non-school). The book and its high-involvement model suggested that a great deal was known about how to improve the effectiveness of organizations, and the findings seemed to be quite applicable to public schools.

The book's conclusions were especially compelling because I read them on a return trip from a meeting at which I had been strongly criticized for supporting a recommendation of an education reform commission for more decentralized management of schools. Both staff and some commission members argued that research on school-based management offered little support for its validity as a means to better school performance, and felt that such a significant change in school governance and management should be bolstered by stronger research knowledge.

Although Lawler's book did not derive from research in education, it nevertheless identified how several other types of organizations had successfully employed a decentralized management approach to improve their performance. The CEO research had shown that when work was complex, best done in teams, and faced an uncertain environment, it was most productively accomplished through a high-involvement organization and management approach. The high-involvement approach enhanced organizational outcomes when power, knowledge, information, and rewards were decentralized.

When the CPRE Finance Center was awarded a three-year grant to study the design and impacts of school-based management, the project director, Priscilla Wohlstetter, enticed a senior research scientist with CEO, Susan Albers Mohrman, to work with her on the study. She believed that such a collaboration would expand the disciplinary perspectives with which the project could examine decentralized management of schools, and felt it was the right time for education to learn from other sectors that had been successful in dramatically improving organizational outcomes. Not only did the high-involvement model appear to include the key issues that had arisen in standard education analyses of school-based management, but also the framework raised several new issues that potentially could expand education's understanding of the conditions under which school-based management and shared decision making could work to improve the schools.

This book is one of the first products of that collaboration. It substantially expands the issues and topics that typically are part of discussions about school-based management, discussions that have centered almost totally on the degree to which budget, personnel, and curriculum have been decentralized to schools. These are issues of power, and they are addressed in this book from several perspectives. The further issues of knowledge, information, and rewards are also discussed from different angles. The chapters in Part One especially provide new insights into the degree to which various strategies in education have decentralized power, knowledge, information, and rewards, as well as the multitude of mechanisms that have been crafted to produce those decentralized resources.

While the high-involvement framework should not be used as a recipe for designing decentralized management of schools (nor private-sector organizations, for that matter), the analyses in all chapters are nevertheless enriched by their use of the broader high-involvement framework. Not only does the book show that the framework can both broaden and deepen our understandings of decentralized management of schools, but it does so through assessments of recent decentralized management efforts that have not been discussed in previous research. These newer efforts have been more ambitious than most efforts up to 1990, and they entail many but not all of the elements of the high-involvement approach. Collectively, they convey a more optimistic portrayal of the potential efficacy of current decentralization efforts, although empirical work conducted by the overall research project from 1993 to 1995 ultimately will show whether such efforts indeed improve school performance.

With Part Two discussing the difficult process of transforming schools to organizations managed through high involvement, the book offers several lessons about how to make school-based management more effective. The chapters show that education needs to move away from viewing school-based management as simply a political issue of changing school governance, and toward a broader perspective that sees it as a means of organizational restructuring designed to produce higher performance, particularly student achievement.

Collectively the chapters conclude that while school-site councils might be appropriate as the overall governance mechanism at a particular school, the real work of organizational restructuring is accomplished through a variety of other decision-making teams. These teams, organized both vertically and horizontally and led by teachers, should, the authors believe, be included in future research on school-based management. Further, these chapters imply that a wide range of new roles for both teachers and administrators flows from a more comprehensive perspective on school-based management, related not only to power, knowledge, information, and rewards but also to the task of orchestrating the complex change process involved in implementing a decentralized management system.

In addition, the chapters argue that school-based management should be conceived as a part of an overall systemic education reform, not as a reform in and of itself, and that decentralized decision making provides the conditions that allow school-site teachers and administrators to design changes in school organization and curriculum that ultimately will improve student achievement. For those outcomes to occur, however, the book emphasizes the importance of clear education goals that focus on student performance. Without such clarity about the purpose of schools, and without good measures of student outcomes, it will be difficult for even a well-designed decentralization strategy to improve school performance.

Finally, the book concludes that restructuring schools toward high performance is a long-term, ongoing process; school-based, high-involvement managing would be a more appropriate phrase. The successful transition to high-involvement management involves creating a learning community within each school that engages in ongoing processes of continuously improving and redesigning the school as both education goals and student enrollment change over time.

Scholars, practitioners, and policy makers who read this book will gain a new, richer, and more comprehensive understanding of the organizational dynamics involved in creating high-performance school organizations. While the book is not full of answers, it is packed with new understandings, new ideas, new strategies, and new mechanisms that have high potential for making our country's schools more productive. The book helps expand the reach of what should be included in school-based management design and suggests that when it comes to dramatically improving school performance in the 1990s, lessons can be learned from sectors outside education. Susan Albers Mohrman and Priscilla Wohlstetter have tapped the minds of several outstanding education scholars who together have provided a rich array of new understandings about school organization, management, and performance. As the country continues its journey to make its schools more effective, the material in this book should serve as a valuable new resource for accomplishing that task.

ALLAN ODDEN

Professor of Educational Administration
and Director, The Finance Center of
The Consortium for Policy Research in Education,
School of Education, University of Wisconsin,
Madison, Wisconsin

Preface

The world that surrounds our organizations has changed. American organizations that were performing well during most of the twentieth century are finding themselves operating in a radically new environment with dramatically changed expectations and requirements. Organizations are now being forced to redesign themselves to ensure their prosperity in the new global order. School organizations are no exception, and this is serious business. At stake is the ability of our schools to contribute to a thriving economy that provides jobs, opportunity, and the basis for a satisfactory standard of living for the citizenry. The societal stake in the improvement of education includes preparing citizens to participate in a community, in the democracy, and in the economy of an increasingly complex society.

School-based management (SBM) is a popular political approach to redesign that gives local school participants—educators, parents, students, and the community at large—the power to improve their school. It modifies the governance structure by moving authority to the local school. By moving governance and management decisions to local stakeholders, those with the most at stake are empowered to do something about how the school is performing. School-based management has great appeal, as witnessed by the large numbers of school districts that are trying some form of it. Its results, however, have been less impressive. The SBM approach takes a long time to implement, does not always focus on educational issues, and often results in friction rather than collaboration between stakeholders. Is the theory flawed? Is the current wave of decentralization just another swing of the pendulum?

This book explores the possibility that results from SBM have been limited because it has been inadequately conceptualized. Too much has been expected from simply transferring power. For local stakeholders to use power to improve the education that occurs in schools, the design of the organization must change in many ways to support the informed and skilled application of this power, and to provide incentives for people to make fundamental changes in how they enact their roles. We argue that a true test of school-based management requires that it be implemented as part of a systemic change. SBM must include the development of an organizational design that supports and values high levels of involvement throughout the organization, with a simultaneous focus on fundamental change to the educational program that supports new approaches to teaching and learning.

The Purpose of the Book

This book aims to take a new look at school-based management through the lens of an organizational model originally used in the private sector. Called the high-involvement model, it has been used successfully to help members of organizations become involved in improving organizational performance. This model, which stems from the work of Edward E. Lawler and his colleagues, stresses creating the capability for meaningful involvement in the organization and a stake in its performance. Such organizations also are designed to get people focusing on the ongoing improvement of performance.

Early efforts in the private sector to create participative structures and to empower employees encountered serious barriers and achieved little. Some organizations retreated from the high-involvement approach. Others persevered, and have gradually put in place the design features required to enable meaningful employee involvement. The changes have been deep and pervasive. We argue that high-involvement management, and by implication school-based management, requires large-scale, fundamental changes for all involved.

There are many obstacles. Educational stakeholders do not agree on what constitutes good performance or how to measure it. Union contracts constrain the freedom of schools to make changes. Many stakeholders are threatened by the changes and they cannot agree on who should have the most power. Perhaps it would be easier to retreat to a more centralized model and to find and impose technical solutions on schools. However, there is ample evidence that teachers can undermine change that they do not agree with and parents can organize to oppose changes that they do not like. Without high levels of involvement, can fundamental change truly occur?

The problems facing schools are systemic. They will not be resolved by returning to the old conditions. School populations will not become more homogeneous. At least in the short term, the nuclear family will not thrive. Social problems will continue to find their way into the school. The process of finding approaches to deal with these and many other issues will require and benefit from the involvement of all stakeholders and participants. We believe that the decision for schools is not whether to involve local stakeholders, but how.

The contributors to this book have graciously consented to look at issues in their areas of expertise using the lens of the high-involvement model. The analyses are their own, but left to their own devices they may not have used that model as an analytical device. The editors, on the other hand, chose this model as the analytical foundation for the book because we were interested in expanding the dialogue about school-based management to include concepts of organizational design for high involvement.

Overview of the Contents

The book is divided into two main parts. Chapters Two through Seven examine the relationship between school-based management and high performance. Lawler's high-involvement framework is used as a template against which to view SBM and its role in high performance. Chapter Two begins with an overview of the high-involvement model as it has been applied in the private sector. Application has been uneven, but its components have been articulated. The chapter does not claim that private-sector organizations have fully succeeded in establishing a new paradigm, nor that practices in the private sector can be transported readily or in the same form into educational institutions. The power of the high-involvement model is that it provides a skeletal framework on which each sector will have to put its own flesh and form. It is that skeletal framework that will guide much of the discussion throughout the book.

In Chapter Three, Ogawa and White present an overview of SBM research to date and comment on the areas where SBM has not been implemented in a manner consistent with a full-blown high-involvement model. SBM implementations have assumed many forms, but attention has been concentrated largely on power, neglecting the other three dimensions of knowledge and skills, information, and rewards.

Wohlstetter and Smyer (Chapter Four) examine several approaches to improving school performance: Effective Schools, the School Development Program, Accelerated Schools, and Essential Schools. They investigate the extent to which the underlying organizational requirements for educational improvement that are addressed by these models are consistent with the high-involvement framework, and they find in these models validation for using high involvement as a framework for thinking about the design issues faced by schools.

In Chapter Five, Johnson and Boles examine SBM through the lens of teacher professionalism. They expand our understanding of the integral nature of information, knowledge, and skills to the involvement of teachers in improving the effectiveness of teaching and learning. They call for an understanding of SBM as nested in an organization that permits two-way influence between administration and teachers.

In Chapter Six, Wohlstetter examines the most extreme of the decentralization approaches in schools—the charter school phenomenon. This chapter cannot help but raise the issue of school-site capacity, for many levels of influence and support are removed from the context in which charter schools operate. They are empowered to make fundamental changes, constrained only by the contract developed by the school and approved by the funding agency.

Chapter Seven integrates the preceding chapters by using the private-sector approaches as a springboard for generating SBM guidelines. The conclusion is that SBM as a method of organizational change has been narrowly understood and narrowly applied and has led to involvement by too few in a constrained domain. This partial implementation may explain the lack of evidence to date that SBM has led to performance improvements.

Part Two addresses the change process required for creating high performance. In Chapter Eight, Mohrman presents three change frameworks that are useful for conceptualizing and guiding the large-scale transition to high involvement. One framework looks at the stage dynamics of such changes. A second provides a roadmap for understanding the redesign process, and the third examines the contextual issues of change.

In Chapter Nine, Marsh reviews a host of literature on change in schools, and extracts learnings useful in thinking about implementing SBM as a high-involvement, performance-improvement strategy. His perspective is that SBM is a pathway to the improvement of schools, and that it is best implemented in conjunction with a new vision of the teaching and learning processes. He advocates planning backward from these new views.

Chapter Ten presents an integration of the points made in the preceding two chapters in the form of implications for understanding and managing the change process. It advocates breaking out of the limited thinking that SBM transfers power primarily by setting up a governance council. Because SBM is part of a systemic change, many opportunities for involvement should be created. This chapter advocates rethinking the appropriate role for different stakeholders in the transition, and suggests that the transition be viewed not as the installation of a council and a new way of governing but as the redesign of the organization for high involvement and high performance.

The final chapter closes with a restatement of the need to go beyond understanding SBM as a change in governance and to view it as a change in organizational design. Successful SBM depends on the development of a shared understanding of the new way of operating. The challenge is to design an organization that enables educators to engage in the extensive learning required to adopt new approaches to teaching and learning, involves them in the continuous improvement of performance, fits with the requirements of the emerging core technologies of teaching and learning, and promotes community involvement and responsiveness of the school to the diverse needs of its community.

The chapter focuses on some new directions that may enhance the impact of SBM. These include expanding the domain of decision making, expanding the improvement approaches that are used, clarifying scope of authority at different levels, and clarifying the role of management. High performance will not magically result from the simple transfer of decision-making power, nor from attention to any other single aspect of the organizational system. Thus,

SBM must be seen as part of an organizational system whose pieces must all be designed to support high performance.

Audience

This book is intended for policy makers, practitioners, and scholars who deal with educational administration and policy. It will serve as a source of ideas for educators who are struggling to create meaningful involvement in educational improvement. It will also be useful for policy makers and scholars who are muddling through the place of SBM in the constellation of efforts that constitute systemic school reform, and for those who are looking for an enriched understanding of SBM that goes beyond its political conceptualization and beyond the statement of faith that moving control to local participants will result in decisions to improve education. Deeper understanding of these issues, we believe, will ultimately produce more sustained and effective SBM approaches that create high involvement in improving school performance.

Acknowledgments

These chapters were written as part of a research project conducted by the Finance Center of the Consortium for Policy Research in Education (CPRE). The project is part of the Studies of Education Reform program, funded by the U.S. Department of Education, Office of Educational Research and Improvement. The program supports studies and disseminates practical information about implementing and sustaining successful innovations in American education. The school-based management study also has received generous support from the Carnegie Corporation of New York and the Finance Center of CPRE.

Many people contributed in different ways to the creation of this volume. The support, encouragement, and collegiality of Allan

Odden were very significant gifts. He supports with enthusiasm and interest, and is always willing to interact with new ideas. His belief in public education and his fervor for its improvement are inspirational. The intellectual support of Edward Lawler has been a guiding light, and we appreciate his willingness to free up Susan Albers Mohrman for three years from obligations at the Center for Effective Organizations.

Our contributors have been patient and diligent, first in creating review papers that constituted the initial application of the high-involvement management framework to the analysis of SBM, and then by doing significant revisions of their work to make them suitable to this book. We thank Susan Moore Johnson and Katherine Boles, Rodney Ogawa and Paula White, and David Marsh for their contributions.

Susan Klein, a senior staff member at the Office of Educational Research and Improvement and the project officer for the school-based management study, also provided important direction during the revision process. Roxane Smyer's contribution as coauthor and research assistant has been significant, and Kerri Briggs provided research assistance and support during the final preparation of the book. We owe a special thanks to Paulette Seagraves, who has managed the manuscript through many iterations with great skill and diligence. Others who provided invaluable support in the preparation of the book include Liza Starr, Alice Mark, and Eric Shaw Quinn.

Last but not least, we would like to thank our families—Monty, Jeremy, and Gregory Mohrman, and Ted, Alison, and Ned Sonnenschein. They have graciously tolerated deadline behavior and preoccupation with details that probably mattered not a whit to them. Their love and support mean a lot.

Los Angeles, California Susan Albers Mohrman
August 1994 Priscilla Wohlstetter

The Authors

The Editors

Susan Albers Mohrman is senior research scientist at the Center for Effective Organizations in the Graduate School of Business at the University of Southern California. She has taught in the management department at USC and the School of Administrative Sciences at Ohio State University. She is author of *Self-Designing Organizations: Learning How to Create High Performance* (1989, with T. Cummings) and *Employee Involvement and Total Quality Management: Practices and Results in Fortune 1000 Companies* (1992, with E. Lawler and G. Ledford). She is co-editor of *Doing Research That Is Useful for Theory and Practice* (1985, with E. Lawler and others); *Large-Scale Organizational Change* (1989, with A. M. Mohrman and others); and *Managing Complexity in High Technology Organizations* (1990, with M. A. Von Glinow). She and others are currently completing a book on the design of organizations that house knowledge work. Her work in the area of school-based management is an opportunity to test the applicability of the frameworks for organization design and change in the educational sector and to enrich those frameworks.

She is active in the Academy of Management, and has performed research and design consulting in over thirty major corporations and a number of public-sector organizations. She received her B.A. degree in psychology from Stanford University (1967), M.Ed. from the University of Cincinnati (1970), and her Ph.D. in organizational behavior from Northwestern University (1979).

Priscilla Wohlstetter is associate professor of politics and policy in the School of Education at the University of Southern California. She also serves as a senior research fellow with the Consortium for Policy Research in Education (CPRE) and directs CPRE's study of school-based management (SBM), on which this volume is based. Her current research interests are in the area of alternative governance models for education, including SBM and charter schools. In the last several years, she has conducted several national studies focused on the politics and fiscal policies of SBM and an international study comparing charter schools in the United States with England's grant-maintained schools.

Before assuming her position at the University of Southern California, she was a postdoctoral fellow with CPRE at the RAND Corporation, where she studied legislative oversight of state education reforms. From 1975 to 1980, Wohlstetter worked as a policy analyst with the U.S. assistant secretary for education, the mayor of Boston, and various consulting firms. She received her B.A. degree (1975) in education and government from Simmons College, her M.Ed. degree (1976) in administration, planning, and social policy from Harvard University, and her Ph.D. (1984) in policy studies from Northwestern University.

The Contributors

Katherine C. Boles is a visiting scholar at the Harvard Graduate School of Education. After a twenty-year career as a public school teacher, she received her Ed.D. degree (1991) in teaching, curriculum and learning environments from Harvard University. Her work focused on school restructuring initiated by teachers. In 1987, while she was teaching in the Brookline, Massachusetts, public schools, Boles cofounded the Learning/Teaching Collaborative, a school-college partnership that links seven Boston and Brookline public schools with Wheelock College and Simmons College. She is the recipient of a 1993 National Academy of Education Spencer post-doctoral fellowship to continue her study of teacher-initiated school restructuring.

Susan Moore Johnson is a professor and academic dean at the Har-vard Graduate School of Education, where she teaches about edu-cational policy, organizational behavior, and administrative practice. A former high school teacher and administrator, Johnson holds a B.A. degree (1967) from Mount Holyoke College and an M.A.T. degree (1969) and Ed.D. degree (1982) from Harvard University. Her research centers on teacher policy, school reform, and school leadership. Johnson is the author of *Teacher Unions in Schools* (1984), which examines the impact of collective bargaining on pub-lic education, and *Teachers at Work* (1990), which considers the school as a workplace from the perspectives of exemplary teachers. She is currently completing a book about new school superinten-dents and leadership.

David D. Marsh is the Robert A. Naslund Professor of Curriculum Theory at the University of Southern California and principal investigator on projects connected with the Coalition of Essential Schools and the National Alliance for Restructuring Education. Each summer, he directs an International Institute for Leadership in School Restructuring with colleagues from England and Aus-tralia, and recently was a Fulbright Fellow in India, where he worked with the central government on improving high schools. He has published widely on the process of change in educational organizations, school leadership, the nature of school transformation, and secondary school reform. He holds three degrees from the University of Wisconsin: a B.S. in Asian studies, an M.A.T. in history/education, and a Ph.D. in curriculum and instruction.

Rodney T. Ogawa is associate professor of education at the University of California, Riverside, where he also is an associate director of the California Educational Research Cooperative. Ogawa's research focuses on the application of organization theory to the study of schools and school leadership. He received his B.A. (1970) from the University of California, Los Angeles, in history, his M.A. (1972) from Occidental College in education, and his Ph.D. (1979) from Ohio State University in educational administration.

Roxane Smyer is a doctoral candidate in the policy and organization Ph.D. program at the University of Southern California. Prior to coming to USC, she was the program evaluator for Drug-Free Schools in the Austin, Texas, public schools. She earned a B.A. (1987) in psychology from Trinity University and an M.A. (1990) in educational psychology from the University of Texas, Austin.

Paula A. White is senior research associate at the Consortium for Policy Research in Education, University of Wisconsin, Madison. She has published in the areas of school restructuring, teacher empowerment, high school course-taking patterns, and graduation requirements. Her current work investigates the impact of efforts to upgrade high school mathematics for lower-achieving students. She received her B.A. degree (1983) in humanistic studies from the University of Wisconsin, Green Bay, her M.A. degree (1984) in political science, and her M.A. (1986) and Ph.D. (1990) degrees in educational policy studies from the University of Wisconsin, Madison.

School-Based Management

Chapter One

Introduction: Improving School Performance

Susan Albers Mohrman

Priscilla Wohlstetter

Many of those who have a stake in America's public schools have declared school performance inadequate to meet the requirements of the world we live in. Our schools have been found not to be developing the skills and knowledge that today's students need to be employees in a globally competitive economy (U.S. Department of Education, 1991; National Commission on Excellence in Education, 1983). Our achievement levels lag our major competitors, particularly in math and science (National Assessment of Educational Progress, 1990). This issue is becoming more critical as experts predict that the skills required for tomorrow's (and increasingly today's) workforce will be substantially higher overall than in years past (National Center on Education and the Economy, 1990). Our schools are not meeting the needs of a large segment of our population. The achievement gap between majority, socioeconomically advantaged students and minority students is extreme; so is the gap in their prospects for meaningful employment and economic self-sufficiency.

School reform has been actively pursued for several decades, and that activity now has a heightened sense of urgency. The call for reform comes from many quarters. Educators themselves have pronounced that American schools do a poor job of engaging the majority of students in serious learning (for example, Goodlad, 1984; Sizer, 1984). It is believed that a school system that is designed to teach reasoning and ways of learning to students who are being raised in an era of explosive information availability and automation will look quite different from the current system, which has retained many of the same characteristics for almost a century (David, 1990; Elmore and Associates, 1990; Cohen, McLaughlin, and Talbert, 1993). A number of states, including California, Georgia, Kentucky, South Carolina, Texas, and Vermont, have engaged in statewide reform efforts, driven by the recognition that their economic viability depends upon the caliber of their educational base. States have been heavily involved in significant experimentation by requiring districts, for example, to provide remedial education for public school graduates now working whose employers are dissatisfied with their levels of basic skills.

Even as the demands increase and acknowledgment of need for change becomes more widespread, schools are encountering resource constraints that threaten their ability to respond. Although the amount of resources available to schools has grown slightly in the last few years, districts are now being squeezed by the rising numbers of handicapped, poor, immigrant, and other special-need populations that require high-priced extra help (Odden and Conley, 1992), and so increases that become available are being used to fund existing operations. Funds are not growing at a rate adequate even to maintain per-student expenditures. Schools are competing for scarce resources with many other state services (Harp, 1992) and budget cutting is often the result, despite the desires of many legislatures to increase educational funding.

The need for high performance from our schools has never been greater, at the same time that the demands placed on the schools are growing. This same pattern—increasing demands and constrained resources—has been experienced in many segments of our economy, both private and public, during the past two decades. First in basic industrial organizations, then in high technology, and finally in service-delivery organizations such as health care, banking, and transportation, the pressure to deliver new kinds of services more quickly, with higher quality and at lower cost has jolted the foundations of traditional, bureaucratic organizations. Many of our best-known corporations, such as General Motors, IBM, Hewlett-Packard, and General Electric, have embarked on massive restructurings as they have discovered that they are unable to meet the more stringent requirements of their marketplaces doing business as usual.

Firms have ultimately recognized that response to the new performance demands requires a redesign of the entire organization (Mohrman and Cummings, 1989; Nadler, Gerstein, and Shaw, 1992; Galbraith, 1994). Organizational innovations, whose concepts originated as a way to boost competitiveness in the manufacturing industry, have been adapted and spread into all parts of the economy, including high-technology research and design and professional service settings such as health care. A new organizational paradigm has developed, one that shares many of the concepts that abound in the literature on educational reform: decentralization, flattening, multistakeholder decision making, flexibility, innovation, lateral networks, teams, and new forms of pay and accountability. Although organizations house different kinds of work and each can rightfully claim to be unique, the emerging models of management bear a strong similarity to one another. In addition, these organizations face similar challenges stemming from the need to overcome the inertia that is built into large, complex organizations populated by people who have become experts in the status quo.

This book examines educational reform activity, in particular the current trend toward decentralization using school-based management (SBM), through the lens of a framework that captures the essence of the organizational renewal activity that has been occurring in many sectors of our economy. The framework, which will be referred to in this volume as high-involvement management, has been delineated by Lawler (1986, 1992) and is closely related to the model of high-commitment work systems depicted by Walton (1985) and to notions of empowerment advocated by Block (1990) and others. Embedded in these notions of organization is the underlying belief that high performance is possible only when all employees are deeply involved in ongoing improvement of organizational capability and in the success of the enterprise. With SBM, the notion of empowerment has focused most recently on teachers; however, the 1960s decentralization movement sought to transfer power beyond professional educators to local communities (David, 1989).

The purpose of this book is to enrich the discussion of SBM by using the high-involvement framework to expand the aspects of organizational design that are considered. Our perspective is that SBM is a component of an emerging paradigm of the high-performance school and that it must be examined in the context of other aspects of school reform. The premise is that high-performing schools are highly involving schools and that SBM, if viewed as an element of systemic change, can be instrumental toward that end. Large-scale, systemic change aims at altering the fundamental capabilities of an organization (Mohrman, Mohrman, Ledford, Cummings, and Lawler, 1989)—both in the private sector and in education. A focus in this book will be the change process for creating high-involvement schools, in this case for implementing SBM in a way that involves organizational members strongly in improving school performance.

Our conclusions will not be novel. We will stress, as have many others, the systemic nature of the changes that are required and are being advocated in education, and the need to place school-based management in that systemic context. The contribution of the book lies in moving the focus of discussion beyond the political arena that is implied when SBM is seen solely as an issue of governance, and depicting the challenge as one of organizational design for high performance. We are not advocating that the political perspective be abandoned; nor do we feel it would be possible to do so, for political processes determine the ends that our schools shall serve. At stake in the political process is the very definition of effectiveness and the extent to which schools will be responsive to their many stakeholders. We do advocate, however, that the design of the school organization be seen as more than a political decision of who shall have control. Designing school organizations to achieve high performance should be a central part of the dialogue that shapes the restructuring of our schools.

High Performance, High Involvement, and School-Based Management

High-performing organizations are able to accomplish their mission by continually improving their capacity to deliver highly valued outcomes to their stakeholders, and in return to continue to receive the resources required for ongoing performance. This view of high performance combines some of the classic elements of the definition of an effective system. Organizations have to accomplish their mission and they have to provide products and services that are valued by the stakeholders in their environment so that they have access to an ongoing stream of the resources necessary for their own survival (Katz and Kahn, 1978; Pfeffer and Salancik, 1978). This definition assumes that the environment will provide resources to an organization only if the organization fulfills its mission and delivers valued goods and services. Resources will gravitate to alternative organizations if they are better able to meet society's needs for value.

Two elements of high performance are particularly emphasized in the new paradigm of organizations. First, organizational survival is related to the value of outcomes as determined by the stakeholders, who provide the resource stream that supports the organization, not by the organizational members. Second, high performance is not a steady state but rather a moving target of ever-increasing standards of performance (Deming, 1986; Juran, 1989). Learning processes enable organizations to continually increase the value of their outcomes (Senge, 1990; Mohrman, Lawler, and Mohrman, 1992). The design challenge is how to organize for high performance and for the ongoing learning processes that will determine performance levels through time.

The content and quality of organizational outcomes and the efficiency with which they are produced determine their value. Part of the jolt felt by American organizations in the past two decades is that their customers are limited in what they can or will pay for high-quality products and services and that their task is to simultaneously optimize cost, quality, and speed. Thus, learning how to provide higher-quality outputs while consuming fewer resources has become the essence of high performance.

Another lesson learned by many American organizations is that they must simultaneously respond to differentiated requirements from different stakeholders. No one car fits all markets. Different subpopulations need different kinds of telephone services or medical care.

Furthermore, not only must organizations differentiate the products or services they offer, but they have to do so while simultaneously capitalizing on economies of scale and maintaining an overall integrated strategy. Companies have to be able to offer customized services and products at commodity prices. Thus, they must become extremely good at calculating their economies of scale and determining which decisions should be organizationwide and which are best located within subunits designed to respond to a particular customer base. They have to learn to be big when it is good to be big (such as to gain purchasing power and to support research and development) and to be small when it is good to be small and focused (such as in customizing products or establishing a relationship with a particular community or customer) (Galbraith, 1994). The designs that are now prevalent in many sectors of the organization contain a complex and flexible mixture of centralization and decentralization, all geared toward optimizing performance.

These elements of high performance seem applicable to schools as well. School performance depends on achieving its mission by delivering highly valued outcomes to its stakeholders. Schools have multiple stakeholders, each with different expectations for valued outcomes from the school. School performance is multifaceted and schools serve an increasingly heterogeneous population. In addition, the stakeholders of schools are demanding ever-increasing levels of performance without a commensurate increase in resources. Thus, it becomes extremely important that school organizations achieve economies of scale by performing some functions at the district level while devolving to school sites some decisions and activities required for delivery of high-quality services. School organizations must determine at what levels (district, school, grade, subject) different kinds of value are best added in order to achieve their mission most efficiently. Furthermore, with research on more effective and efficient ways for teaching and learning being validated, many schools likely will respond to environmental pressures by adopting these new strategies. How schools organize for this purpose will be critical.

In the private sector, it has been learned that the only true competitive advantage is the ability to execute better than others—for example, high performance. High performance is a function of the design of the organization: for example, the organizational processes and structures and their configuration (Galbraith, 1994). This has been referred to as the "architecture" of the organization (Nadler, Gerstein, and Shaw, 1992). It includes such issues as the technologies used; the units that house those technologies and are the building blocks of the organization; how the building block units are aggregated into larger organizational units; what tasks get done centrally (on an organizationwide basis) and what tasks get done in subunits; the manner in which the organization links to its suppliers, customers, and other stakeholders; selection criteria and processes; development processes; information and accountability systems; rewards, appraisal, and career systems; and decision-making processes and structures. High performance results when these design features are mutually reinforcing and when they fit with the organization's strategy and market, with the core technical requirements of the work, and with the needs of the people who work in and consume the outputs of the organization.

Although competitiveness has not historically been viewed as an organizational survival issue for schools, there is no reason to assume that schools as organizations will not face similar survival pressures as have been faced by organizations in other sectors. One only has to think about the current massive changes occurring in health care to realize that providing a social service delivered by highly trained professionals does not yield immunity from environmental threat. The sacred cows of health care professionals have rapidly come under fire, and large-scale transformation is underway in organizations that deliver health care services, largely because existing institutions have failed to deliver the value the public demands at a cost society can afford.

Some of the recent societal debates concerning choice (Raywid, 1990) and efforts such as open-enrollment plans, charter schools, and public-private school vouchers (which recently appeared on ballots in several states) may eventually introduce serious competition into the educational arena. Despite the ideologically based debate over the desirability of these new approaches, it is not inconceivable that public education as we know it may face competition from the marketplace. Already we have charter school laws in eight states that allow schools to redesign themselves; if at the end of the contract period, performance falls short of goals, the school is put out of business.

Fifteen years ago, organizations that housed such public goods as transportation, telephone, and other utilities were publicly protected and felt immune to competition. Through deregulation, they were dragged kicking and screaming into the world of competition, all the while proclaiming that quality of service and equal access would deteriorate. Instead there have been major changes in the design of these companies, as they were forced to respond to a service and quality imperative. It is not inconceivable that some form of choice will also put public schools into a competitive situation that will threaten the viability of their current design. It stands to reason that if organization design has a major impact on the performance levels of other organizations, it also is a factor in school system performance.

The high-involvement model (Lawler, 1986; 1992) provides a set of principles for designing organizations so that their members are more likely to become involved in improving performance and contributing to the success of the organization. It emphasizes the need to alter the logic of the organization so that there is a less distinct demarcation between the work that produces the products or delivers the services and the work of developing strategies and plans, allocating resources, and controlling performance. It leads to an examination of all aspects of an organization's design to ensure that knowledge, skills, and information are spread throughout the organization and that people on the front lines are empowered to deliver high-quality services or products and to influence the decisions that determine the context within which work is done. Finally, the framework includes the alignment of rewards with performance, to ensure that all organizational members have a personal stake in the successful performance of the organization.

High-involvement approaches have been found to be most applicable to organizations where the work is highly complex and uncertain. Complexity of work raises the likelihood that different types of expertise will be required; in such an environment, effective performance is facilitated when the organization is designed so that people integrate their efforts. Here the term *uncertainty* refers to the inability to preprogram the work because it involves many different and unique situations or because the knowledge base concerning the work technology is incomplete. Both these aspects of work demand judgment at the point of service delivery or production.

Schools are very high on both the complexity and uncertainty dimensions. They would seem to be prime candidates for high-involvement approaches (Mohrman, Lawler, and Mohrman, 1992). In fact, the traditional school design has of necessity vested a great deal of discretion in the role of the classroom teacher. On the other hand, teachers have not traditionally had a great deal of influence on organizationwide decisions or on designing the larger context in which they work. Also, classrooms where the work of teachers is rarely integrated are known to nurture teacher isolation.

The response of schools to demands for higher levels of performance must include the involvement of many stakeholders in determining, executing, and supporting better ways to deliver educational services, and organizing work settings and organizational units for higher performance. A prominent theme in the literature on educational reform is the essential role of teachers in improving teaching and learning processes. Almost as frequently stressed is that many other stakeholders—including administrators, parents, the business community, governments, universities, and foundations—have important roles to play. At the extreme is the Chicago School Reform, passed by the state legislature in 1988, which endows local community members, not professional educators, with the balance of power in running the city's public schools.

High-involvement approaches to design include the use of work teams that have complete responsibility for producing a product or delivering an integrated set of services to a defined population of customers. These teams may manage their own performance within a set of organizationally determined constraints, such as budget or personnel policies. Other approaches include the use of task teams and improvement teams to address organizationwide issues and develop changes to the work processes used. An array of human resource practices such as multiskilling, cross training, flexible scheduling, skill-based career paths, team hiring and firing, and multidirectional appraisals are common in high-involvement organizations. Rewards accrue to individuals who develop increased knowledge and more ways of contributing to the organization, and to teams and organizational units for their measurable achievement of goals. Information sharing and accountability systems are a key component of a high-involvement organization.

Most of the elements described above are found somewhere in the current approaches to educational reform. One element that deals explicitly with the power dimension of high involvement is the current widespread adoption of school-based management. Although SBM takes many forms, it generally involves devolving power over budget and personnel from the central offices to the schools, generally to a school-site council, which often includes principals, teachers, community members, and sometimes students in its composition (Wohlstetter and Odden, 1992).

The SBM literature has differed from the high-involvement literature in that it has viewed SBM largely as a political reform rather than an issue of organizational design. Viewed as a governance reform, SBM has been analyzed along a centralization-decentralization continuum that reflects the tension between centralized governmental units that view the mission of schools as accomplishing the public good and local communities and families that view the mission of schools as meeting their needs. Indeed, proponents of SBM argue that when decisions are made by those at the school site who are closest to the students, the results are better decisions tailored to student needs. Another aspect of the analysis is the tension between the determination of educational processes by professional educators using professional expertise and the lay control of schools to promote the values and ends determined by community members (for an excellent discussion of these issues, see Hannaway and Carnoy, 1993).

Thus, arguments for changes to the structural design of the organization have been based on preferences for a particular mechanism of governance. Structure has been resolved by determining who should decide the mission and values of the school rather than what is the most effective way to accomplish a particular mission and deliver a particular set of services. It is a political pawn in the game of who controls what, a game often settled by compromise. In fact most commentators agree that the swings of the pendulum regarding centralization and decentralization have had little impact on what actually happens in the classroom and consequently on the quality of teaching and learning that occurs (Hannaway and Carnoy, 1993).

The underlying tensions of mission and governance will always be with us, and their active resolution is essential to the fabric of American society. However, we argue that the discussion of SBM should be approached as the issue of how to design organizationally for high performance. The question is how best to deliver services that accomplish the societal mission, meet the needs of the community, and are efficient and effective. This design solution includes the structures for governance, but goes beyond that to include the technology and design of work and the other aspects of organization design that must complement each other in a mutually reinforcing system that involves all stakeholders in organizational success.

The need to go beyond simplistic answers to the decentralization issue has been pointed out by Elmore, who argues that "the central policy question should not be whether to centralize or decentralize authority, but rather what should be loosely controlled from any given level of government and what should be tightly controlled" (1993a, p. 51). When taken to the level of district and school, this becomes a question of organizational design. The challenge is not unlike that faced by private-sector organizations deciding when to be big and when to be small.

Viewed in this manner, school-based management is not an either-or proposition where the schools are automatically given control over all aspects of education or control is fully vested in the district. Rather, it is a set of design choices. Furthermore, SBM is not simply a set of decisions about the governance system; rather, it is the creation of a whole set of organizational design features that enable the school-level participants to greatly enhance their influence and their involvement in the creation of high-performing schools. In addition, SBM needs to be integrally related to other elements of school reform, for example in the areas of teaching and learning, in order for student performance to improve.

This book will use the framework of high-involvement management to examine the extent to which mutually reinforcing design features are embodied in current SBM efforts and in other parts of the school reform movement. We argue that the tendency to cast SBM primarily as a political reform may help explain limited implementation and consequently limited success of the reform.

School Reform and School-Based Management

There is widespread recognition in the educational community of the need to make fundamental changes in our schools. Pressure to enhance performance stems from two sources. First, outcome standards are being developed to encourage higher levels of skills and knowledge that will be required of tomorrow's adults as they find their places in a society where jobs require lifelong learning, complex problem solving, and the ability to deal in a technologically sophisticated world. Adding to the outcome performance pressure is the emergence of the global economy, which means that our economic viability and hence ability as a society to offer employment opportunities to our citizens depends on our employee base being as well educated as that of our foreign competitors.

The second source of performance pressure is on the input side of the system. Here, schools are facing an increasingly diverse student body, speaking multiple languages, bringing different cultural values into the classroom, and in many cases bringing many social problems springing in part from the breakdown of the nuclear family. As a result, the task of educating is increasingly complex and uncertain, not to mention sometimes discouraging. All this at a time when another key input—financial resources—is becoming increasingly strained.

The systemic reform movement (Fuhrman, Massell, and Associates, 1992; Fuhrman, 1993) is a call for coherent policy in addressing these challenges. It calls for alignment around common outcomes among the various institutions and governmental bodies that constitute the intricately connected network within which schooling occurs and that have a stake in whether and how schools adapt to their changing environment. It also calls for comprehensive change that addresses many aspects of the educational system, including performance goals, assessment, curriculum content and pedagogical approaches, school governance, and teacher professional training. In *Designing Coherent Education Policy* (1993), Fuhrman and others describe the role that state policy on outcome standards, assessment, and curriculum frameworks can play in stimulating systemic reform (the top-down role) and the bottom-up role of schools. They discuss the importance of school-site governance in determining how to carry out state and district policies and to introduce new approaches to teaching and learning. In that same volume, Elmore argues that districts have taken a largely reactive role in instructional reform, but that their role needs to be examined and a context created in which they can become leaders in improvement (1993b).

Implicit in the discussion of systemic reform are the organizational design questions of what decisions should be made at what system level for optimal performance and improvement. For example, should the decision to use manipulatives in teaching math be made at the state, district, building, grade, or classroom level? In addition, the need for changes in many aspects of the system (for systemic change) is quite explicit. The organization of teaching would have to change to support the amount of educator learning that would be required to make the change and to enact the new approaches to teaching and learning (Cohen and Spillane, 1993). Such change, of course, would have broad implications for schools of education and other institutions in the business of training new and experienced teachers.

An umbrella term that describes the new approaches to teaching and learning that are being advocated is *teaching for understanding* (Cohen, McLaughlin, and Talbert, 1993). The goal is to enhance student abilities of problem solving, critical analysis, and deep or flexible understanding of subject matter; for example, higher-order thinking skills. These approaches require moving away from the teacher-dominated classroom to the coconstruction of knowledge with learners who are actively trying to make sense of a subject area. They require new ways of relating learning to life, including cross-discipline treatments of issues and new connections between school and work. The school organization must include new mechanisms for linking the school to its community, students to their learning experiences, and educators to one another.

Much has been written about the challenge of the transition that will be required to move to the new ways of teaching and learning that are implied by "teaching for understanding" and the changed roles and behaviors that will be required (for example, Ball and Rundquist, 1993; McCarthey and Peterson, 1993). To support the transition, there will need to be enhanced collaboration among educators and large amounts of professional development. Calls abound for finding time in the day for teachers to collaborate in the learning process, to plan together, and to develop the needed new approaches. In addition, there are a number of articulations of restructured schools that call for new structures such as teams (Comer, 1980), cadres (Levin, 1987), and houses (Sizer, 1992). Again, there is much discussion of the appropriate roles of different players in the educational organization and different levels in the system in supporting changes in practice (Cohen and Barnes, 1993; Talbert and McLaughlin, 1993). In other words, achieving teaching for understanding will require a redesign of the school, certainly to support the immense amount of learning that must underpin the changes in the core technology, but most probably also to enable the application of the new methods and approaches.

The literature on teacher professionalism is concerned with creating the career rewards to attract and retain teachers with the necessary intellectual quality to teach in new and more complex ways, and with promoting teaching excellence, continuous improvement, and commitment through new organizational practices that promote teacher interaction and support (Sykes, 1990). School-based management that involves teachers in school-level decisions can provide a vehicle for enhancing teacher professionalism. The literature underscores the need for teachers to become more collaborative in their learning and in the manner in which they deliver their services, and more influential in their own staff development processes. In addition, it stresses the importance of an increased teacher role in the governance of the school, including the conditions and methodologies of teaching and learning. The creation of new roles and alternative career tracks for teachers is also advocated (Johnson, 1990).

Viewed through lenses focusing on increased teacher professionalism, school-based management supports such teacher participation in governance and provides mechanisms for teachers to affect key school decisions and the manner in which teaching is conducted. It opens up new roles for teachers. However, more is implied than simply a change in governance. Creating a professional culture that instills collaboration among teachers in learning new, more effective approaches to teaching and in the way they conduct their professional assignments will certainly imply more fundamental changes than simply setting up a representative decision-making council. Once again, an implied question is how best to design the school to enable such collaboration to occur and more effective teaching and learning to go on. Through SBM, teachers and other stakeholders theoretically have mechanisms to become influential in redesigning their school and introducing innovative approaches to teaching and learning.

The advocacy of school-based management has been related to a number of these themes of educational reform. First and foremost is the argument that SBM moves resources and the decisions about tradeoffs to the school level, where they can be tailored to the needs of the particular students being served. In this sense, SBM has been depicted as a way to bring decision making closer to individual school communities, so that education can be more responsive to local needs.

Sometimes the concept of community control of schools, with parents and other community members included in the governance process, predominates; other times the notion of teacher empowerment is the major theme and teachers assume a key role in governance. Another underlying notion is that if external controls on schools are loosened, such as by granting waivers from district regulations, teachers will be encouraged to experiment and innovate, and thus the transition to new forms of teaching and learning will be furthered. Thus, SBM, if implemented in a manner that leads to increased collaboration of teachers in crafting and adopting new approaches, will enable and perhaps catalyze greater teacher professionalism.

Obviously, the ultimate purpose of all these streams of reform, SBM included, is to improve the performance of schools in delivering value to society. Although there is great room for debate among educators and the public about what constitutes value, we will loosely describe valued outcomes as preparation of a diverse population of students with the skills and knowledge they will need to be productive members of society. Value is enhanced when educational services are delivered in an equitable fashion, attending to the learning needs of all students, and in a manner that makes efficient use of society's resources.

The design challenge faced by the educational establishment is to arrive at an organizational configuration that involves the various stakeholders in improving performance. SBM is only one piece of the puzzle, and must fit with the other strands of systemic reform, new approaches to teaching and learning, and enhanced teacher professionalism. Furthermore, SBM is only one piece of the design challenge; a complex network of institutions must be designed to support large-scale change in the capabilities of our schools to deliver value.

This book focuses on SBM and its role in creating high performance. Much of the discussion of SBM has dealt with control and whether yielding control to this group or another will lead to innovative teaching and learning, more responsiveness to stakeholders, and better school performance. Our contention is that for SBM in particular and school reform in general to make a difference, strategies must focus on how to design school organizations for high performance.

Clearly, new educational methods and processes will be at the core of higher performance. Just as certainly, the institutional and policy context in which schools and districts are embedded will have to change to support extensive reform processes and new ways of delivering services. Already we see evidence of this as politicians and educators debate the role of local school boards in the context of systemic reform (Danzberger and Usdan, 1994). Our focus, however, is on SBM, and how it might be reconceived as an approach to involving stakeholders in the continual improvement of school performance.

References

Ball, D. L., and Rundquist, S. S. (1993). Collaboration as a context for joining teacher learning with learning about teaching. In D. K. Cohen, M. W. McLaughlin, and J. E. Talbert (Eds.), *Teaching for understanding: Challenges for policy and practice* (pp. 13–42). San Francisco: Jossey-Bass.

Block, P. (1990). *The empowered manager: Positive political skills at work.* San Francisco: Jossey-Bass.

Cohen, D. K., and Barnes, C. A. (1993). Pedagogy and policy. In D. K. Cohen, M. W. McLaughlin, and J. E. Talbert (Eds.), *Teaching for understanding: Challenges for policy and practice* (pp. 207–239). San Francisco: Jossey-Bass.

Cohen, D. K., McLaughlin, M. W., and Talbert, J. E. (Eds.). (1993). *Teaching for understanding: Challenges for policy and practice.* San Francisco: Jossey-Bass.

Cohen, D. K., and Spillane, J. P. (1993). Policy and practice: The relations between governance and instruction. In S. H. Fuhrman (Ed.), *Designing coherent education policy: Improving the system* (pp. 35–95). San Francisco: Jossey-Bass.

Comer, J. (1980). *School power.* New York: Free Press.

Danzberger, J. P., and Usdan, M. D. (1994). Local education governance: Perspectives on problems and strategies for change. *Phi Delta Kappan, 75,* 366.

David, J. L. (1989). Synthesis of research on school-based management. *Educational Leadership, 46*(8), 45–53.

David, J. L. (1990). Restructuring in progress: Lessons from pioneering districts. In R. F. Elmore and Associates (Eds.), *Restructuring schools: The next generation of educational reform* (pp. 209–250). San Francisco: Jossey-Bass.

Deming, W. E. (1986). *Out of the crisis.* Cambridge, MA: MIT Press.

Elmore, R. F. (1993a). School decentralization: Who gains? Who loses? In J. Hannaway and M. Carnoy (Eds.), *Decentralization and school improvement: Can we fulfill the promise?* (pp. 33–54). San Francisco: Jossey-Bass.

Elmore, R. F. (1993b). The role of local school districts in instructional improvement. In S. H. Fuhrman (Ed.), *Designing coherent education policy: Improving the system* (pp. 96–124). San Francisco: Jossey-Bass.

Elmore, R. F., and Associates. (Eds.). (1990). *Restructuring schools: The next generation of educational reform.* San Francisco: Jossey-Bass.

Fuhrman, S. H. (Ed.). (1993). *Designing coherent education policy: Improving the system.* San Francisco: Jossey-Bass.

Fuhrman, S. H., Massell, D., and Associates. (1992). *Issues and strategies in systemic reform.* New Brunswick, NJ: Rutgers University, Consortium for Policy Research in Education.

Galbraith, J. (1994). *Competing with flexible lateral organizations* (2nd ed.). Reading, MA: Addison-Wesley.

Goodlad, J. (1984). *A place called school.* New York: McGraw-Hill.

Hannaway, J., and Carnoy, M. (Eds.). (1993). *Decentralization and school improvement: Can we fulfill the promise?* San Francisco: Jossey-Bass.

Harp, L. (1992). Report documents new round of state fiscal lows. *Education Week, 11*(32), 17.

Johnson, S. M. (1990). Redesigning teachers' work. In R. F. Elmore and Associates (Eds.), *Restructuring schools: The next generation of school reform* (pp. 125–151). San Francisco: Jossey-Bass.

Juran, J. M. (1989). *Juran on leadership for quality*. New York: Free Press.

Katz, D., and Kahn, R. L. (1978). *The social-psychology of organizations* (2nd ed.). New York: Wiley.

Lawler, E. E. (1986). *High-involvement management*. San Francisco: Jossey-Bass.

Lawler, E. E. (1992). *The ultimate advantage*. San Francisco: Jossey-Bass.

Levin, H. M. (1987). Accelerated schools for disadvantaged students. *Educational Leadership, 44*(6), 19–21.

McCarthey, S. J., and Peterson, P. L. (1993). Creating classroom practice within the context of a restructured professional development school. In D. K. Cohen, M. W. McLaughlin, and J. E. Talbert (Eds.), *Teaching for understanding: Challenges for policy and practice* (pp. 130–166). San Francisco: Jossey-Bass.

Mohrman, A. M., Mohrman, S. A., Ledford, G. E., Cummings, G. F., and Lawler, E. E. (1989). *Large-scale organizational change*. San Francisco: Jossey-Bass.

Mohrman, S. A., and Cummings, T. G. (1989). *Self-designing organizations: Learning how to create high performance*. Reading, MA: Addison-Wesley.

Mohrman, S. A., Lawler, E. E., and Mohrman, A. M. (1992). The performance management of teams. In W. J. Bruns (Ed.), *Performance measurement, evaluation, and incentives*. Boston: Harvard Business School Press.

Mohrman, S. A., and Mohrman, A. M. (1993). Organizational change and learning. In J. Galbraith and E. E. Lawler (Eds.), *Organizing for the future: The new logic for managing complex organizations* (pp. 87–108). San Francisco: Jossey-Bass.

Nadler, D., Gerstein, M. S., and Shaw, R. B. (1992). *Organizational architecture: Designs for changing organizations*. San Francisco: Jossey-Bass.

National Assessment of Educational Progress. (1990). *America's challenge: Accelerating academic achievement*. Princeton, NJ: Educational Testing Service.

National Center on Education and the Economy. (1990). *America's choice: High wages of low skills*. Rochester, NY: Author.

National Commission on Excellence in Education. (1983). *A nation at risk*. Washington, DC: U.S. Government Printing Office.

Odden, A. R., and Conley, S. (1992). Restructuring teacher compensation systems. In A. Odden (Ed.), *Rethinking school finance: An agenda for the 1990s*, (pp. 41–96). San Francisco: Jossey-Bass.

Pfeffer, J., and Salancik, G. (1978). *The external control of organizations: A resource dependence perspective*. New York: Harper & Row.

Raywid, M. A. (1990). Rethinking school governance. In R. F. Elmore and Associates (Eds.), *Restructuring schools: The next generation of school reform* (pp. 152–205). San Francisco: Jossey-Bass.

Senge, P. (1990). *The fifth discipline: The art and practice of the learning organization.* New York. Doubleday.

Sizer, T. (1984). *Horace's compromise: The dilemma of the America high school.* Boston: Houghton Mifflin.

Sizer, T. (1992). *Horace's school: Redesigning the American high school.* Boston: Houghton Mifflin.

Sykes, G. (1990). Fostering teacher professionalism in schools. In R. F. Elmore and Associates (Eds.), *Restructuring schools: The next generation of school reform* (pp. 59–96). San Francisco: Jossey-Bass.

Talbert, J. E., and McLaughlin, M. W. (1993). Understanding teaching in context. In D. K. Cohen, M. W. McLaughlin, and J. E. Talbert (Eds.), *Teaching for understanding: Challenges for policy and practice,* (pp. 167–206). San Francisco: Jossey-Bass.

U.S. Department of Education. (1991). *America 2000: An Education Strategy.* Washington, DC: U.S. Government Printing Office.

Walton, R. E. (1985). From control to commitment in the workplace. *Harvard Business Review, 63*(2), 76–84.

Wohlstetter, P., and Odden, A. (1992). Rethinking school-based management policy and research. *Educational Administration Quarterly, 28*(4), 529–549.

Part One

School-Based Management and High Performance

High-Involvement Management in the Private Sector

Susan Albers Mohrman

Private-sector organizations in the United States are in the midst of slow and often painful transitions in the way they are designed and managed. These transitions have been triggered by a host of environmental forces that demand new kinds and levels of performance in order for organizations to survive and prosper. Increased levels of competition, the globalization of many markets, and the deregulation of previously protected industries have jolted these organizations out of complacency. The rapid evolution of telecommunications and computer technologies has provided new, powerful work tools that have enabled the distribution of knowledge and information throughout an organization and created a highly knowledgeable set of customers who demand nothing but the best, for the lowest price, and in the shortest time frame. These new technologies are calling for a more highly skilled workforce; at the same time that workforce is coming to organizations with exalted expectations for meaningful work and dignified treatment and bearing very diverse backgrounds.

A major international study by a group of researchers at the Massachusetts Institute of Technology has found a number of root causes of the slippage in the competitive posture of American industry. The group highlighted the importance of the design of organizations and the management of human resources. It called on industry to invest more in the capabilities of its people, to establish partnerships with employees and other organizational stakeholders, to tear down the functional boundaries that divide people within organizations, and to provide more meaningful work and more opportunity for employees to make a difference in organizational performance (Dertouzos, Lester, and Solow, 1989).

In response to these pressures to do more with less, organizations are gradually shedding the trappings of the centralized bureaucracies that have been the underpinnings of American management in the twentieth century. A new framework for management is slowly being defined: one that moves away from centralized control-oriented practices toward approaches that foster initiative and self-management throughout the organization. Although private-sector organizations have led the way in this transition, some public-sector organizations have also begun to use these approaches, including areas of the federal government, some city governments, and the military. In the educational sector, school-based management (SBM) is a related phenomenon in that it promotes moving decisions to the units and performers where the work is being done.

Using the framework defined by Lawler in his book entitled *High-Involvement Management* (1986) and further developed in *The Ultimate Advantage* (1992), this chapter examines practices that move information, knowledge, power, and rewards downward and throughout the organization. It reports findings of a recent study of high-involvement management practices by the 1,000 largest service and manufacturing firms in the United States (Lawler, Mohrman, and Ledford, 1992) and relates the adoption of these practices to effectiveness. It is not the intent of this chapter to carry a message that "if it works in the private sector, schools should do it too." Rather, the chapter provides the framework for a possible reconceptualization of SBM and for examining the extent to which it has been implemented consistently with this employee involvement framework. Chapter Three will examine this latter issue in some detail.

The transition to new organizational forms and ways of managing is an area where practice is preceding research. Consequently, there is a paucity of systematic research studies examining either the occurrence of these forms or their impact. There is, however, a long tradition of prescriptive works, varying in rigor from thoughtful research-based work to casual advocacy pieces. There is also a vast array of descriptive case studies, again varying tremendously in rigor. Only a very few comparative research studies have examined organizations employing these new forms. This chapter will rely primarily on one longitudinal study of practice patterns, but will also refer to a number of solid works that both describe and study high-involvement management.

Overview of High-Involvement Management

The High-Involvement Model

Advocacy of participative organizations dates back to the 1930s (see Weisbord, 1987, for a review). However, these concepts did not receive attention from U.S. practitioners until the 1960s, when the works of Chris Argyris (1964), Douglas McGregor (1960), and Rensis Likert (1961) established the concept of *participative management* as part of the consciousness of American managers through inclusion in the curricula of most management education programs. These works primarily advocated changes in the behavior of managers within a traditionally designed bureaucratic organization. The advocacy of participative management was based primarily on values of human growth and development, and to some extent on laboratory and field studies supporting the notion that participative managers achieved greater productivity and employee satisfaction.

During approximately the same period, a participative approach to the design of manufacturing plants was originating in Europe.

The sociotechnical systems approach (Trist and Bamforth, 1951; Cummings, 1978; Pasmore, 1988) emphasized the participative design of organizations to optimize both the social needs of employees and the technical requirements of the work, and to create highly participative work settings characterized by self-regulation or self-management. Case studies of plants using this approach showed them to be more productive than comparable plants, although the quality of the research was in some cases suspect (Cummings and Molloy, 1977). This approach was imported to the United States, and by 1985 it was reported that at least 40 major corporations had at least 200 plants that were sociotechnically designed and participatively operated (Walton, 1985).

These plants have been called new-design plants (Lawler, 1978), high-commitment work systems (Walton, 1985), and high-performing work systems (Hanna, 1988). Both Lawler and Walton have outlined the design features of these plants and contrasted them with traditional plants. New-design plants have flat organizational structures, enriched and often team-based jobs, cross training, sharing of information at all levels of the organization, self-direction at the lowest level, few status differentiators between ranks, pay for performance and skills, and employee input into a wide variety of policies and practices, organizational goals, and methods used to improve performance.

During the 1980s the concepts and practices embodied in new-design plants slowly began to be applied in white-collar service and knowledge work components of some organizations. Exploration of their applicability in these arenas was motivated by increasing recognition that American manufacturing organizations were competitively disadvantaged by the high burden of white-collar overhead and that their managerial, service, administrative, and technical components needed the same kind of reconceptualization as was occurring in their blue-collar components. Service organizations also started to invest heavily in high-involvement transitions once it became clear that these approaches could be adapted to fit nonmanufacturing settings.

The conceptual underpinnings of the application of these practices in these new settings have been provided in part by scholars working to understand the nature of knowledge-based and information-based work (Pava, 1983; Zuboff, 1984) and to apply sociotechnical principles to it (Pasmore, 1988). Their basic premise is that in knowledge work, effectiveness depends on applying knowledge and information to decision making, and therefore improving effectiveness requires changes in the way information is used and decisions are made. In addition, the rapid advances in computer and telecommunications technology have led researchers to conceptualize the proper split of work between man and machine and the implications of new technological capabilities for organizational design (for example, Walton, 1989). Continuing this stream of work, an eleven-company study of the design of knowledge work has yielded a design model based in part on the empirical finding that the effectiveness of a business unit is greater when the conditions for employee involvement are in place (Mohrman, Cohen, and Mohrman, 1994).

In the 1980s, the momentum of change was enhanced by the popularization of total quality management (TQM) (Crosby, 1979; Deming, 1986; Juran, 1989). TQM consists of a set of practices designed to provide employees with systematic tools for improving quality and work process and to create problem-solving forums for employees. In these forums workers representing various organizational perspectives come together to define and generate solutions to quality problems and to improve work processes. A key aspect of TQM is that quality is defined through the eyes of the customer. High quality is meeting the requirements of the customer—a definition in full alignment with the survival needs of the organization.

The paradox of TQM is that it has not questioned the trappings of the bureaucratic design of organizations and that it has relied on a top-down approach to implementation; at the same time, its success depends on unraveling that bureaucracy in order to empower people to work across organizational boundaries to initiate and implement change. This issue is now being recognized. Process reengineering, the most recent addition to the tools for organizational redesign, addresses head-on the need to redraw the organization's boundaries (Hammer and Champy, 1993). It entails the identification of the whole set of activities (processes) involved in delivering value to the customer, and reorganizing so the activities of all contributors to the entire process are integrated. In most cases this entails moving away from a functional, discipline-based organization, and establishing cross-functional work units.

Lawler (1986) has provided a framework for understanding the essence of high-involvement management that transcends particular organizational settings and can serve as a set of general design principles for any organization embarking on a transition. According to this framework, getting people involved in the success of their organization depends upon increasing their ability to influence their jobs and work settings, to participate in identifying and solving problems in the organization, and to understand and contribute to organizational success. This requires increasing the availability of the following four resources downward and throughout the organization:

1. *Information* that enables the individual to participate and influence decisions with understanding of the organization's environment, strategy, work systems, performance requirements, and level of performance.
2. *Knowledge and skills* required for effective job performance and for effective contribution to the success of the organization.
3. *Power* to influence decisions about work processes, organizational practices, policies, and strategy.
4. *Rewards* that align the self-interest of employees with the suc-

cess of the organization because they are based on performance and linked to contribution to organizational success.

The premise behind this framework is that the design of the
organization shapes the behaviors and performance of the people
in it. By distributing these four resources, organizations will increase
people's capacity and motivation to perform effectively. Such an
approach to defining high involvement allows organizations to follow general principles in designing high-performing work settings,
rather than implementing a well-defined, cookie-cutter design. A
number of different design features can be employed to develop
these resources deep in the organization, depending on the nature of
the work. Examples of approaches that have been used extensively
in the private sector will be presented in this chapter; however, the
organizations need to design specific practices to fit their particular
context.

The Systemic Nature of High-Involvement Management

Studies of the implementation of high-involvement management
have indicated that making the transition is not accomplished
simply by changing a few practices in the organization. Nor is it
accomplished by moving only one or two key resources. High-
involvement management represents large-scale change, change
that is deep and pervasive. As such, it entails a redesign of many if
not most aspects of the organization (Lawler, 1986; Mohrman and
Cummings, 1989; Mohrman, Mohrman, Ledford, Cummings, and
Lawler, 1989). It is not a set of practices; rather, it is a new way of
functioning that is shaped and supported by the way the organization is designed. Consequently, the transition involves designing
ways to share knowledge, information, power, and rewards that fit
with each other and fit with the nature of the work.

The systemic nature of the transition was confirmed in the

research that serves as the foundation for the remainder of this chapter (Lawler, Mohrman, and Ledford, 1992). This study examined the patterns of adoption of an assortment of practices designed to redistribute knowledge, information, power, and rewards. The 500 largest manufacturing firms and the 500 largest service firms in the United States constituted the sample for the 1990 study.

A cluster analysis was then performed to discover whether there are clusters of organizations with similar patterns of adoption. With one exception, organizations clustered with respect not to *which* practices they implemented but rather *how extensively* they were implementing the high-involvement practices in general. Companies clustered into high adopters (7 percent), average adopters (34 percent), and low adopters (36 percent) (the remaining 16 percent could not be classified). The exception to this pattern were the 7 percent of companies who appeared to be using their reward systems as their lead variables. They were more likely than the other companies to base pay on performance and skills, but average in their application of approaches to redistribute power, information, and knowledge. This finding reflects the fact that pay for performance is a concept equally at home in a traditional or innovative work system.

The finding that change is a systemic process is not surprising. The field of organizational theory has been partially built on the notion of open systems, which specifies the importance to organizational effectiveness of "fit" between the various elements of the system (Leavitt, 1965; Nadler and Tushman, 1988; Katz and Kahn, 1978). Although an organization can withstand minor changes to various aspects of its system while maintaining an equilibrium, significant changes will entail a realignment of all or most elements of the system. Thus, for example, smaller units may be created to heighten performance accountability and responsibility. That is a major structural change, and it will need to be reinforced very quickly by changes in measurements, rewards, and other practices.

The Effectiveness of High-Involvement Management

Early advocates of participative management emphasized the human growth and development that would result. One school of thought still argues that high-involvement practices should be adopted for ethical reasons because they contribute to human satisfaction (Sashkin, 1984). The argument that seems to be driving today's organizational change efforts, however, is that high-involvement organizations are more effective. In the study by Lawler, Mohrman, and Ledford, more than two-thirds of the firms reported that they were adopting high-involvement practices to improve productivity and quality, while only one-fifth were doing it for ethical and value reasons (multiple responses were permitted). Improving employee motivation (52 percent), reducing costs (46 percent) and adapting to future environmental changes (45 percent) were other reasons commonly reported. Thus, businesses are clearly being motivated to change because they want to achieve the higher levels of organizational performance required in the changing environment.

The question of effectiveness is whether creating the organizational conditions for high involvement actually leads to employees performing their jobs more effectively and making improvements in how work gets done. Companies with more extensive involvement features reported qualitative change such as better decision making and more effective change implementation. The real question, however, is whether outcomes are improved (Lawler, Mohrman, and Ledford, 1992). These companies apparently believe that they are accomplishing their objectives. More than two-thirds of them reported that they were experiencing positive impact on the quality of products and services, level of customer service, and work satisfaction. At least half reported positive impact on employee quality of work life, productivity, and competitiveness. Although company motivation is heavily weighted toward business objectives, the adoption of these practices is seen as enhancing both business and employee outcomes.

Only a few studies have systematically compared companies that are characterized by high involvement with those that are not. These offer support for the claim that high-involvement practices contribute to organizational effectiveness. Three studies (Denison, 1984, 1990; Mitchell, Lewin, and Lawler, 1990; Kravetz, 1988) found that companies that operate with an involvement-oriented model obtain superior economic performance when compared with companies using more traditional practices. In addition, hundreds of studies looked at the effectiveness of various practices, such as gain sharing, job enrichment, or self-managing teams, that are common ways of moving knowledge, information, power, and rewards downward in an organization. The weight of these studies supports the argument that high-involvement practices contribute to effectiveness (Cummings and Molloy, 1977; Lawler, 1986).

A major review of studies of the relationship between participation and economic performance (Levine and Tyson, 1990) found that there is a weak, short-term relationship in general, but that participation involving *substantial* organizational influence relates to long-term significant performance improvements. This finding was further substantiated in the study by Lawler, Mohrman, and Ledford, which found that companies in the cluster of high adopters achieved above-average impact on both productivity and quality of goods and services. These were the companies that had more ways of involving their employees, had been altering their practices toward high involvement for a longer period of time, and directly involved a greater percentage of employees.

These results confirm the large-scale, systemic nature of the change to a high-involvement system. Some positive results accrue to companies that have made minor changes in organizational systems. In the study by Lawler, Mohrman, and Ledford, these companies also reported that they had begun their transition more recently. The biggest payoff was being experienced by organizations that had been at it longer and had made more significant changes.

The systemic nature of change is also pointed out by the finding that organizations stressing a reward approach to change reported the least impact on productivity. They were less likely to be making the across-the-board design changes needed to foster true involvement. Aligning self-interest is insufficient, because it does not follow that the organization will then make the changes required to allow employees to make a difference.

Who Are the Adopters?

The study of the Fortune 1000 companies confirmed what has been very evident in the literature: the transition to high involvement is more advanced in manufacturing than service companies. Service companies lag manufacturing in many practices that develop information, knowledge, power, and rewards through the organization. The few exceptions to this will be noted in the next section of the chapter. Service companies are not only less advanced in their application of high-involvement approaches, they also report less positive outcomes. Given the systemic change argument, this finding is to be expected. Positive outcomes begin to accrue when the organization has made significant changes.

A corollary to this finding is that even within manufacturing firms, the transition has proceeded at a slower pace in the management and white-collar components. It is only in the past ten years that significant attention has been given to the need to improve performance in these sectors. Before that, the perceived crisis in our economy was lack of worldwide competitiveness of manufacturing capabilities.

The companies that have moved furthest in implementing high-involvement practices are those that are experiencing very clear performance challenges: foreign competition and decreasing product life cycle. The former creates pressures for reduced cost and high quality simultaneously; the latter puts a premium on speed: time to market, cycle time, or response time. These performance pressures require organizations to get out from under the weight of their top-down bureaucracy and to develop approaches where decisions are made deep in the organization among the people who have to work together to do the job (Mohrman, Mohrman, and Lawler, 1992).

High-involvement practices have their biggest payoff in organizations where work is uncertain, complex, and interdependent (Cummings, 1978; Lawler, 1986). Complexity and uncertainty require a great deal of discretion by the people who carry out the core technology of the organization. Such work cannot be preprogrammed and controlled from a distance. Uncertainty is present when cause-effect knowledge is incomplete, requiring on-line learning and adapting of work processes. Complexity could mean that the characteristics of the raw materials vary greatly, or that customer requirements differ dramatically from one another. The need to respond to unique customers leads many organizations to adopt high-involvement practices. Such tailored response cannot easily be controlled hierarchically. Work is interdependent when the output of one work group affects others, requiring on-line coordination and integration. In settings where work has those three characteristics, organizational performance can be enhanced by approaches that involve people and that empower them to make decisions close to the work through lateral rather than hierarchical means.

Some service companies, including data processing and financial services, are beginning to feel the pressures of foreign competition. Others, however, are simply facing an environment of scarcer resources—having to provide better service at lower costs. These performance pressures are leading them to explore high-involvement management principles, recognizing that approaches used in blue-collar settings will have to be modified to fit the nature of the work they do. Service companies such as insurance, financial services, and health care are beginning to use empowered multifunctional service teams to address the needs of customers. They have also been leaders in business process reengineering—rethinking the processes they use to do their work, eliminating low-value activities, finding new ways to deliver value to the customer, and applying information technology to greatly extend employee capabilities (Davenport, 1993; Hammer and Champy, 1993).

Decentralization Strategies

The transition to high involvement requires systemic change that increases the amount of all four of the key resources—information, knowledge, power, and rewards—lower in the organization. This section will describe some main approaches being used in the private sector to increase this movement downward.

Two caveats are in order. First, some of these approaches have been used for a long time to create more participation within traditionally designed organizations; consequently, they are more prevalent, but they do not constitute as large a step toward high involvement since they are more compatible with traditional control-oriented designs. For example, profit sharing is an age-old tool used in many companies. It rewards employees a bonus based on success of the business. It can exist quite well in top-down, bureaucratic settings. On the other hand, team and business unit rewards for performance require that teams and business units be measured and empowered to improve their own performance. This moves the organization further along the continuum to high involvement.

Second, the design approaches that are discussed are those that have been used primarily in the private sector. They have mostly been developed in manufacturing settings; however, variants of these and new approaches altogether are beginning to crop up in knowledge work and service organizations. Thus, it is more important to focus on the intent of the design approach rather than on the particular form it takes.

The Fortune 1000 study, for example, asked organizations whether they were using a particular approach and what percentage of their employees were involved in it. Organizations often begin their transitions in portions of their operations, sometimes because the managers learn about different approaches and decide to apply them. Even when the transition is being officially led and encouraged from the top, different units will adopt practices at different rates. Plants or other business units are often the level at which innovative approaches are first adopted (Beer, Eisenstat, and Spector, 1990). As mentioned, the white-collar components of firms often lag the blue-collar components.

Decentralizing Information

For employees to be involved in the success of the organization, they need to know and understand the organization's mission, strategy, plans, and goals; the key success factors and how they are measured; and how their own performance can contribute to organizational success. In addition, they need ongoing feedback about how well the organization as a whole and their unit in particular are performing; only with feedback about results can employees identify areas where corrective action is required.

In the private sector, feedback about how the organization is performing in comparison to competitors is critical to improving competitiveness. As the American automobile industry discovered, a company can be continually improving its own historical performance, and at the same time slipping farther behind competitors. Sharing competitor performance provides an external benchmark.

Creating an open information environment is a way of building trust among employees about the intent of the company. People often resist performance improvement for fear they will work themselves out of a job. This can be partially offset by making sure that employees are fully informed about company plans, including the plans for introducing new technologies and all the new approaches that will affect them.

Lawler and his associates found that although three-quarters of companies shared overall company operating results with all employees, only about half broke those results down to operating units. In general, workers feel they have more ability to affect more proximate results; the "line of sight" to companywide results is often too distant (Lawler, 1981). The performing unit that employees feel they can affect is most likely the business unit or the work team.

Less than one-fifth of companies shared competitor performance, consequently depriving the employees of an understanding of how their results compared with others. Almost half shared business plans and goals; on the other hand, only one-quarter shared information about new technologies that would affect employees. It is a mixed picture whether organizations are providing employees with the information they need about how they will need to change and develop relevant skills, and what standards will be required to keep the organization viable through time.

The most advanced high-involvement firms regularly share all these kinds of information with the employees. They use a number of approaches, including face-to-face, all-hands meetings, regular videotaped presentations from company officers, and display boards that provide up-to-date performance information and often include trends and data on competitor gaps. Companies effective at sharing information use multiple media and even redundancy. They have eliminated the old "need to know" guideline; the burden of proof is now on those who advocate withholding information. They have also made good communication a clear accountability for all managers.

Decentralizing Knowledge and Skills

Sharing information with employees is only a first step toward enabling them to contribute more effectively to organizational success. A number of knowledge sets and skills are also required by involved employees, so that information can be understood and processed in a manner that leads to better decisions and better results. Several domains of knowledge and skills are especially important: job skills, social skills, and organization or business skills. In addition, many of the performance improvement methodologies require participants to use statistical quality analysis and other problem-solving techniques. Job skills are the *sine qua non* of effective performance; they are obviously important even in a traditionally designed organization. Yet study after study shows American organizations are badly lagging international competitors in their investment in people (for example, Dertouzos, Lester, and Solow, 1989). The Fortune 1000 study supports this conclusion. Only one-third of companies reported that more than 60 percent of employees had received job skills training in the past three years. This contrasts with Japanese companies, for example, where several weeks of training per year is the norm. Indeed, some of our most advanced involvement companies have been aggressive in this area, requiring several weeks a year of training and education.

Cross training is another area of job skills development that has implications for high involvement. As people learn more and more aspects of the company's work, they can be more flexibly employed. As important, they have a broader perspective on the work of the organization, can contribute more knowledgeably to decisions and problem solving, and can interact more effectively with others in the organization. Cross training is a fundamental underpinning of self-management in manufacturing settings. Teams in these settings have sufficient skill redundancy to flexibly deploy their members to the tasks at hand. Two-thirds of companies report that more than 40 percent of employees are cross-trained.

Social-skills training is a key component of high involvement because working with and influencing others is critical to working in teams and to many approaches to performance improvement. Historically, only managers have received social-skills training. Team problem solving and decision making are underpinnings of process and organizational improvement. Relying less on hierarchical control implies being more effective at resolving issues and making decisions laterally. Training in group decision making and problem solving, team building, and leadership is frequently part of the implementation of efforts such as total quality management or the creation of work teams or mini-enterprise units (smaller, self-contained units within a bigger business unit). However, American organizations seem to be developing these skills sparingly. Approximately half have trained 20 percent or more of their employees in these skills in the past three years. Organizations investing the most in the transition to high-involvement management, however, often provide social-skills development for 100 percent of employees.

Finally, contributing to the success of the organization requires understanding its business elements, including its financial systems, accounting practices, sources of revenue and expense, and the various constraints and requirements placed upon it by its different stakeholders. Again, this is an area where historically only managers have received training. Only if employees understand these issues are they able to make competent decisions that take the business realities and imperatives into account. About two-fifths of companies had trained 20 percent or more of their employees in these skills, but some companies are giving all employees training in budgeting, planning, and competitive factors.

A special kind of business skill is knowledge of how to apply statistical analyses and other systematic analytic techniques to the improvement of business processes. These skills are the underpinnings of total quality management. It is not unusual for companies that seriously implement this approach to embark on wholesale training of all employees in the basic tools. On average, however, we find a similar pattern to other skills, with two-fifths of companies having trained 20 percent or more of their employees during the past three years.

Although companies have invested a great deal of resources in training employees so they can be effectively involved in the business, the general pattern is that it is one-shot training and involves only a small percentage of employees. Companies with a limited training investment have also achieved limited outcomes. Again, the most advanced companies have gone beyond this minimal training, and are committing to the continual development of employee skills and knowledge.

Decentralizing Power

Possessing information, knowledge, and skills is critical but insufficient to the exercise of influence in an organization. They may permit influence over one's own job domain or may enable more effective application of informal influence. In organizations, however, decisions are often formally vested in positions, units, or committees, often making it difficult for those who are not in those positions or those forums to exercise influence. Procedures and policies are often determined centrally, by specialized groups, and imposed on the rest of the organization with little chance for stakeholder input and influence. Decentralizing power therefore requires the creation of forums that enable the exercise of influence, or the redesign of work and of the organization to vest increased influence in the people doing the work. Both approaches are being used in the private sector.

The first approach involves creating special groups or holding special meetings to give various stakeholders the opportunity to identify issues, solve problems, and generate new and better ways of doing things. This approach often is parallel (Ledford, Lawler, and Mohrman, 1988) to the functioning of the primary organizational structure; that is, these involvement forums are not the primary mechanism for doing the work that transforms organizational inputs into products or services.

Three main approaches have been used in the private sector to create forums for employee input. The oldest and most established is survey feedback, where an organizational survey is administered and then fed back to problem-solving groups. Survey feedback is not strictly a parallel approach, since intact work groups tend to be the units that receive the data and generate ideas. This often leads, however, to the establishment of special task teams to work the problems and suggest solutions. Survey feedback has been used for decades in some organizations, and is able to coexist with a traditional organizational structure and provide opportunities for participation within that structure. Lawler, Mohrman, and Ledford (1992) found that this is the most frequently used approach to getting employee input; three-quarters of private-sector organizations use it. Survey feedback is also the most likely to be used with the entire employee base. Periodic all-company surveys are administered in 16 percent of companies.

Another parallel approach is the establishment of participation groups. One of the best known is the quality circle: a small group of employees constituted to identify problems and to use statistical process analysis skills to find root causes and generate solutions. Although the heyday of quality circles is past (Lawler and Mohrman, 1987), two-thirds of companies report using quality circles in at least some parts of the organization.

Quality circles have tended to be replaced or supplemented by other kinds of participation groups, including quality improvement teams (QITs), which are advocated within the TQM movement. QITs differ from quality circles in that the problems that they address are often identified by management, which then sets up a team of relevant employees to solve them. Other forms of participation groups include task teams and councils. Eighty-five percent of companies report participation group activity, although most companies involve less than half of their employees.

The popularity of participation groups is in part based on the fact that they can be established and function quite well even in traditionally structured organizations. Their use entails a very small departure from the traditional control-oriented culture. Another reason for popularity, however, is that participation groups can bring together people from quite different parts of the organization, and can thus serve to integrate across the organization. When used in this way, they are a step toward replacing hierarchical control with lateral integration.

In unionized settings, union-management committees are often employed to begin to develop collaboration between the institutional union and management that can lead to an environment where employees become even more involved in the business. It is not unusual for union-management committees to cosponsor employee problem-solving teams and other decentralization approaches. Forty percent of unionized companies have some union-management committees.

The second major approach to decentralization of power is to redesign the organization or jobs to change the way authority is formally vested. The underlying principle is to move control and accountability as close as possible to the people doing the work. Three approaches are being used: job enrichment or redesign, self-managing teams, and the establishment of mini-enterprise units.

Job enrichment entails the redefinition of jobs to include as much discretion and authority over a complete task as possible. This approach has been in existence for several decades, and has primarily been used to increase the motivation potential of routine tasks by adding variety and responsibility to the job (Hackman and Oldham, 1973). The long history of this approach is evidence that it can exist in traditionally managed organizations. There has been a recent upsurge in interest, however, with more than three-quarters of companies employing job enrichment in some parts of the organization (Lawler, Mohrman, and Ledford, 1992). The current upsurge might best be understood as bringing the philosophy that underpins the way jobs are defined into alignment with the high-involvement philosophy.

It is often difficult to build discretion and authority over a complete task into individual jobs. The complete task may require the contributions of many different people who bring to bear many different skills and knowledge bases. In this case, involvement may best be achieved in a team setting, by vesting discretion and authority in the team. Self-managing teams are also referred to as semi-autonomous work groups, self-regulating work teams, or simply work teams. The work team, sometimes without a supervisor, is responsible for a whole product or service and makes decisions about task assignments and work methods. It may also be responsible for its own support services and may perform certain personnel functions such as hiring and firing team members and determining pay increases. Thus, the support units of an organization and the management structure get smaller because their skills are developed or moved into the teams. If this is not possible, support services and managers are given a service mission so that they view the teams as customers rather than seeing their role as regulating teams.

The concept of self-managing teams was first developed in the sociotechnical systems movement of work design, which advocated that the definition of a team and its functions should be based on a thorough analysis of the work performed and the characteristics of the surrounding social system. This design feature is at the heart of many companies' approach to the implementation of high-involvement management. Only about half of the 1,000 companies surveyed by Lawler and associates used self-managing teams in 1990, but this percentage represented a large increase in prevalence compared to earlier studies (Lawler, Mohrman, and Ledford, 1992). Most companies apply this design feature in only a small part of their organization, partly because its application depends on the work being suitable to a team approach.

Mini-enterprise units are relatively small self-contained organizational units within a larger business unit, which produce their own product or service and operate in a decentralized manner as a small business. A product line within a plant, for example, might be constituted as a minienterprise, be given relative autonomy, and be held accountable for results. This is one of the newest innovations being used to create high involvement; in 1990 mini-enterprise units were used in only one-quarter of companies. The

Fortune 1000 study found that companies that used self-managing work teams and mini-enterprise units were also highly likely to use a number of parallel approaches to high involvement. These companies have a fundamental commitment to change, and are high adopters of high-involvement practices in general. Work team and parallel approaches are complementary; a complete implementation of high-involvement management would entail redesigning the basic jobs and units of the organization in order to move authority to the lowest possible level, and also providing forums for input and initiation of change in the way things are done.

Decentralization of Rewards for Performance

While the decentralization of information, knowledge, and power gives employees the ability to exercise influence, the decentralization of rewards for performance gives them a personal stake in the success of the organization. It provides the reinforcement for exercising influence in a manner that leads to greater performance. If rewards for performance are to have their intended impact, there must be a clear definition of the desired performances and how they will be rewarded. Rewards can be linked to performance at any level in the organization, from individual pay for performance to companywide profit sharing. Intermediate-level pay for performance approaches are most relevant to high-involvement management.

Profit-sharing and stock-ownership programs reward people for the company's financial performance. These programs have been around for a long time, and have often been adopted for reasons such as tax advantage that have nothing to do with creating a high-involvement organization. Most important, however, the line of sight between the individual and corporate financial performance is so distant that it is difficult for individual employees to see the connection between their performance and corporate profitability or stock price. These programs do, however, have the impact of linking self-interest to company performance, and are thus supportive of the basic notion of high-involvement. They also create a sense of belonging to the enterprise and concern with how well it is doing. Almost two-thirds of companies have profit-sharing and stock-ownership programs, often applied to all employees (Lawler, Mohrman, and Ledford, 1992).

Individual incentives are used to some extent in 90 percent of companies. They focus on individual performance, and generally do little to tie the individuals to the success of the business. In fact, they often lead individuals to suboptimize by focusing too narrowly on their own set of activities out of context of the overall process of delivering the service or making the product. If an individual's job can be performed completely independently, however, individual rewards create the closest line of sight.

Midrange performance-based pay approaches such as team incentives or gain sharing tie together the people in a performing unit and reinforce collaborative efforts to improve unit performance. Team incentives work particularly well to reinforce performance where work is assigned to teams that are accountable for measurable outcomes and when value to the customer depends on integrated effort by multiple contributors. Sixty percent of companies report that they have team incentives in place in at least part of the organization.

Gain sharing rewards all employees for performance improvement in a unit that is usually larger than a team and smaller than the corporation. Used in about two-fifths of companies, this approach is closely identified with high involvement since it stresses involvement in improvement efforts as a way to increase the performance of the organizational unit (Lawler, Mohrman, and Ledford, 1992). Rewarding performance at this level motivates employees to use shared resources efficiently and coordinate their work.

One individual approach that is fully consistent with high involvement is the use of skill- or person-based pay. When pay is based on the knowledge and skill of the person rather than on an arbitrary evaluation of a job or years of experience, it rewards capability and flexibility of contribution. Furthermore, it promotes cross training and the development of broader understanding of the organization (Ledford, 1990). In 1990, half of companies applied skill-based pay in some parts of the organization. This number is substantially higher than was found in previous studies, indicating an upsurge in this approach (Lawler, Mohrman, and Ledford, 1992). Skill-based pay is especially associated with the use of work teams in which members are cross-trained to provide flexibility. They are granted pay increases as they master more aspects of the work done in the team.

Conclusion and Implications for School-Based Management

The high-involvement management framework provides a way of understanding and guiding the multiple facets of the decentralization of authority in an organization. It involves redesigning an organization's practices and processes to transfer information, knowledge, power, and performance-based rewards downward and throughout the organization. Although only a small percentage of companies are well advanced in their adoption of these high-involvement practices, the vast majority of large companies in the United States have begun to implement some of them.

Private-sector organizations are implementing high-involvement management practices for business reasons. They have found that the performance pressures being posed by the environments in which they operate are so extreme that they can achieve these new levels of performance only by rethinking in a fundamental fashion the way they do business. In particular, they are finding it necessary to break up the logjam of the bureaucracy and move decision making closer to the people who do the work and to the customer.

This chapter presented an overview of the major design features that are being employed to foster high involvement. Some approaches to involvement can be used within a traditional organization. Others entail more fundamental changes to formally vest authority lower in the organization. Skill-based pay, gain sharing, cross-functional teams, and organizational restructuring to create self-managing work teams and mini-enterprise units are among the design features particularly characteristic of organizations that have moved the furthest toward the high-involvement model. Broad sharing of information and a significant commitment to ongoing training and development of employees at all levels provide the tools that permit involvement mechanisms to be effective.

The current approaches to high-involvement management have been shaped in manufacturing settings. Service and white-collar organizations are currently in the process of tailoring them to meet the requirements of the kind of work they do. The basic principles do not change—these organizations also find it necessary to decentralize information, knowledge, power, and performance-based rewards to more fully involve employees in the success of the organization. The particular design approaches that are used look somewhat different where the work is not similar to manufacturing work.

Education, like other sectors of the economy, houses work that is in many ways unique. However, it is work that is complex, uncertain, and interdependent (the work of various educators may impact the same child or group of children). The principles of high-involvement management therefore seem to fit the work that is done in the field of education. School-based management (SBM) has a great deal of conceptual overlap with high involvement, although it has not necessarily been implemented with a systemic set of design heuristics. Taking a systematic design approach to SBM may help unlock the potential of this approach.

What forms will the distribution of knowledge, information, power, and rewards take in educational organizations? Although a lot of ideas can be generated by examining the experiences of other kinds of organizations that are making the transition, schools are evolving their own approaches, approaches that fit with the nature of the work they do and the societal context in which they exist.

The transition to a high-involvement organizational model is a large-scale, systemic change. Ultimately many, if not most, of the processes and design features of the organization will have to be modified to be congruent with the logic of an organization where decisions are made close to the work and lateral organizational dynamics are as important as hierarchical dynamics. Various stakeholders, including teachers, administrators, students, and parents, will have to learn new roles and begin to understand their schools much differently.

The transition itself entails a substantial commitment of time and money for staff development, innovation, and the development of the organizational infrastructure to support this new way of functioning. Will educational institutions feel sufficiently challenged to embark on this journey? Will they find the resources, both financial and human, to proceed? Many are already moving along this path. For them, the question is whether they will persevere to get to the point where enough aspects of the school organization have changed to provide an environment where people can make a difference.

The next chapters of this book consider the applicability of the high-involvement framework to education by examining learnings to date from SBM implementation and other approaches to school improvement. Looked at from the perspective of the high-involvement framework, what can we learn about SBM? Does the application of this framework yield insight into the role of SBM in the improvement of education? The systemic nature of the transition will be examined in greater detail in Part Two of the book.

References

Argyris, C. (1964). *Integrating the individual and the organization*. New York: Wiley.

Beer, M., Eisenstat, R. A., and Spector, B. (1990). *The critical path to corporate renewal*. Boston: Harvard Business School Press.

Crosby, P. B. (1979). *Quality is free.* New York: McGraw-Hill.

Cummings, T. G. (1978). Self-regulating work groups: A socio-technical synthesis. *Academy of Management Review, 3,* 625–633.

Cummings, T. G. and Molloy, E. J. (1977). *Improving productivity and the quality of work life.* New York: Praeger.

Davenport, T. H. (1993). *Process innovation: Re-engineering work through information technology.* Boston: Harvard Business School Press.

Deming, W. E. (1986). *Out of the crisis.* Cambridge, MA: MIT Press.

Denison, D. (1984). Bringing corporate culture to the bottom line. *Organizational Dynamics, 13*(2), 4–22.

Denison, D. (1990). *Corporate culture and organizational effectiveness.* New York: Wiley.

Dertouzos, M. L., Lester, R. K., and Solow, R. M. (1989). *Made in America: Regaining the production edge.* Cambridge, MA: MIT Press.

Fuhrman, S. H. (1993). *Designing coherent education policy: Improving the system.* San Francisco: Jossey-Bass.

Hackman, J. R., and Oldham, G. R. (1973). *Work redesign.* Reading, MA: Addison-Wesley.

Hammer, M., and Champy, J. (1993). *Reengineering the corporation: A manifesto for business revolution.* New York: HarperBusiness.

Hanna, D. (1988). *Designing organizations for high performance.* Reading, MA: Addison-Wesley.

Juran, J. M. (1989). *Juran on leadership for quality.* New York: Free Press.

Katz, D., and Kahn, R. L. (1978). *The social-psychology of organizations* (2nd ed.). New York: Wiley.

Kravetz, D. J. (1988). *The human resources revolution: Implementing progressive management practices for bottom-line success.* San Francisco: Jossey-Bass.

Lawler, E. E. (1978). The new plant revolution. *Organizational Dynamics, 6* (3), 2–12.

Lawler, E. E. (1981). *Pay and organization development.* Reading, MA: Addison-Wesley.

Lawler, E. E. (1986). *High-involvement management.* San Francisco: Jossey-Bass.

Lawler, E. E. (1992). *The ultimate advantage: Creating the high-involvement organization.* San Francisco: Jossey-Bass.

Lawler, E. E., and Mohrman, S. A. (1987). Quality circles: After the honeymoon. *Organizational Dynamics, 15* (4), 42–54.

Lawler, E. E., Mohrman, S. A., and Ledford, G. E. (1992). *Employee involvement and total quality management.* San Francisco: Jossey-Bass.

Leavitt, H. (1965). Applied organizational change in industry. In J. March (Ed.), *Handbook of Organizations.* Skokie, IL: Rand McNally.

Ledford, G. E. (March, 1990). Effectiveness of skill-based pay systems. *Perspectives in Total Compensation, 1* (1), 1–4.

Ledford, G. E., Lawler, E. E., and Mohrman, S. A. (1988). The quality circle and its variations. In J. P. Campbell, R. J. Campbell, and Associates (Eds.), *Productivity in organizations: New perspectives from industrial and organizational psychology.* San Francisco: Jossey-Bass.

Levine, D. L., and Tyson, L. D. (1990). Participation, productivity, and the firm's environment. In A. S. Blinder (Ed.), *Paying for productivity: A look at the evidence.* Washington, DC: Brookings Institute.

Likert, R. (1961). *New patterns of management.* New York: McGraw-Hill.

McGregor, D. (1960). *The human side of enterprise.* New York: McGraw-Hill.

Mitchell, J. B., Lewin, D., and Lawler, E. E. (1990). Alternative pay system, firm performance and productivity. In A. S. Blinder (Ed.), *Paying for productivity: A look at the evidence.* Washington, DC: Brookings Institute.

Mohrman, A. M., Mohrman, S. A., and Lawler, E. E. (1992). The performance management of teams. In W. J. Bruns (Ed.), *Performance measurement, evaluation, and incentives* (pp. 217–241). Boston: Harvard Business School Press.

Mohrman, A. M., Mohrman, S. A., Ledford, G. E., Cummings, G. F., and Lawler, E. E. (1989). *Large-scale organizational change.* San Francisco: Jossey-Bass.

Mohrman, S. A., Cohen, S. G., and Mohrman, A. M. (1994). *Designing team-based organizations for knowledge work.* (Technical Report). Los Angeles: University of Southern California, The Center for Effective Organizations.

Mohrman, S. A., and Cummings, T. G. (1989). *Self-designing organizations: Learning how to create high performance.* Reading, MA: Addison-Wesley.

Nadler, D. A., and Tushman, M. (1988). *Strategic organization design.* Glenview, IL: Scott, Foresman.

Pasmore, W. A. (1988). *Designing effective organizations: The sociotechnical systems perspective.* New York: Wiley.

Pava, C. (1983). *Managing new office technology: An organizational strategy.* New York: Free Press.

Sashkin, M. (1984). Participative management is an ethical imperative. *Organizational Dynamics, 12*(4), 5–23.

Trist, E. L., and Bamforth, K. W. (1951). Some social psychological consequences of the longwall method of goal-setting. *Human Relations, 4,* 3–38.

Walton, R. E. (1985). From control to commitment in the workplace. *Harvard Business Review, 63* (2), 76–84.

Walton, R. E. (1989). *Up and running.* Boston: Harvard Business School Press.

Weisbord, M. R. (1987). *Productive workplaces: Organizing and managing for dignity, meaning, and community.* San Francisco: Jossey-Bass.

Zuboff, S. (1984). *In the age of the smart machine: The future of work and power.* New York: Basic Books.

Chapter Three

School-Based Management: An Overview

Rodney T. Ogawa

Paula A. White

American public education has of late been involved in reform efforts of unprecedented scope. Where previous reforms sought simply to improve the existing structure and operation of public school systems, this latest wave is aimed at overhauling, or restructuring, public schools.

School-based management (SBM) is one form of restructuring that has gained widespread attention. Like others, it seeks to change the way school systems conduct business. It is aimed squarely at improving the academic performance of schools by changing their organizational design. Drawing on the experiences of existing programs, this chapter describes how SBM is being implemented.

Themes in the Literature on School-Based Management

Comprehensive reviews of the literature on SBM have revealed several broad themes (see Malen, Ogawa, and Kranz, 1990; David, 1989b). Four have particular relevance to this chapter:

1. The lack of evidence on the efficacy of school-based management.
2. The popularity of the reform.

3. The diversity of school-based management.
4. The difficulty of defining the concept.

Efficacy of School-Based Management

Evidence on the efficacy of SBM programs is not compelling. A comprehensive literature review (Malen, Ogawa, and Kranz, 1990) concludes that there is little evidence that SBM has significantly enhanced conditions in schools and districts or improved students' academic performance.

A recently published evaluation of the School-Based Management/Shared Decision Making Program in the Dade County, Florida public school district, which began piloting the program in 1987 in thirty-two schools (by 1989 all schools participated), is not any more encouraging (Collins and Hanson, 1991). On the one hand, evaluators reported statistically significant differences between project schools and nonproject schools for the overall district on some measures. Project schools had higher scores on more than half of the ten factors assessed by the Purdue School Climate Evaluation. Student attendance in project schools was somewhat better than in nonproject schools. In addition, the evaluation showed that suspension rates in project schools were lower than the district in general. Also, dropout rates in project high schools declined over the three-year period of the project.

On the other hand, the evaluation showed that little or no difference existed between project schools and nonproject schools on other important measures. Project schools fared no better than nonproject schools on school report cards, staff attendance was no better, and student performance on standardized achievement tests did not change during the project.

The lack of evidence of SBM's capacity to enhance the performance of students, schools, and school districts provides an important focal point for this chapter. It is our hope that this chapter will provide an initial step toward understanding how school-based management can serve as an effective approach to educational reform. By systematically describing and analyzing the practices of existing programs, we identify their strengths and weaknesses. If the strengths are reinforced and the deficiencies are corrected, then SBM may finally provide an effective approach to educational reform and the improvement of academic achievement.

A Popular Reform

The popularity of school-based management as a reform is evident in how widespread it is. Approximately one-third of the nation's school districts, located in every corner of the United States—from Maine to California and from Washington to Florida—have SBM programs (Hill and Bonan, 1991; National Education Association, 1991). A few districts, such as Dade County (Florida), Salt Lake City (Utah), and Hammond (Indiana), implemented decentralization plans in the 1970s and early 1980s; the number of districts that have adopted SBM programs has mushroomed since 1986 (Ogawa, 1993).

Diversity of Forms

While literally thousands of school districts have decentralized decision making under the banner of school-based management or other closely related labels, decentralization takes many different forms. Malen, Ogawa, and Kranz (1990) and David (1989b), for example, conclude that SBM programs vary on several dimensions: the level of authority delegated to schools, the domains over which school-level decision makers have discretion, the groups of stakeholders involved on decision-making bodies, and the purposes served by school-level decision-making bodies.

The popularity and diversity of SBM provide a frame of reference for this chapter and a rich pool of strategies from which to draw examples. The large number of programs also reveals that the limitations of current practice are widespread. Further, the diversity of programs suggests that the documented limitations of SBM may be the product not of specific strategies but of the mix of strategies that have been adopted.

Defining School-Based Management

Like so many terms in the educational lexicon, school-based management has a variety of definitions. Given the many forms SBM has taken, the variety of definitions should come as no surprise. In some instances, SBM documents note that such ambiguity is intentional, based on the belief that school-level actors should determine how SBM programs will operate.

After reviewing many and often ambiguous definitions, Malen, Ogawa, and Kranz (1990, p. 290) derived the following comprehensive, if cumbersome, definition:

> School-based management can be viewed conceptually as a formal alteration of governance structures, as a form of decentralization that identifies the individual school as the primary unit of improvement and relies on the redistribution of decision-making authority as the primary means through which improvements might be stimulated and sustained. Some formal authority to make decisions in the domains of budget, personnel and program is delegated to and often distributed among site-level actors. Some formal structure (council, committee, team, board) often composed of principals, teachers, parents, and, at times, students and community residents is created so that site participants can be directly involved in school-wide decision making.

Participatory Management: A Conceptual Framework

The perspective adopted in this chapter is based largely on a framework of participatory management developed by Lawler (1986) and

expanded upon by Mohrman, Lawler, and Mohrman (1992), arising from extensive research and experience in corporate settings.
Mohrman, Lawler, and Mohrman (1992) claim that participation
is positively associated with organizational effectiveness. They identify four elements of participatory management: power, information,
rewards, and knowledge and skills. They advise that the presence
or absence of these features at lower levels in the organization is
essential in determining the effectiveness of a participatory management program. According to this framework, then, each of these
four elements must be present for a participatory management program to be effective. Mohrman and others add that the extent to
which an organization is involved in a participatory system is a fifth
telling point.

Decentralizing Power

Power, according to Mohrman, Lawler, and Mohrman's (1992)
framework, is a key element of participatory management. Thus, it
is fitting that power and its delegation lie at the heart of school-
based management. In a centrally organized school district, the
source of most administrative decisions is the central office (Tucker
and Ziegler, 1980; Campbell, Cunningham, Nystrand, and Usdan,
1985). Decentralized school districts, in contrast, implement SBM
with the expressed purpose of improving schools' academic performance by delegating decision-making authority to the school-level
actors, namely principals, teachers, and parents (Clune and White,
1988; Moore, 1991; Etheridge, Hall, Brown, and Lucas, 1990).
In fact, many SBM plans emphasize the power element to the
near exclusion of the other three elements of participatory decision
making.

In large part this rests on the assumption that school-level
actors are better positioned than district officials to make decisions
for their schools (Northwest Area Foundation, 1985; Hill and
Bonan, 1991). According to this reasoning, teachers, principals,

and parents better understand the needs of the students and communities served by their schools. Moreover, teachers possess the professional knowledge to make decisions about curriculum and instruction.

The emphasis on the decentralization of power is reflected in definitions of school-based management. The definition cited earlier is both a compilation and clarification of other published definitions. The focus is clearly on decentralizing decision-making power, the point at which SBM is initiated. Next, the domains in which that decision-making power is to be plied are identified. Finally, the vehicles through which that power operates and the participants are selected are included in these definitions. The other elements of participatory management are not mentioned.

Three issues, then, arise in the distribution of power in SBM programs: the vehicles for distributing power, the domains in which power is distributed, and the removal of constraints that can limit power.

The vehicle for distributing power in most SBM programs is the school-level council. Numerous school districts delegate decision-making power to school councils, which vary widely in their composition and delegated powers. Some of the more common models are (Hill and Bonan, 1991; Wohlstetter and McCurdy, 1991):

- Community control, which implies community governance of schools; for example, the Chicago School District.

- Administrative decentralization, which implies a dominant role for both teachers and principals; used in, for example, Dade County (Florida), Los Angeles, Rochester, and Santa Fe.

- Principal control, where the locus of authority lies with the principal, such as in Edmonton (Alberta, Canada) or Prince William County (Virginia).

Community members constitute the majority of the membership on Chicago's local school councils; the eleven-member councils comprise six parents, two teachers, two community representatives, and the principal (Moore, 1991). In districts such as Dade County, teachers and administrators share equal representation on the councils. In Rochester, New York, teachers make up the majority of the members on the council. The Los Angeles school district reserves half of the school council seats, which range in number from six to sixteen depending on the level of the school, for teachers, including the school's teacher union representative. The other seats are distributed among the principal, nonteaching staff, parents, and community representatives (Wohlstetter and Odden, 1992). SBM plans operating in Chicago and Hammond provide representation not only to teachers, administrators, and parents, but also to nonparent residents of the school community and to students (Casner-Lotto, 1988; White, 1989; Etheridge, Hall, Brown, and Lucas, 1990; Moore, 1991). In some SBM programs, the formation of school councils is optional. For example, Edmonton's SBM plan requires only that the principal consult with school-level personnel, but does not require the formation of formal school-site councils (Wohlstetter and Buffett, 1992).

The councils are directed by a variety of leaders. Those in Chicago are headed by parent representatives (Moore, 1991). In Kalispell, Montana, and Rochester, New York, the principal serves as chair; in Poway, California, and Winona, Minnesota, the chairperson is a teacher (Koppich, 1992; White, 1992). Some school districts have uniform policies about the composition of the councils (Malen and Ogawa, 1988; David, 1989a; Etheridge, Hall, Brown, and Lucas, 1990; Moore, 1991; Van Meter, 1991). Others allow each school to determine the makeup of its council (Monroe School District, 1986; David, 1989a; Hannaway, 1992). Little published documentation exists on the varieties of school councils in districts where schools have the authority to devise their own governance systems. The sizes of school councils in these districts may vary widely. For example, councils in the Dade County School District range in size from nine to thirty-two (Wohlstetter and McCurdy, 1991).

The type of governance and composition of the councils are linked to politics. For example, Chicago's SBM plan was imposed externally by the state legislature as the result of rigorous lobbying by community organizations and business groups (Wohlstetter and McCurdy, 1991). Since outside players have a strong role in Chicago's educational power structure, it is not surprising that laypeople constitute the majority on Chicago's local school councils. The influence of nonprofessionals on the Chicago councils is exemplified by voting procedures: only six votes (the number of parent members on the council) are required to retain a principal, while seven votes are needed to approve the hiring of a new principal (Wohlstetter and Odden, 1992).

In contrast to Chicago's plan where community and business organizations sought state mandates to bring about school decentralization, SBM plans in Dade County, Hammond, and Los Angeles have been internally motivated, through collective bargaining negotiations. In those three districts, strong union leadership has influenced the development of a teacher contract that calls for all teachers to participate in school-based planning. Teachers make up the majority on these councils (Koppich, 1992; Smylie and Tuermer, 1992; Wohlstetter and Buffett, 1992).

The process for selecting council members varies from district to district. School-site council representatives may be appointed by the principal or selected through an election or on a volunteer basis. Most recent SBM plans call for the election of council members by their specific constituent groups. For example, in Kentucky's SBM projects, parents elect parent representatives and teachers elect teachers (Wohlstetter and Buffett, 1992). Districts in Hammond and Salt Lake City have undergone a conversion in school-site council governance. The Hammond School Improvement Councils, initiated in 1986, were replaced in 1990 by a school-based restructuring process that redefined the roles and responsibilities of council members (Smylie and Tuermer, 1992). Salt Lake City's shared governance program shifted from a focus on administrative control to control shared by teachers, administrators, and parents (Malen and Ogawa, 1988).

Some SBM programs require each school to have more than one council. For example, in the Salt Lake City school district, teachers and the principal usually make up one committee; parents join the teachers and principal to make up a second committee (Malen and Ogawa, 1988). In the Chicago school district parents have their own, separate committee (Chicago Panel on Public School Policy and Finance, 1990). In Memphis, Tennessee, in addition to parent, teacher, and community representation on a school-site council, participating schools also have a professional advisory committee composed of department heads and grade-level chairpersons. Specific guidelines, however, have not been developed as to how these two groups should coordinate their decision making (Etheridge, Valesky, Horgan, Nunnery, and Smith, 1992).

SBM programs delegate different levels of power to school-level decision makers, ranging from making binding decisions to advising or giving consent. The distinctions, moreover, are not always made clear by SBM plans (Northwest Area Foundation, 1985). In some school districts, the power varies between types of participants. For example, SBM programs in Monroe County, Florida, and Edmonton, Alberta, are not explicit about the level of power delegated to teachers, noting that the final responsibility lies with the principal (Monroe School District, 1986; Hill and Bonan, 1991). In Dade County, teachers and staff members make decisions about school programs, while parents and community members only advise (Dade County Public Schools, 1989).

Another issue involves the domain in which power is delegated. Of the many possibilities (Wallace, 1988), the literature highlights three as key domains: budget, personnel, and instructional programs (Clune and White, 1988; Malen, Ogawa, and Kranz, 1990). Clune and White (1988) provide an overview of SBM programs in over thirty school districts and note that the programs generally delegate decision-making power in those three areas.

However, that same overview concludes that the decentralization of authority within school districts falls into four categories: those that decentralize power in all three domains, those that decentralize budget and personnel decisions, those that decentralize only budget decisions, and those that have elements of decentralized management but have no formal, structural vehicle for decentralization. SBM programs continue to reflect a similar range of strategies. Plans in Chicago, Dade County, and Duval County, Florida, decentralize decisions on budget, personnel, and instructional programs (Clune and White, 1988; Chicago Panel on Public School Policy and Finance, 1990; Etheridge, Hall, Brown, and Lucas, 1990; Hill and Bonan, 1991). Santa Fe's plan decentralizes curriculum and personnel decisions but not budget (Carnoy and MacDonnell, 1989), and districts such as San Diego, Cleveland, and Jefferson County, Colorado, decentralize budget and personnel decisions but not curriculum (Clune and White, 1988; Wohlstetter and McCurdy, 1991).

Upon closer examination, we can see that SBM programs employ a variety of strategies within the three general domains. A study of five urban districts' budgeting practices under school-based management is revealing (Wohlstetter and Buffett, 1992). It focuses on several stages of the budgeting process and uncovers variation in strategies in each stage. For example, school boards and district administrators in four districts (Chicago, Dade County, Detroit, and Los Angeles) play limited roles in formulating school budgets. Instead they provide information and technical assistance to enable schools to develop revenue estimates and derive budget items from performance goals. However, in the fifth district (Edmonton), area superintendents and district administrators are more involved; district-level administrators consult with school-level personnel in developing performance goals.

Even more telling differences are revealed by rules governing the allocation of funds to schools in the five districts. In Los Angeles, the most restrictive case, the schools control expenses for instructional supplies and substitute teachers, which account for less than a quarter of the schools' total budgets. In the less restrictive cases of Chicago, Dade County, and Edmonton, officials maintain control over all funds committed by district contracts, which includes teachers' salaries and benefits. However, school councils in these districts have some control over even these funds because they have the discretion to alter staffing arrangements and increase class size. Finally, in Detroit, the least restrictive case, schools receive lump sums based on enrollment counts and control fully 80 percent of their budgets.

SBM programs also vary in the amount of latitude school councils have in making personnel decisions. Schools in all five urban districts determined the experience level of teachers but not the number of teachers; that was controlled by district policies on teacher-pupil ratios. In addition, school councils in Chicago have the authority to hire and fire principals (Moore, 1991). Another study reveals that each school in a southern California school district (unnamed in the study) is authorized to determine its staffing arrangement based on its plan for implementing the district's curriculum (Hannaway, 1992).

SBM programs also use different strategies in curriculum and instruction, ranging from district control of curriculum to almost complete autonomy for school-level personnel. In Cleveland and San Diego, for example, curriculum remains a district responsibility (Clune and White, 1988). Teams of teachers work with administrators to develop districtwide curriculum, while schools make budget and personnel decisions based, in part, on their plans to implement that curriculum. In the Chicago program, curriculum is developed at the school level by teachers and adopted by school councils (Moore, 1991); curriculum decisions are monitored by the board of education and district administration.

A final issue that affects the distribution of power is the web of constraints under which school-level decision makers operate. Schools are subject to district policies, teacher contracts, and state and federal policies. In most instances, school districts require that school-level decisions comply with district and state policies. State and district guidelines or union contracts regarding teacher salaries, standardized curricula, maximum class size, and length of the school day may serve to restrict school-based management and reduce the amount of flexibility that schools are allocated.

Increased involvement of school staff and community members in school policy decisions may conflict with state mandates prescribing curriculum and content. For example, Florida has imposed legislative action about curriculum standardization and some districts with SBM programs have requested special status to diverge from the state requirements (National School Boards Association, 1988). SBM plans in Dade County and Louisville enable schools to seek waivers from district and state policies (Kerchner, 1992; Etheridge, Hall, Brown, and Lucas, 1990; Dade County Public Schools, 1989).

Decentralizing Information

Information, the second element of participative management, has two dimensions: flow and type. Information can flow in several directions throughout an organization. Conventional approaches to management tend to emphasize the downward flow of information from top management to other employees. For example, in a traditionally governed school district, decisions are made at the top and implemented down through the chain of command (Tucker and Ziegler, 1980; Campbell, Cunningham, Nystrand, and Usdan, 1985). This downward flow gives the central office a clearly defined role in the control of a school's budget, curriculum, and personnel. However, as Lawler (1986) notes, the upward flow of information is the other half of the story. In participatory management, both the downward and upward flow of information are crucial.

The types of information that flow through organizations are an important consideration in decentralizing authority. Lawler (1986) identifies two important types: information concerning ideas and information concerning performance. The former concerns issues such as improvements in the way tasks are completed and in employees' attitudes. The latter involves issues such as operating results and overall organizational performance.

SBM programs have focused less on information than on power. Consequently, we know little about the strategies used to channel information. The little evidence that exists suggests that SBM facilitates the flow of information both downward from districts to schools and upward from schools to districts.

Information strategies vary markedly across SBM programs. The superintendent of the Monroe County school district in Florida, for example, has an administrative team that holds bimonthly meetings with the district's principals (Monroe School District, 1986). During the meetings, information is shared by district administrators and principals and decisions about districtwide issues are made. Thus, principals are the key communication link. In the Chicago school district, the board of education and district administrators monitor the curriculum decisions of school councils and assess school effectiveness (Moore, 1991). The Chicago school board and district administrators are largely responsible for the flow of information between schools and the district.

In the decentralization of decision making, the flow of information within schools is as important as the flow of information among schools. SBM councils create opportunities for interaction both within and among schools as well as across grade levels and subject areas. According to Little (1981), the most successful schools appear to be those where school staff frequently exchange ideas about teaching. For example, in the ABC unified school district in Cerritos, California, the SBM councils provided a communication link that teachers never had before (Sickler, 1988). By participating in decisions about school budget, curriculum, and staff, school staff and community members have opportunities to develop areas important to teaching.

SBM programs provide only scattered and sketchy descriptions of the content of information transmitted through school systems. They tend to emphasize information about whether the school councils' decisions comply with district and state policies. For example, in the Chicago school district, local school councils have the authority to adopt curriculum, while district officials monitor the councils' decisions on curriculum issues for compliance with broad, district standards (Moore, 1991). In a southern California school district, school councils must clear proposals for programs that require major structural alterations with the district board (Hannaway, 1992). In that same system, district officials monitor budgets and school plans adopted by school councils for compliance with state regulations.

Less evidence is available on the transmission of other types of information. SBM programs in a few districts communicate information about school or district performance. For example, district administrators in Columbus, Ohio, and Edmonton, Alberta, assess the progress of individual schools in meeting student performance goals (Hill and Bonan, 1991). However, Clune and White (1988) report that few SBM programs monitor district or school progress toward specified objectives.

Decentralizing Rewards

Rewards, the third element of participatory decision-making programs, are important because they can affect the motivation of organizational members. As with information, Lawler (1986) identifies two dimensions of rewards: type and distribution. Two types of rewards are generally acknowledged in the organizational behavior literature: extrinsic, or external, rewards (financial compensation, praise, and awards) and intrinsic, or internal, rewards (those that stem from the work itself). The way rewards are distributed across organizations is an important issue, particularly where participatory management practices are employed.

In centrally managed systems, districts typically do not reward successful schools with more resources and schools receive services regardless of their performance (Wohlstetter and Buffett, 1992; Mohrman, Lawler, and Mohrman, 1992). In decentralized school districts, individuals at the school site may expect increased rewards when they exert greater power and have more information, especially if they believe that their participation has positively affected organizational performance.

Thus far, SBM programs generally have not focused on rewards. However, when they do, they use a variety of methods and are met with varying responses. SBM programs have introduced monetary incentives such as career ladders, lead teacher programs, and peer appraisal systems. Another approach is rewarding with budgetary flexibility, which allows schools to save in one budget area and use the savings in another area. Detroit's SBM program provides financial awards to participating schools that demonstrate improved performance (Wohlstetter and Buffett, 1992). In Kentucky's statewide SBM program, the staff members of schools receiving rewards determine how the money will be spent to support future improvements (Van Meter, 1991). However, other plans such as New York's state reform efforts have not provided schools with monetary rewards for the work required to implement school-based changes or for the student outcomes that those changes may produce (Kelley, 1988).

Efforts to reward schools for high performance have met with resistance from teacher unions and parent organizations. These groups question the fairness of evaluation systems because rewarding successful schools implies providing less support to failing schools. While responses to monetary awards are mixed, Firestone (1991), in a study of merit programs and reward systems, suggests that reward systems that are school-based rather than district-based will allow individual schools to develop systems compatible with their own needs.

At the onset of this chapter we discussed the lack of evidence of the relationship between school-based management and improved student achievement. Since the outcomes of school-based management are entangled with other trends at the school site, or at local, state, or national levels, it is difficult to draw a cause-and-effect relationship between SBM and student achievement (White, 1989). However, some school districts that have decentralized decision making have identified improved classroom practice and student achievement. For example, the ABC unified school district in Cerritos, California, which began to decentralize decision making in the 1970s, has reported improvements in student test scores. In 1970, students scored below the 15th percentile on standardized achievement tests; by 1975–76 they were in the 62nd percentile in math and the 60th percentile in reading. By 1986, they were in the 72nd percentile in math and the 62nd percentile in reading. In addition, both student and teacher absenteeism have declined.

The discussion of employee morale and motivation in the SBM literature touches on implicit rewards that individuals might gain from participation (Malen, Ogawa, and Kranz, 1990). It is widely claimed that teachers who participate in SBM programs enjoy enhanced morale and motivation. As McNeil (1987) stated, if teachers have more input in designing curriculum they are more likely to reach a better balance between student knowledge and the knowledge that students need to know about the world. Studies of school districts such as Dade County, Florida, Kalispell, Montana, Poway, California, and Winona, Minnesota, report that teachers, in fact, do initially gain a sense of greater professionalism from their involvement on school councils (Dade County Public Schools, 1988a; White, 1992). However, these initial positive responses are often counteracted by situational factors, such as the time-consuming character of council participation (Clune and White, 1988; David, 1989a; White, 1992), the difficulty of actors' having to learn new roles (Northwest Area Foundation, 1985) and the resentment of some participants at not being able to make what they deem important decisions (Jenni, 1988).

Firestone's (1991) study of mentor programs and reward systems concluded that for individuals at the school site to gain implicit rewards through decentralization, teachers need to have more time for preparation, improved curriculum, and additional staff development. Seen in Mohrman, Lawler, and Mohrman's framework, Firestone's findings indicate that to improve school performance, the decentralization of rewards must be accompanied by decentralization of power, information, and knowledge and skills—the next element of participatory management to be discussed.

Decentralizing Knowledge and Skills

Knowledge and skills constitute the fourth element of participatory management. This element has received less attention in SBM programs than information or rewards.

In centrally organized school districts, some kinds of knowledge and skills are concentrated at the top, and school staffs are expected to comply with directives from above (Johnson, 1987; Mohrman, Lawler, and Mohrman, 1992). With the decentralization of knowledge and skills, teachers and administrators share knowledge and skills on new instruction strategies, on planning and organizing meetings, in developing school goals, and in designing staff development plans (David, 1989a; Wohlstetter and Odden, 1992).

Lawler (1986) defines three types of knowledge and skills: the work that employees engage in, the process of sharing in decision making, and the overall operation of organizations. For employees to participate fully in decision making, they should possess all three types. The importance of information, as Lawler indicates, raises the related issue of training provided to employees by the organization.

SBM programs emphasize two of the three types of knowledge—instruction and decision-making process—and tend to ignore the third, knowledge about the overall operation of districts. In regards to the first type, SBM programs emphasize contrasting aspects of knowledge about teaching and learning. Districts such as Dade County focus on the need for teachers to be more actively involved in decision making for the very reason that they possess professional expertise on instructional matters (Sang, 1988; Dade County Public Schools, 1988a, 1988b, 1989; Lieberman and Miller, 1990). Other programs emphasize that teachers cannot be assumed to know enough about instructional matters to make decisions (Maeroff, 1988; Hill and Bonan, 1991; Taylor and Levine, 1991).

The second type of knowledge to which some SBM programs attend concerns the process of shared decision making. This type receives the most attention in SBM programs, but unfortunately descriptions are often vague about the specific aspects in which participants need to be knowledgeable. For example, many programs simply make a general reference to the need for participants to understand the process of shared decision making (Kelley, 1988; Etheridge, Hall, Brown, and Lucas, 1990).

Most reports on SBM programs mention a training component. While the descriptions are often ambiguous, it does appear that SBM programs use different strategies to deliver training. The array of training is quite varied, as is the range of funding sources: statewide professional organizations, foundation grants, and diverting funds from other areas.

Schools with school-based budgeting have diverted money to staff development by conserving costs in other areas. For example, an Edmonton school used a previous year's surplus of $30,000 to send teachers and aides to conferences and to provide substitute time to send teachers to visit other schools (Brown, 1990). The ABC unified school district in Cerritos, California, reduced the district management and secretarial positions by twenty-two between 1983 and 1988 and made these funds available for school-level improvements (Sickler, 1988). Some districts rely on statewide professional organizations or foundations for technical support. For example, the Carnegie Corporation of New York has provided assistance to New Orleans' Effective Schools Project and the Matsushita Foundation, provided funding to Dade County, Jefferson County, and Santa Fe for teacher release time to talk to other school districts implementing decentralization plans (Carnoy and MacDonnell, 1989; David, 1989a).

Some school districts sponsor districtwide workshops for teachers and other SBM participants. In Dade County and Santa Fe, for example, outside consultants are hired to lead workshops (Carnoy and MacDonnell, 1989; Dade County Public Schools, 1989). Dade County provided each school with $6,250 to train staff on shared decision making, including school-based budgeting and conflict resolution. Teachers in Dade County, New Orleans, Poway, California, and Kalispell, Montana, school districts have piloted innovative programs and led workshops for other teachers in their district (David, 1989a; White, 1992).

As part of its professional development offerings, the Dade County school district gives teachers minisabbaticals. The sabbaticals run for nine weeks and enable teachers to attend seminars and clinics, participate in internships, or conduct research (Dade County Public Schools, 1989). The Dade County district also offers a three-day conference during which teams of teachers and principals develop shared decision-making skills.

SBM programs vary in the amount of discretion schools have in selecting or designing training programs. In Dade County, Kalispell, New Orleans, and Poway, districtwide committees of teachers design and offer staff development workshops (David, 1989a; White, 1992). In Dade County, Edmonton, and Hammond, school councils control training budgets, which enables councils to purchase or design programs based upon the needs of their schools (Hill and Bonan, 1991; School City of Hammond, 1991). Local school councils in the Chicago school district can purchase training from the district or from independent consultants (Moore, 1991). Councils in the Hammond school district can use funds to pay for substitute teachers to free up teachers to attend workshops (School City of Hammond, 1991).

Extent to Which the Organization Is Involved

Mohrman, Lawler, and Mohrman (1992) identify a final issue that can bear on the effectiveness of shared management: the extent to which an entire organization is actually involved. They note that a great deal of variation exists in the degree to which organizations engage in participatory management. Some programs involve only a few individuals or groups, while others engage the entire organization. Mohrman and colleagues suggest that a shared management system is more likely to be successful if a large proportion of the organization is involved.

The extent to which the school district is involved in its SBM program varies across districts. In some school districts SBM has been a joint effort, with central-office administrators, the school board, teachers' union, and external consultants involved to varying degrees. In the 1988–89 school year, Glenview school district in Glenview, Illinois, developed a constitutional agreement between the teachers and school board establishing procedural guidelines on budget, curriculum, and staffing decisions (National School Boards Association, 1988). In several districts SBM was initiated in a joint effort by the district and a grant-sponsoring agency, which also monitored the projects. For example, the Northwest Area Foundation provided funding for SBM programs in eight school districts, including one in Oregon, two in Washington, and five in Minnesota (Northwest Area Foundation, 1985).

The degree of grassroots involvement is not ordinarily given much attention by school districts considering school-based management. Districts such as Hammond, Indiana, established a committee of approximately twenty teachers and several administrators, parents, students, and community members to create the district's SBM plan (National School Boards Association, 1988). Parents and teachers are often left out of the process to develop procedures and goals in the initial SBM planning stages. Top-down implementation of a reform to have decentralized decision making is less likely to acquire grassroots support than when the movement has grown from the bottom up (Elmore and McLaughlin, 1988).

Brown (1990) has identified three variations on the method of involving schools in school-based management:

1. Move to 100 percent decentralization at once.

2. Permit individual schools to volunteer to participate.

3. Phase the program in over time.

School districts often incorporate both methods 2 and 3; initiating SBM in several schools on a volunteer basis with the intention of eventually phasing the program into all schools. The first method was used by the Chicago school district, which implemented SBM in 1988–89 in all 600 schools (Moore, 1991). Dade County, Louisville, and Prince William County, Virginia, used the second method: only a portion of the schools began piloting SBM (Dade County Public Schools, 1989; Hill and Bonan, 1991; Van Meter, 1991). In its first year of implementation in Dade County, 32 schools participated in school-based management; by the fourth year, all the district's 260 schools participated. The third method was used in Memphis, Tennessee, where only a small percentage of schools volunteered to participate in school-based management, and the rest continued to operate under district direction (Etheridge, Hall, Brown, and Lucas, 1990).

The length of time that a district takes to implement the changes also has important implications. For example, Chicago's SBM plan was implemented on a large scale within a short period of time, without acquiring the full support of the school community. Principals in the district remain the strongest opponents to the plan. Under Chicago's program, principals lose their tenure and their replacements are selected by school councils composed of at least six parents, two teachers, and two community members (Snider, 1989). Such a large-scale simultaneous conversion may entail many unanticipated side-effects. More generally, the popularity of SBM may result in rapid changes without the development of clearly defined goals and high expectations may lead to dissatisfaction with results.

Conclusions

Having described and assessed SBM strategies to distribute crucial elements, we arrive at three general conclusions. First, descriptions of SBM programs remain ill-defined and ambiguous. Second, they use a wide variety of strategies. Third, they emphasize one element of participatory management—power—over the three other elements and over the degree to which a school district is involved. Taken together, these three conditions make it difficult to evaluate school-based management and to determine how existing SBM programs might be changed to enhance their ability to affect the academic performance of schools.

Areas of Ambiguity

Earlier examinations of school-based management indicate that both the concept and descriptions of the programs are often vague or ambiguous. Despite the recent widespread adoption of SBM by school districts in the United States, this problem continues. Mohrman, Lawler, and Mohrman's conceptualization of participatory management (1992), which was used to frame this book, reveals several areas in which the literature is unclear.

Even though most SBM programs are similar in their emphasis on decentralizing power, vagueness on several aspects of the distribution of power remains. For example, in school districts where each school is allowed to determine its own decision-making system, reports often fail to specify which decisions are delegated to different types of participants. Many documents do not precisely report the domains in which school-level actors are delegated decision-making authority (Conley and Bacharach, 1990). SBM programs have focused relatively little attention on the other elements of participatory management and on the extent to which an organization is involved. We know little about the flow or content of information in SBM programs; we know even less about the distribution of rewards; we possess only spotty evidence on the type of knowledge or training that is provided; and in many instances we cannot be sure about the degree to which a district is involved in its SBM program.

This ambiguity makes it difficult to assess the relative effectiveness of variously configured SBM programs. Without a clear understanding of the practices being employed, making meaningful comparisons between different programs and their abilities to affect the performance of schools will be extremely difficult.

Variety of Practice

The research on SBM programs reveals that this approach to educational reform takes many different forms (Clune and White, 1988; David, 1989b; Malen, Ogawa, and Kranz, 1990). With regard to the decentralization of power, for example, programs employ several different configurations of participants. These configurations vary not only across school districts but also within districts where policies allow each school to determine how to set up school-based management. Consequently, SBM programs delegate varying levels of decision-making authority over different domains. In addition, while most SBM programs require that school-level decisions comply with district and state policies, a few grant waivers based on higher-level policies (Fernandez, 1990).

Less is known about the decentralization of information, rewards, and skills and knowledge. SBM programs use various types of communication channels to transmit different types of information. Few programs reward schools for meeting performance standards; most make no mention of such a practice. Programs emphasize the importance of different types of knowledge, although many seem to assume the expertise of teachers and use different arrangements to provide training. Finally, school districts vary in the degree to which the district is involved in school-based management. On one extreme are districts where all schools have been involved since the outset. On the other are districts where only a small proportion of schools will ever be involved.

The variety of strategies employed in the name of school-based management presents difficulties in assessing the relative effectiveness of both general programs and specific strategies. These variations, combined with the problem of ambiguity, help to explain the lack of broad, comparative assessments of SBM programs. In addition, these variations in strategies suggest that an alternative research strategy may be warranted. For instance, researchers working closely with policy makers and practitioners in a series of action studies may be the best way to examine the effectiveness of a variety of practices in different settings. While critics might doubt the scientific validity of such research, such an activity would at least provide comparative findings, something that is almost impossible with more conventional approaches to research.

Need for a More Balanced View

We have noted at several points in this chapter that SBM programs emphasize power rather than the other elements of information, rewards, and knowledge and skills. While this emphasis may be due to the assumptions on which SBM is based, the failure to focus on all four elements may have produced a damaging though unintended consequence.

Mohrman, Lawler, and Mohrman (1992) suggest that the degree to which all four elements are decentralized can affect the performance of participatory decision-making programs. They add that participatory programs may perform better when a greater proportion of the organization is involved. The failure to focus on all elements may explain why available evidence does not point to the effectiveness of existing SBM programs. If the programs are not designed and implemented with a mind to decentralizing all four elements and to involving large segments of school districts, their potential effectiveness may be greatly compromised.

To enhance the potential of SBM programs as vehicles for improving schools and their academic performance, we offer three recommendations. First, designers of current SBM programs need to consider how their programs address the four elements and the extent to which their districts are involved. Second, by reviewing effective restructuring in the private sector, policy makers and architects of future programs need to reassess how they define SBM. Third, researchers who document the implementation of SBM programs should clearly record if and how the four elements are addressed and the extent to which the school districts are involved.

References

Brown, D. J. (1990). *Decentralization and school-based management.* Bristol, PA: Falmer Press.

Campbell, R. F., Cunningham, L. L., Nystrand, R. O., and Usdan, D. M. (1985). *The organization and control of the American schools* (5th ed.). Columbus, OH: Charles Merrill.

Carnoy, M., and MacDonnell, J. (1989). *School district restructuring in Santa Fe, New Mexico.* New Brunswick, NJ: Rutgers University, Center for Policy Research in Education.

Casner-Lotto, J. (1988). Expanding the teacher's role: Hammond's school improvement process. *Phi Delta Kappan, 5,* 349–353.

Chicago Panel on Public School Policy and Finance. (1990). *Chicago school reform: What it is and how it came to be.* Chicago: Chicago Panel on Public School Policy and Finance.

Clune, W. H., and White, P. A. (1988). *School-based management: Institutional variation, implementation, and issues for further research.* New Brunswick, NJ: Rutgers University, Center for Policy Research in Education.

Collins, R. A., and Hanson, M. K. (1991). *Summative evaluation report: School-based management/shared decision making project: 1987–88 through 1989–90.* Miami, FL: Dade County Public Schools.

Conley, S., and Bacharach, S. B. (1990). From school-site management to participatory school-site management. *Phi Delta Kappan, 71,* 539–544.

Dade County Public Schools. (1988a). *School-based management. Shared-decision making 1987–88.* Miami, FL: Dade County Public Schools.

Dade County Public Schools. (1988b). *Superintendent's report: Dade County Schools 1987–88.* Miami, FL: Dade County Public Schools.

Dade County Public Schools. (1989). *Professionalization of teaching/education: Update 1988–89*. Miami, FL: Dade County Public Schools.

David, J. L. (1989a). *Restructuring in progress: Lessons from pioneering districts.* Washington, DC: National Governors Association.

David, J. L. (1989b). Synthesis of research on school-based management. *Educational Leadership, 46*(8), 45–53.

Elmore, R. F., and McLaughlin, M. W. (1988). *Steady work: Policy, practice, and the reform of American education.* Santa Monica, CA: RAND Corporation.

Etheridge, C. P., Hall, M. L., Brown, N., and Lucas, S. (1990). *Establishing school based decision making in seven urban schools in Memphis, Tennessee: The first year.* Memphis, TN: Memphis State University, College of Education, Center for Research in Educational Policy.

Etheridge, C. P., Valesky, T. C., Horgan, D. D., Nunnery, J., and Smith, D. (1992, April). *School based decision making: An investigation into effective and ineffective decision making processes and the impact on school climate variables.* Paper presented at the annual meeting of the American Educational Research Association, San Francisco, CA.

Fernandez, J. A. (1990). Dade County Public Schools' blueprint for restructured schools. In W. H. Clune and J. F. Witte (Eds.), *Choice and control in American education: Volume 2* (pp. 223–250). Philadelphia: Falmer Press.

Firestone, W. A. (1991). Merit pay and job enlargement reforms: Incentives, implementation, and teacher response. *Educational Evaluation and Policy Analysis, 13*(3), 269–288.

Hannaway, J. (1992, April). *Decentralization in education: Technological demands as a critical ingredient.* Paper presented at the annual meeting of the American Educational Research Association, San Francisco, CA.

Hill, P. T., and Bonan, J. (1991). *Decentralization and accountability in public education.* Santa Monica, CA: RAND Corporation.

Jenni, R. W. (1988). *School based management: Implementing an innovation in education.* Minneapolis: University of Minnesota, Strategic Management Research Center.

Johnson, S. M. (1987). *Teachers as decisionmakers.* Discussion paper prepared for the National Education Association.

Kelley, T. (1988). *Small change: The comprehensive school improvement program.* New York: Educational Priorities Panel.

Kerchner, C. T. (1992). *Louisville: Professional development drives a decade of school reform.* Claremont, CA: Claremont Graduate School, Claremont Project VISION.

Koppich, J. E. (1992). *The rocky road to reform in Rochester.* Claremont, CA: Claremont Graduate School, Claremont Project VISION.

Lawler, E. E. (1986). *High-involvement management.* San Francisco: Jossey-Bass.

Lieberman, A., and Miller, L. (1990). Restructuring schools: What matters and what works. *Phi Delta Kappan, 71*, 759–764.

Little, J. W. (1981). *The power of organizational setting: Schools norms and staff development.* Paper presented at the annual meeting of the American Educational Research Association, Los Angeles, CA.

Maeroff, G. I. (1988). The principles of teacher empowerment. *NASSP Bulletin, 72*, 52–60.

Malen, B., and Ogawa, R. T. (1988). Professional-patron influence on site-based governance councils: A confounding case study. *Educational Evaluation and Policy Analysis, 10*(4), 251–270.

Malen, B., Ogawa, R. T., and Kranz, J. (1990). What do we know about school-based management? A case study of the literature—A call for research. In W. H. Clune and J. F. Witte (Eds.), *Choice and control in American education, Volume 2* (pp. 289–342). Philadelphia: Falmer Press.

McNeil, L. M. (1987). The politics of Texas school reform. In W. L. Boyd and C. T. Kerchner (Eds.), *Politics of excellence and choice in education* (pp. 199–216). Philadelphia, PA: Falmer Press.

Mohrman, S. A., Lawler, E. E., and Mohrman, A. M. (1992). Applying employee involvement in schools. *Educational Evaluation and Policy Analysis, 14*, 347–360.

Monroe School District. (1986). *School-based management.* Key West, FL: Monroe School District.

Moore, D. R. (1991, April). *Chicago school reform: The nature and origin of basic assumptions.* Paper presented at the annual meeting of the American Educational Research Association, Chicago, IL.

National Education Association. (1991). *Site-based decisionmaking: The 1990 NEA census of local associations.* Washington, DC: National Educational Association.

National School Boards Association. (1988). *Communicating change: Working towards educational excellence through new and better school district communication.* Alexandria, VA: National School Boards Association.

Northwest Area Foundation. (1985). *School-based management: An interim report, 1985.* St. Paul, MN: Northwest Area Foundation.

Ogawa, R. T. (1993, April). *The institutional sources of educational reform: The case of school-based management.* Paper presented at the annual meeting of the American Educational Research Association, Atlanta, GA.

Sang, H. (1988). *School-site management: The key to educational excellence.* Jacksonville, FL: Duval County Public Schools.

School City of Hammond. (1991). *School city of Hammond strategic planning committee: School-based restructuring process.* Hammond, IN: School City of Hammond.

Sickler, J. (1988). Teachers in charge: Empowering the professionals. *Phi Delta Kappan, 5,* 345–356, 375.

Smylie, M. A., and Tuermer, U. (1992). *Hammond, Indiana: The politics of involvement v. the politics of confrontation.* Claremont, CA: Claremont Graduate School, Claremont Project VISION.

Snider, W. (1989). Chicago's principals fight loss of tenure in reform-law suit. *Education Week,* September 6, pp. 1, 33.

Taylor, B. O., and Levine, D. U. (1991). Effective schools project and school-based management. *Phi Delta Kappan, 72,* 394–397.

Tucker, H. J., and Ziegler, L. H. (1980). *The politics of educational governance: An overview.* Eugene: ERIC Clearinghouse on Educational Management, University of Oregon.

Van Meter, E. J. (1991). The Kentucky mandate: School-based decision making. *NASSP Bulletin, 75,* 52–62.

Wallace, R. C., Jr. (1988). *The instructional cabinet and shared decision making: A position paper.* Unpublished paper.

White, P. A. (1988). *Resource materials on school-based management.* New Brunswick, NJ: Rutgers University, Center for Policy Research in Education.

White, P. A. (1989, September). An overview of school-based management: What does the research say? *National Association of Secondary School Principals,* pp. 1–8.

White, P. A. (1992). Teacher empowerment under "ideal" school-site autonomy. *Educational Evaluation and Policy Analysis, 14*(1), 69–82.

Wohlstetter, P., and Buffett, T. (1992). Decentralizing dollars under school-based management: Have policies changed? *Educational Policy, 6,* 35–54.

Wohlstetter, P., and McCurdy, K. (1991). The link between school decentralization and school politics. *Urban Education, 25,* 391–414.

Wohlstetter, P., and Odden, A. (1992). Rethinking school-based management policy and research. *Educational Administration Quarterly, 28,* 529–549.

Chapter Four

Models of High-Performance Schools

Priscilla Wohlstetter

Roxane Smyer

High-performance schools are those that continually improve their level of performance and the efficiency with which they consume resources. Based on what we already know from the private sector, the way an organization is structured is key to high performance. There is evidence that a high-involvement approach where control over power, knowledge, information, and rewards is decentralized can boost organizational performance and productivity.

In this chapter we examine four models of high-performance schools that advocate restructuring school organizations in various ways in order to improve performance. The four models are Effective Schools, the School Development Program, Accelerated Schools, and Essential Schools. We hope to determine the extent to which these models complement the high-involvement approach and to learn from them strategies that may be helpful in making the connection between school-based management and high performance.

Private-sector management research has linked decentralized control in the four areas of power, knowledge, information, and rewards to organizational effectiveness and productivity (Lawler, 1986). Control in these areas entails:

- *Power* to make decisions that influence organizational practices, policies and directions. The two major power authorities are those over budget and personnel.

- *Knowledge* that enables employees to understand and contribute to organizational performance. Knowledge includes both technical knowledge to do the job or provide the service, and managerial knowledge.

- *Information* about the performance of the organization, including revenues, expenditures, and unit performance.

- *Rewards* based on the performance of the organization and the contributions of teams and individuals. Rewards include the compensation structure, which may also feature incentives or a shift to a knowledge- and skills-based pay structure.

Various Approaches to High-Performance Schools: An Overview

Effective Schools, the School Development Program, Accelerated Schools, and Essential Schools are models of high performance that restructure the school organization in order to better meet students' needs. All four models try to create a unique culture at the school to foster student learning.

The culture of the Effective School centers on the belief that all students can achieve. The principal often functions as a strong instructional leader with responsibility for motivating staff to have high goals for student performance. The School Development Program strives to improve communication between the school and the home. Parental involvement is seen as essential to high student performance. Accelerated Schools deliver a challenging, thinking-oriented curriculum to all students to enable them to catch up with or get ahead of what they must learn. The object is to accelerate rather than remediate students. Essential Schools place greater emphasis on the relationship between staff and students, and devise structures that allow teachers to get to know students as individuals, rather than as members of a large group. The four models are discussed in more detail in this section.

Effective Schools

The Effective Schools movement began in the late 1970s and early 1980s with studies by Ronald Edmonds of Harvard University. Edmonds defined Effective Schools as schools in which student achievement scores (and other indicators of student success) did not vary by socioeconomic status. He associated five characteristics with Effective Schools:

1. Strong leadership by the principal.
2. High expectations of student performance.
3. An emphasis on basic skills.
4. An orderly and controlled atmosphere.
5. Frequent testing of student performance.

Much of the subsequent research on Effective Schools, conducted largely in inner-city schools (Eubanks and Levine, 1983), examined the extent to which these characteristics were present and suggested various ways they could be implemented in school settings. The few additional characteristics that were uncovered in later studies served mainly to embellish Edmonds' original research by refining the nature of an Effective School.

School leadership was an important aspect of the Effective School. Power often was centralized in the principal, who served as the instructional leader for the school, but leadership also could include teachers and community members. The person in the leadership role communicated goals, such as achievement test scores for student performance, to staff; identified problems that were present in the school; and motivated both teachers and students.

Effective Schools also tended to have school climates similar to one another, with school staff who were devoted to student learning and students who knew what was expected of them. Effective Schools exhibited a professional work environment with staff development, collaborative planning, excellent teaching, and low staff turnover. The Effective School climate also featured commonly shared goals and high expectations for the students (Edmonds, 1979; Purkey and Smith, 1983; Wilson and Corcoran, 1987).

Another facet of the Effective School climate was that schools emphasized basic skills instruction and closely monitored student progress in order to promote student learning. In addition, the learning environment of Effective Schools was characterized by curriculum articulation and an organizational structure that maximized learning time, in a setting that was both orderly and disciplined. Finally, Effective Schools made an effort to recognize academic success (Edmonds, 1979; Purkey and Smith, 1983; Wilson and Corcoran, 1987).

Effective Schools also had positive relations with the communities they served. The parents especially were knowledgeable about and involved in the functioning of the school (Purkey and Smith, 1983; Corcoran and Wilson, 1986; Wilson and Corcoran, 1987). In addition, each school was regarded as a member of the community it served. That sense of community helped to reduce alienation between the school and the community and to increase student achievement.

Because much of the research on Effective Schools was conducted in inner-city schools, the student populations tended to be minority or disadvantaged. Two of the three remaining high-performance models also focused on creating a challenging learning environment for disadvantaged students: the Comer School Development Program and Levin's Accelerated Schools.

The School Development Program

The School Development Program is a school-based decision-making model developed by psychiatrist James Comer as a joint effort between the Yale University Child Development Center and the New Haven Public Schools (Comer, 1980, 1988). The plan was developed originally as a way to improve the education of lower-income students; however, Comer (1986) has since argued that many aspects of the program also would be valuable to middle- and upper-income students.

The first School Development schools began in New Haven in 1964. The four pilot schools had student achievement far below other schools in the district, but by 1988, with no change in student demographics, these same schools had some of the highest achievement scores in the district (Comer, 1988). More recently, another Comer school, Columbia Park Elementary in Prince Georges County, Maryland, also showed remarkable progress by boosting achievement test scores from the 35th to the 98th percentile during a six-year period from 1986 to 1991 ("School development," 1991). The network of Comer schools now includes more than 250 schools nationwide (Olson and Rothman, 1993).

Comer's model is a shared-governance approach that seeks to "develop patterns of shared responsibility and decision making among parents and staff" (Comer, 1980, p. 68). The model requires that three structures, or teams, be established at the school site: a school planning and management team, which is primarily responsible for developing a school improvement plan with input from the whole school community; a mental health team, which works to prevent behavior problems and to create an environment of orderliness, mutual respect, and success; and a parent program team, which works to involve parents actively in the school (Anson, 1991). The three structures working together are intended to promote a school-based community focused on continuous improvement.

A school-based community, Comer argues (1980), is necessary for improving student behavior and academic performance and for drawing parents deeper into the educational process. The three teams contribute by providing a sense of direction to the school; by helping to create feelings of shared ownership and responsibility; by promoting implementation of the improvement plan; and by helping to create a cohesiveness within the community (Anson, 1991). Developing a direction for the school and creating a successful school climate are processes that the School Development Program shares with Effective Schools. Also like Effective Schools, Comer schools conduct regular assessments to monitor progress toward school goals (Schmoker and Wilson, 1993).

The community feeling is promoted further by how teams conduct business and how the school campus functions in general. Three primary principles, advocated by Comer, are "no fault" problem solving, collaboration, and decisions by consensus rather than vote. The "no-fault" policy and decisions by consensus help assure that in times of stress no one is able to point the finger of blame. Consensus means that all policies are mutually agreed upon by school constituents. As a result, no one person or group of persons is at fault should an innovation fail. Instead all parties involved in the school must work together collaboratively to solve the problem (Comer, 1989). This process fosters a sense of community within the school by reducing factions that might develop. Agreement by consensus rather than vote also eliminates taking sides. It reduces ownership of ideas and contributes to the success of the no-fault policy, since all members share responsibility equally. Together these three principles help to establish a cohesive, collegial environment at the school that focuses attention on setting and achieving goals aimed at improving student learning.

Accelerated Schools

Henry Levin of Stanford University, who created the Accelerated Schools model, also was concerned about fostering high performance among disadvantaged, at-risk students. Students in Accelerated Schools participate in a challenging curriculum that in the past often was reserved for gifted students. Schools are encouraged to pay special attention to developing students' language skills, both reading and writing (Levin, 1987). Currently, 300 schools in 25 states are pursuing the Accelerated Schools model (Brandt, 1992).

Like Effective Schools and the School Development Program, Accelerated Schools strive to define a new culture and a new set of practices for schools (Levin, 1991a). All three models also advocate creating a schoolwide goal that plainly establishes the direction of the school—what Levin calls "unity of purpose"—and the pursuit of constant improvement.

According to Levin, there are two other important principles of Accelerated Schools. First, empowerment must be coupled with responsibility: school staff are able to effect school change but also are held accountable for results. Second, schools must base improvements on the existing strengths that students and teachers bring to the classroom.

Two distinct change processes, termed Big Wheels and Little Wheels, are involved in creating an Accelerated School (Brunner and Hopfenburg, 1992). Big Wheels are major changes that alter school culture and practice; because of their scope, they generally entail group decision making that represents the school as a whole. An example of a Big Wheel would be a schoolwide goal or a mission statement. Little Wheels, on the other hand, involve smaller change practices. They can be instigated by an individual or a group because they are small, focused projects. Informal innovations, spin-offs, and small creative experiments are examples of Little Wheels. Little Wheel practices are critical to success because they allow for quick action, everyone is eligible to initiate change, and, if successful, they may influence Big Wheels. Big Wheel practices can be viewed as the major, ongoing change process that is focused on moving the school slowly toward its goal. Little Wheels, on the other hand, are day-to-day activities that contribute to the larger change. An Accelerated School is a balance between Big Wheels and Little Wheels.

Results from Accelerated Schools suggest the model is able to turn schools around quickly and improve levels of student achievement. Scores on standardized tests at Daniel Webster Elementary in urban San Francisco went from 69th to 23rd in the district in only three years. At Hollibrook Elementary in Houston, Texas, where 85 percent of the students enter without speaking English, fifth graders raised their reading and language arts scores from the 3.7 level to the 5.3 level between 1988 to 1991. Hollibrook staff accomplished this by emphasizing "hands-on programs and enrichment" and they did it with "no infusion of funding to make the difference" (Schmoker and Wilson, 1993, p. 393).

Essential Schools

Not all models of high-performance schools target the needs of at-risk or low-performing students. Theodore Sizer of Brown University has designed a model, called Essential Schools, that offers a set of common principles to guide change at individual school sites. The nine principles are (Sizer, 1992):

1. An *intellectual focus* directed at helping students to use their minds well.
2. *Simple goals* related to students mastering a limited number of skills and knowledge.
3. *Universal goals* for all students in the school.
4. *Personalization* through decreasing the number of students a teacher teaches.
5. Viewing the *student-as-worker* rather than passive receptor of information.
6. *Student exhibitions* that indicate a grasp of knowledge and skill acquisition.
7. An *attitude* that stresses trust and decency.
8. A *staff* who are generalists first and specialists second.
9. A *budget* that does not exceed traditional schools' expenditures by more than 10 percent.

All Essential Schools adopt these principles but each school develops a unique solution, so that the way they are embodied on the campus varies depending on the needs of a particular school. In 1984, the Coalition of Essential Schools, a nationwide network of schools sharing a common belief in what good schooling practices are and a common method of putting those beliefs into practice, was formed (Sizer, 1984). Since then, it has grown to include 400 schools (Muncey and McQuillan, 1993).

The Essential Schools model attempts to correct what Sizer perceives to be fundamental flaws of American schools, especially high schools. Essential Schools aim to simplify the school day and emphasize content over coverage. Traditional high schools structure school days into seven class periods with seven teachers for each student. In Essential Schools, a common change is to divide a single grade level of students into smaller cohorts, called houses, and then to have them instructed by a team of teachers. The house becomes the basic working unit of the school, and the team of teachers is jointly responsible for the learning of students in its house. Like the three models discussed previously, Essential Schools also stress the establishment of schoolwide goals. Furthermore, these goals, argues Sizer, must be simple and focused narrowly. An example would be "all kindergarten students will know the alphabet before first grade" rather than "all children will come to school ready to learn."

These four models of high-performance schools are distinctive in how they propose to redesign the organization of schools. However, there are similarities across the models. For instance, all emphasize the development and delivery of a quality curriculum that resembles the idea of "teaching for understanding" with its focus on active, engaged, constructive learning for both students and teachers (Perkins and Blythe, 1994). The four models also strive to create a defining school culture centered on student learning, and parents are encouraged to participate actively in the school.

Such school characteristics have been isolated as significant to educational success by other groups interested in fostering a qualified and educated population. One example is the Business Roundtable, which has developed nine essential components of a successful school (National Alliance of Business, 1991). Several of the characteristics are also found in the models of high-performance schools, including the belief that all students can learn at higher levels, that curriculum content must reflect high expectations for all students, that pedagogy should reflect the varied needs of students, and that school staff should have a major role in instructional decisions.

The remainder of this chapter is devoted to the restructuring strategies of the four models, especially those that can be used to promote high-involvement management in schools. How each of the four models decentralizes control over power, knowledge, information, and rewards offers policy makers and practitioners alternative ways to implement high involvement and boost school performance.

Not surprisingly, the models of high-performance schools vary in their attention to and concern with the four resources; however, across all models strategies to decentralize power predominate. Power strategies usually entail giving a wider audience a voice in running the school. Decisions tend to focus around curricular issues at the school site. Though less common, the need for staff development also is acknowledged. Training is sometimes expanded to include all stakeholders involved in restructuring the school, including parents. Strategies to decentralize information are almost exclusively concerned with informing school constituents about the performance and nature of the school. For the most part, individual school performance was not compared to other schools. The least common strategy is to decentralize control over rewards. Where mentioned, reward strategies most commonly deal with rewarding students for performance.

Strategies for Decentralizing Power

In service organizations, such as schools, power includes the ability to make decisions over budget and personnel, including hiring and firing staff (Lawler, 1986). Empowered employees are ones who are able to make both operational decisions—how the organization functions—and strategic decisions—why the organization will take a particular course of action. Power is likely to be what comes to mind when one thinks of leadership and decision making, since powerful people have the authority to make decisions and to ensure compliance with their decisions. Power, within the context of school-based management, is moved away from the district's central office and vested in individual school sites.

All four models of high-performance schools alter power structures within the school organization. The models typically focus on devolving power from the principal in the front office to groups of teachers and community members, especially parents. The one exception to this is the Effective Schools model, which advocates that there be a strong central leader who serves as instructional leader for the school.

To empower school staff, Comer, Levin, and Sizer often advocate shifting decision-making responsibilities from the principal to teams of staff and sometimes community members. For example, a fundamental aspect of Comer's School Development Program is group empowerment, which is promoted through the creation of three teams that practice shared decision making. The team structure gives specific power to members of the school community other than the school principal. It uses the empowerment process as a means of creating a cohesive school community that is dedicated to improving student learning. As noted earlier, the membership of each team includes both school staff and parents. Each team has unique leadership, goals, and responsibilities. The school planning and management team, for example, is composed of parents, teachers, administrators, and other school professionals, and the principal serves as the team leader. The team is responsible for soliciting input from the whole school community that is used to create a school improvement plan and goals. Comer argues that with various stakeholders participating in decision making, no one group is perceived to be in control and so stakeholders work closely together to strive for consensus. The principal, too, must share power, allowing the teams to decide (through consensus) proper goals and courses of action for the school. The decision-making process, Comer adds, helps reduce feelings of distrust, conflict, and alienation that center on power (Comer, 1980).

In Comer schools, as in the other models, teacher groups also may play a role in restructuring schools. Teachers work closely with the consumers of education—the students—and therefore may be best able to assess the realities of the campus. In restructured schools, teacher groups often are central actors in the chain of empowerment and are given opportunities for responsibility, choice, and authority (Lightfoot, 1983). Classroom teachers frequently are involved in evaluating the school, assessing needs, and shaping the educational environment. Sizer (1984) suggests that in Essential Schools teacher teams should help establish the direction of the change process. School Development Schools also view teachers as important resources in curriculum development and so there is a strong commitment to professional development and to providing teachers with opportunities to direct the educational program for the school (Comer, 1980).

Teachers also can be involved in curriculum reform on campus. In Accelerated Schools, teachers are given greater control over the classroom and are able to introduce innovations they find appropriate. As a result, many teachers feel freed from the constraints of the traditional structure and feel encouraged to implement radical change in the classroom (Brunner and Hopfenburg, 1992). Schools also may be reorganized to give teachers more responsibility for fewer students. In Essential Schools and Accelerated Schools, teachers work in collegial groups, known as houses or cadres, and are given wide latitude in selecting teaching techniques. At the same time, teachers also assume greater responsibility and accountability for the success of their students.

There also is evidence from restructured schools that empowering the larger school community is important to school success.

Levin's Accelerated School model requires that 80 percent of the entire school community, including custodians, cafeteria workers, secretaries, student representatives, and parent representatives, vote in favor of establishing the model at the school. Thus, from the beginning school constituents are empowered to change the school. Comer's School Development Program makes special efforts to involve parents in the school. Parents are given opportunities to help in classrooms, through membership on teams and in the decision-making process. Comer believes that parents who are aware of and support what is occurring in the school setting are an asset to the improvement process.

While the majority of restructured schools promoted group empowerment, Effective Schools often were characterized by a single leader, usually the principal. The role of the principal was to set clear goals for the school, communicate high expectations to staff and students, and to create a collegial environment that emphasized order and discipline (Purkey and Smith, 1983; Austin and Holowenzak, 1985). In addition, the leader of an Effective School needed to be an instructional leader by exhibiting assertive, instructionally oriented leadership and by creating and implementing a system of instructional objectives and a means of evaluating progress toward these objectives (Shoemaker and Fraser, 1987).

Across restructured schools, changing power structures goes beyond simply rearranging relationships within schools; it allows schools to create a unique, defining school climate. Groups of people involved in the decision-making process were able to create goals for the school, establish priorities, and allocate resources in accordance with those goals. A significant feature in all four models of high-performance schools was the amount of authority the school was given to define itself. Typically, the models dispersed responsibility to both school staff and parents, who were empowered to define the nature and functioning of the school. In effect, the school was given the power to create its own climate, and school-level constituents commonly used that power to develop a cohesive school culture that promoted student learning by providing a safe environment.

As noted in Chapter Three, school-based management plans have focused on decentralizing power over budget, personnel, and curriculum to school sites. The four models of high-performance schools, likewise, advocate that schools should be empowered in these three areas. Although the models pay scant attention to budget issues, there is evidence that some control over the budget is characteristic of restructuring schools.

Some Effective Schools were permitted to reallocate resources once they were received on campus from the district office (Dorman, 1987). This typically involved adjusting staff time or job duties. For example, teachers may be given an extra planning period during the regular school day in exchange for working after school hours to keep the library open. Another method used by Effective Schools was for schools to become entrepreneurial and find additional resources over which individual schools were able to exert control (Miles and Louis, 1990). Regardless of how successful schools are in procuring additional resources, a key budgetary principle of Essential Schools holds that per-pupil expenditure should not be more than 10 percent above per-pupil cost at traditional schools. Consequently, some services available to students in traditional schools may need to be phased down or eliminated in Essential Schools to accommodate innovation. The school community, not the central office, examines budget constraints and allocates resources to determine what services to decrease or eliminate.

Like budgetary decisions, public schools traditionally have little control over who is hired to work at the campus. Staff often must be hired from district-approved lists and in some cases teachers are assigned to campuses. Effective Schools tend to have at least some discretion in hiring and often have a waiting list of teachers seeking employment (Austin and Holowenzak, 1985; Hill, Foster, and Gendler, 1990). All four models feature a clearly defined vision and performance goals, and this information tended to act as a screening device, attracting staff who fit into the school culture and repelling those who did not. Once staff were hired, restructured schools also spent considerable time acclimating them to the school culture and trying to influence teacher performance. This is discussed later in the section on knowledge strategies, which include staff development.

Curriculum decisions concern the school's academic mission, curriculum focus, and instructional materials. Whereas public schools usually have curriculum decisions made in large part for them by the state or local school district, restructured schools generally have the power to personalize the curriculum at the campus level. A central part of the Accelerated Schools model is the belief that all children can benefit from challenging lessons that are usually reserved for gifted students. Hence, teachers are encouraged to create a learning environment that they would like for their own children (Brunner and Hopfenburg, 1992) and are empowered to design learning experiences that best fit the needs of their students. Effective Schools often tried to influence what was being taught by involving parents and the community in curriculum decisions such as textbook selection (Lewis, 1986; Dorman, 1987). In addition, teachers made efforts to fit school practices to student needs by, for example, developing alternative sanctions to student suspension (Dorman, 1987).

Strategies for Decentralizing Knowledge

New roles in the workplace require the acquisition of new knowledge and skills. In high-involvement management organizations where budgetary decisions, for example, are decentralized to work teams, employees need training in accounting. In addition to training for new job tasks, employees need communication and problem-solving skills to help them work effectively in management roles that involve group planning and decision making. Finally, employees need technical skills for the substantive tasks of the work team. In schools, such training might include instructional techniques for teaching a thinking-oriented curriculum. From what we know about high-involvement management in the private sector, employees should be empowered to identify the areas in which training is given and also to arrange for its delivery.

Staff development is a universal occurrence in schools. The traditional model vests control in central-office staff, who define the training needs of schools and deliver the training off-site (perhaps at the district office). By contrast, the four high-performance models generally support staff development that is developed on the school site, that reflects school needs, and that is offered in a collaborative manner (Comer, 1980; Sizer, 1984; Purkey and Smith, 1985; Levin, 1991b). Restructured schools have shown that school-based training has a myriad of benefits. Support for school improvement is greater when staff development focuses on the individual school (Ornstein and Levine, 1990). In addition, the training is more likely to be tied to teacher needs (Purkey and Smith, 1983); and it also is more likely to contain issues relevant to the school organization. Finally, school-based training tends to be less concerned with remediation—fixing problems of individual teachers or administrators—and more focused on building on the expertise and experience of school staff (Purkey and Smith, 1983).

In terms of process, restructured schools encourage teachers and administrators to work together to develop training that fits the specific needs of the campus (Ornstein and Levine, 1990). When training is developed collegially and related to school improvement, then the staff develop a sense of responsibility, not only for the training but also for the creation of a restructured school. Mutual assistance helps improve teacher interest in training and encourages teachers to feel a sense of ownership (Everson, Scollay, Fabert, and Garcia, 1986). Finally, like the private sector, it is considered important to involve staff development participants in the whole process, from planning the training to arranging for its delivery (Everson, Scollay, Fabert, and Garcia, 1986).

In some restructured schools, outside experts help guide and implement the change process. When a school adopts the Accelerated Schools model, all school staff receive five full days and six half days of staff development from outside experts provided through Stanford University (Levin, 1991a). The training is focused primarily on implementation issues so the school can anticipate likely problems. After the initial training tapers off, the school delivers its own training on an as-needed basis.

In addition to training teachers and other campus staff, Comer's School Development Program extends training to everyone involved in the school improvement process, especially parents. Such training typically is designed to help parents understand the academic and social programs of the school, and how to help their children improve performance (Comer, 1986). Parents play a large role in planning the training; however, workshops usually are led by teachers or other school staff.

Strategies for Decentralizing Information

Whereas strategies decentralizing knowledge and skills aim to improve the abilities of employees, information strategies aim to keep employees fully informed about the workings of the organization (Lawler, 1986). In the private sector, employees in high-involvement organizations receive information about the organization's structure, its goals, employee roles, and the organization's position in the market. Such information gives employees a holistic view of the organization. Being fully informed, moreover, is important to high-involvement management because effective decisions are informed decisions; employees have the information to better understand the implications and possibilities of their actions.

Strategies to help disseminate information within schools are frequent in high-performance schools. The nature of these schools seems to dictate an informed environment. The kinds of information available to school staff tend to be campus-based, not comparative. Restructured schools typically do not have routine access to information about how their school fits into the district system or how their performance compares with other schools serving similar populations, information that is standard in high-involvement organizations in the private sector.

One role of information sharing among school staff is to develop a uniform vision of the school and to create agreement on school goals. In essence, information sharing is a way for school staff to agree on what they are doing (Cohen, 1986). Restructured schools typically include instructional goals among the information that was shared (Cohen, 1983). The goals are clear, public, and agreed upon, and they form a basis for learning objectives.

Agreement on school goals in Accelerated Schools and Effective Schools is fostered early in the change process by involving staff during the diagnostic phase to develop a coherent picture of the school (Purkey and Smith, 1983). It has been found that sharing information with all staff increases a sense of both commitment and responsibility to the organization. Furthermore, through a common vision, which identifies selected goals and expectations, the energy and efforts of organizational members can be channeled toward a mutually agreed-upon purpose (Purkey and Smith, 1983), and also individual performance can be adjusted to conform with school norms. In this way, information sharing among school staff helps to align instructional content and learning activities, grade and classroom instructional objectives, school goals, and measures of pupil performance (Cohen, 1983).

As part of their school vision, restructured schools tend to have written mission statements (Comer, 1980; Sizer, 1984; Lezotte, 1989; Levin, 1991b). Typically the statement was created collaboratively by everyone interested in the success of the school (Comer, 1989). The process was data-driven, using appropriate information about the school, such as school district demographics and student achievement test scores, and relevant research about what works in schools (Lezotte, 1989). The statement also contained core values, such as treating each student as an individual, and the goals for the school, usually related to student performance. The statement also laid out rules under which the school operates. For Essential Schools, Sizer (1992) emphasizes the importance of having a mission statement that is narrowly focused.

With a mission statement in place, everyone involved with the school understands the vision of the school and the goals that the school is moving toward, and then works together to achieve the desired ends. In some Effective Schools, the plans also establish leadership practices for the school, define the school organization and its curriculum, and establish assessment practices for students as well as ways to monitor progress toward school goals (Everson, Scollay, Fabert, and Garcia, 1986).

In all four models of high-performance schools, collegial relationships and feedback are used to inform staff about the school and how it is performing (Squires, Huitt, and Segars, 1983). Information sharing helped to support a school climate in which academics were emphasized, order was maintained, and expectations of staff and students were communicated. Academic success was supported by recognizing successful academic performance; by offering teachers feedback on classroom visits; and by allowing communication on instructional issues through workshops, for example, that fostered collegial relationships. In Essential Schools where teachers work in houses and are mutually responsible for the success of the students, they share information about teaching practices and student performance (Sizer, 1984). In Accelerated Schools, teachers often share ideas that they find unusually successful and sometimes combine classes for lessons (Levin, 1991b). Order and discipline in Effective Schools is maintained by messages of praise and by a mix of rewards and encouragement for positive behavior and swift, formal punishment for infractions (Cohen, 1983).

Across all high-performance models, expectations for staff and students were high and were communicated by informing school constituents of school goals and monitoring progress toward those goals. The School Development Program model, by virtue of its team governance structure, encourages collegial sharing among all school constituents. Comer also uses information to help forge a strong bond between the school and home. He stresses the importance of keeping parents informed about what is happening in the school and parental participation is actively encouraged. Accelerated Schools likewise strive to assure that all members of the school community, including parents, are informed about and support changes that are occurring at the school.

Information sharing also allows current practices to influence future changes. For example, Little Wheel changes in an Accelerated School may affect Big Wheel policies. When Levin's staff first began to implement the Accelerated model in schools, they asked school staff to design the best educational program they could for their at-risk students. Levin's staff found that if faculty members were asked to design the best curriculum for their own children, the results were quite different. Curriculum developed for their own children was frequently more complex and exciting than that developed for at-risk students. Since Accelerated Schools attempt to benefit all students through an undifferentiated curriculum, this presented a dilemma (Brunner and Hopfenburg, 1992). To ensure that schools offer a challenging curriculum to all students, staff are now asked to tailor the school program to fit the needs of *their own* children.

Comer's School Development Program, likewise, works to make all concerned aware of current developments. Comer's schools stress ongoing evaluation and assessment of the school program, and this information is used to adjust the program to the changing needs of the children, staff, and parents (Comer, 1989). Effective Schools also emphasize the importance of providing evaluative information, such as student achievement results, to the school community in a timely manner.

Strategies for Decentralizing Rewards

Rewards are motivators to employee performance. High-involvement management requires that employees can influence the determination of rewards, the criteria for attaining them, and the schedules of dissemination. It also depends on rewards being tied to performance for employees throughout the organization.

Strategies to decentralize rewards are rare in restructured schools. Theodore Sizer (1992) in his model of Essential Schools acknowledges the importance of rewards and asserts that schools should be given control over rewards because ultimately rewards are power. However, no strategies for the decentralization of rewards were offered.

Of the four models, Effective Schools is the only one to suggest reward strategies. Effective Schools tend to concentrate resources on rewarding students for academic achievement. It is hoped that these extrinsic motivators will be internalized by the students and will contribute to establishing a school norm that values achievement. The most common strategy for decentralizing rewards to students is to publicly recognize academic success. One method is ongoing, schoolwide recognition of students' academic success (Eubanks and Levine, 1983; Purkey and Smith, 1983, 1985). Recognition fosters excellence and a desire to succeed. In addition to public award ceremonies, sanctions for poor performance are used in some Effective Schools (Wynne, 1981). Sanctions reinforce the message that the school values high performance and encourages student achievement as a way to avoid sanctions.

Another method used in Effective Schools is to focus rewards on the classroom instead of the school. Sometimes classrooms are restructured for a classroom-based reward system. One example would be to place students into mixed academic-level teams, have teams compete against each other in academic games, and then reward the winning teams (Cohen, 1983). In schools where such reward systems have been used, peer tutoring and cooperation among students increased. This approach also shifts classroom norms more toward achievement and collaborative learning, since advanced students have a stake in the performance of slower students.

Educators have been viewed traditionally as responding to intrinsic motivators. Not too surprising, most reward strategies aimed at teachers in restructured schools are concerned with increasing intrinsic motivators that made the practice of teaching more intrinsically rewarding. The most common strategy is to allow teachers greater opportunities to develop collegial relationships. In Effective Schools, collegial sharing is associated with reduced teacher isolation and less competition among teachers. Collegiality also effectively promotes teaching as a "public art" rather than a practice that occurs behind closed doors (Smylie and Smart, 1990).

Conclusion

The four models of high-performance schools use different strategies to achieve the same goal: increased student achievement. For instance, Effective Schools stress the importance of a powerful leader to guide the school, while Comer's School Development Program attempts to fully inform the community about the functioning of the school and involves parents in school reform efforts. There are, however, many similarities across the four models. The similarities can be grouped into three categories: strategies that promote a school culture; strategies that develop learning opportunities for students; and strategies that foster local control. Each group of strategies encourages the efficient use of power, knowledge, or information by the school organization.

Each high-performance model attempts to create a strong school culture, and efforts are directed at fostering a sense of community that helps to define the school. Establishing a shared culture on the campus requires effective communication and information sharing among school constituents. School Development Schools tried to create a school-based community necessary for improving student behavior and academic performance. The community feeling is promoted by the governance structure that encourages all the constituencies involved to achieve consensus and to take joint responsibility for actions. Accelerated Schools have a unity of purpose: constant improvement. The established goal helps focus campus efforts. Effective Schools try to develop an environment centered on student learning. Students are informed of expectations and staff members support students in achieving school goals. Essential Schools try to break down barriers between teachers and students. For example, teaching loads are decreased to foster personal contact between faculty and students.

Each model also focuses attention on student learning. Accelerated Schools present a challenging curriculum, usually reserved for gifted students, to all students. Essential Schools stress content over coverage in class, arguing that it is better to learn one thing well than to be exposed to many things. Effective Schools emphasize basic skills instruction, maximize learning time, and closely monitor student progress. School Development Schools train parents to become more involved with students and the school. Across all four models, knowledge and skill-based training often are provided to staff and parents to assure that they understand and are prepared for the curricular demands placed on students.

Finally, in each model schools are given some degree of control over school operations. School Development Schools establish three teams to govern specific areas of the school environment. Teams are composed of parents, teachers, and school administrators who work together to effect change. Effective Schools encourage creativity in the way campus resources, such as teacher time, are used. Such schools also often have a fair amount of autonomy in staff selection. Accelerated School teachers are encouraged to create an ideal learning environment for students. The school community of an Essential School decides what services to decrease or eliminate to control costs, not the central office. In sum, all four high-performance models empower school constituents with at least some control over shaping the campus environment.

The one decentralization strategy that the four models of high-performance schools tend to neglect is rewards. The culture of American education is such that educators are expected to be motivated by rewards that are intrinsic and personal. As alternative reward structures are introduced into educational settings, it is likely that novel reward structures will be built into high-performing schools.

Taken together, the four models of high-performance schools clearly complement the high-involvement approach to management. The similarities, moreover, suggest implementation strategies that are helpful in using SBM as a route to high performance.

- Schools should be given wide latitude in defining themselves. This means that they should be empowered to set priorities, define their own mission, and tailor curriculum and instructional practices to fit student needs. Such authority will help schools establish an identity and culture centered on student learning.

- Power roles on campus should be extended beyond school staff to include various stakeholders, especially parents. Shared responsibility helps to diffuse the burden of decision making and to engender commitment to the organization. Shared decision making also helps promote information sharing among stakeholders.

- Training opportunities should include knowledge of issues related to self-governance, as well as content and pedagogical knowledge. It also is important for all participants in school-based management—educators and other stakeholders—to be given opportunities for training and that such opportunities be school-based.

• While the use of financial rewards are uncommon in the high-performance models, schools at a minimum should be given some authority to control their own budgets, so that resources can be allocated to promote school priorities.

In an atmosphere of educational reform where school-based management is becoming increasingly common in school districts across the country, the four models of high-performance schools offer some useful strategies for advancing its implementation by applying the high-involvement approach.

References

Anson, A. (1991). The Comer school development program: A theoretical analysis. *Urban Education, 26,* 56–82.

Austin, G. R., and Holowenzak, K. (1985). An examination of 10 years of research on exemplary schools. In G. Austin and H. Garber (Eds.), *Research on exemplary schools.* Orlando, FL: Academic Press.

Brandt, R. (1992). On building learning communities: A conversation with Hank Levin. *Educational Leadership, 75,* 19–23.

Brunner, I., and Hopfenburg, W. (1992, April). *Growth and learning in accelerated schools: Big wheels and little wheels interacting.* Paper presented at the annual meeting of the American Educational Research Association, San Francisco, CA.

Cohen, M. (1983). Instructional, management, and social conditions. In A. Odden and L. D. Webb (Eds.), *School finance and school improvement: Linkages for the 1980s* (pp. 17–50). Cambridge, MA: Ballinger.

Cohen, M. (1986). Effective schools: Accumulating research findings. *American Education, 34,* 13–16.

Comer, J. (1980). *School power.* New York: Free Press.

Comer, J. (1986). Parent participation in the schools. *Phi Delta Kappan, 67,* 442–446.

Comer, J. (1988). Child development and education. *Journal of Negro Education, 58,* 125–139.

Comer, J. (1989, Spring). Racism and the education of young children. *Teacher's College Record,* pp. 352–361.

Corcoran, T., and Wilson, B. (1986). *The search for successful secondary schools: The first three years of the secondary school recognition program.* Philadelphia, PA: Research for Better Schools.

Dorman, G. (1987). *Improving middle-grade schools: A framework for action*. Chapel Hill, NC: Center for Early Adolescence.

Edmonds, R. (1979). Effective schools for the urban poor. *Educational Leadership*, 37(1), 15–24.

Eubanks, E. E., and Levine, D. U. (1983). A first look at effective schools projects in New York City and Milwaukee. *Phi Delta Kappan*, 64, 697–702.

Everson, S. T., Scollay, S. J., Fabert, B., and Garcia, M. (1986). An effective schools program and its results: Initial district, school, teacher, and student outcomes in a participating district. *Journal of Research and Development in Education*, 19, 35–50.

Hill, P., Foster, G. and Gendler, T. (1990). *High schools with character*. Santa Monica, CA: RAND Corporation.

Lawler, E. E. (1986). *High-involvement management*. San Francisco: Jossey-Bass.

Levin, H. (1987). Accelerated schools for disadvantaged students. *Educational Leadership*, 44(6), 19–21.

Levin, H. (1991a). Accelerated visions. *Accelerated Schools*, 1(3), 2.

Levin, H. (1991b). Don't remediate: Accelerate. *Principal*, 70, 11–13.

Lewis, A. C. (1986). The search continues for effective schools. *Phi Delta Kappan*, 68, 187–188.

Lezotte, L. W. (1989). Features of effective school improvement plans. *The American School Board Journal*, 174, 18–20.

Lightfoot, S. L. (1983). *The good high school*. New York: Basic Books.

Miles, M., and Louis, K. (1990). Mustering the will and skill for change. *Educational Leadership*, 47, 57–61.

Mohrman, S. A., Lawler, E. E., and Mohrman, A. M. (1992). Applying employee involvement in schools. *Educational Evaluation and Policy Analysis*, 14, 347–360

Muncey, D. E., and McQuillan, P. I. (1993). Preliminary findings from a five-year study of the Coalition of Essential Schools. *Phi Delta Kappan*, 74, 486–489.

National Alliance of Business. (1991). *The business roundtable participation guide: A primer for business on education* (2nd ed.). New York: The Business Roundtable.

Olson, L., and Rothman, R. (1993, April 21). Road map to reform. *Education Week*, pp. 13–17.

Ornstein, A. C., and Levine, D. V. (1990). School effectiveness and reform: Guidelines for action. *Clearing House*, 64, 115–118.

Perkins, D., and Blythe, T. (1994). Putting understanding up front. *Educational Leadership*, 51(5), 4–7.

Purkey, S. C., and Smith, M. S. (1983). Effective schools: A review. *The Elementary Schools Journal*, 83, 427–452.

Purkey, S. C., and Smith, M. (1985). School reform: The district policy and implications of the effective schools structure. *The Elementary Schools Journal, 85*, 354–389.

Schmoker, M., and Wilson, R. (1993). Transforming schools through total quality education. *Phi Delta Kappan, 74*, 389–395.

School development program newsline. (1991, April). *District News*, p. 2.

Shoemaker, J., and Fraser, H. (1987). What principals can do: Some implications from studies of effective schooling. *Phi Delta Kappan, 69*, 178–182.

Sizer, T. (1984). *Horace's school: Redesigning the American high school.* Boston: Houghton Mifflin, 1984.

Sizer, T. (1992). *Horace's compromise: The dilemma of the American high school.* Boston: Houghton Mifflin.

Smylie, M. A., and Smart, J. C. (1990). Teacher support for career enhancement initiatives: Program characteristics and effects on work. *Educational Evaluation and Policy Analysis, 12*, 139–155.

Squires, D., Huitt, W., and Segars, J. (1983). *Effective schools and classrooms: A research-based perspective.* Alexandria, VA: Association for Supervision and Curriculum Development.

Wilson, B., and Corcoran, T. (1987). *Places where children succeed: A profile of outstanding elementary schools.* Philadelphia, PA: Research for Better Schools.

Wynne, E. A. (1981). Looking at good schools. Phi Delta Kappan, 62, 377–381.

Chapter Five

The Role of Teachers in School Reform

Susan Moore Johnson

Katherine C. Boles

School-based management (SBM) is meant to change the way school districts do business and, through that change, to improve public education. Policy makers often promote site-managed schools in the hope of drawing on teachers' frequently untapped expertise and expanding their professional influence in important matters of curriculum, staffing, and school organization (Carnegie Forum, 1986; Johnson, 1990).

For example, SBM in Hammond, Indiana, rests on the idea that "teacher participation in decision making provides crucial information closest to the source of many problems and opportunities of schooling—the school and classroom. Increased access to and use of this information, the logic goes, improves the quality of ideas and decisions." Moreover, reformers there assume that participating in school-level decisions promotes among teachers a "commitment to new programs and policies and increases motivation to implement them" (Smylie and Tuermer, 1992, p. 6). Therefore, SBM may at once decentralize governance and augment teacher professionalism in the interests of better instruction.

School-based management is attractive in theory and popular in practice. Almost one-third of the 5,747 districts responding to a survey by the National Education Association (1991, p. 1) reported some kind of site-based decision making. Yet, early research suggests that SBM is difficult to implement and its effects hard to trace. In their 1991 review of the literature, Malen, Ogawa, and Kranz concluded that SBM was "empirically, an elusive notion" (p. 296) and that there was "little evidence that [it] alters influence relationships, renews school organizations, or develops the qualities of academically effective schools" (p. 289). Moreover, they found "little evidence that teachers exert meaningful influence" in schools that experiment with SBM (p. 306).

Interpreting the Evidence

Before 1990, those reviewing the SBM literature would likely have pronounced the reform a failure, for there were few positive outcomes to point to, particularly in the area of increased learning for students. Even now, with more encouraging findings emerging about the implementation of SBM in several districts, claims of success remain guarded. Several plausible explanations exist for the scarcity of positive findings.

First, it may be that actual control over budget, program, and staffing has not been transferred to the school site in any substantial way (National Education Association, 1991; White, 1992) and that, in many districts, SBM exists in name only. For example, Wehlage, Smith, and Lipman's evaluation of the Annie E. Casey's New Futures Initiatives in four urban districts led them to conclude that "in more than one city, teachers and principals felt all along that the call for restructuring was hollow because their freedom to explore different alternatives was sharply limited" (1992, p. 88).

Second, even in districts where authority has been decentralized, schools may lack the organizational capacity to implement SBM. Malen, Ogawa, and Kranz (1991, p. 309) found that "sponsoring systems rarely infuse councils with critical resources (e.g., time, technical assistance, independent sources of information, continuous, norm-based training, funds to assess current programs or funds to develop additional programs)." Similarly, Wehlage, Smith, and Lipman (1992) concluded: "Simply providing the time to meet . . . was no guarantee that teachers would know how to work together in ways likely to result in more engaging curriculum and improved student performance" (p. 76).

Third, it simply may be too soon to expect either full implementation or positive change. Hammond, Indiana, initiated its School Improvement Process (SIP) in 1986. Disappointed with the early results, reformers there declared a moratorium on the effort and in 1990 replaced SIP with a new School-Based Restructuring Process (SBRP), which "shifted the focus from 'doing what we do now better' to reconceptualizing schools and the roles and responsibilities of teachers, administrators, students, and parents" (Smylie and Tuermer, 1992, p. 13). The Hammond experience suggests that finding the right model and making it work take time.

Together, these alternative explanations suggest that those at the school sites must have real authority, enhanced knowledge, more extensive support, and greater time for deliberation and experimentation in order to make SBM work as it was intended. They also indicate that it would be premature for researchers to pronounce SBM a failure or for policy makers to abandon it.

However, there remains the possibility that, fully implemented, SBM may not lead to the changes reformers had hoped. School-site councils can make new decisions, control their budgets, and reorganize their schools without improving children's learning. Or schools may become so autonomous that the resulting system is atomized, inefficient, and inequitable. Murphy (1989) warns about pursuing policies of "radical decentralization." If such policies are pursued, he foresees a time some years hence when "strong schools [will] have thrived under the new autonomy, but weak schools [will] have languished, and some [will] have become captives of parochial interests," where there [will be] "growing disparities in school resources, teacher quality, and student outcomes," and "poor children [will be] neglected" (p. 808).

Although there is general agreement that SBM introduces decentralization, as yet there has been little debate about the appropriate relationship between the district and the schools, between autonomy and control, and between self-sufficiency and subordination in a decentralized system (Johnson, 1991).

In this chapter, we address this issue of balance by analyzing the strategies of local districts as they decentralize. Our focus is on the role of teachers in these reforms. We argue that the most promising approaches view SBM as a two-way relationship of mutual influence between the district and the schools.

Revised Model for School-Based Management

Ironically, although SBM is designed to encourage those in the schools to take charge of their own organizations, the prevailing model for achieving this change is a top-down one in which district officials delegate authority and responsibility. Districts may differ in what they choose to delegate to school-site councils (such as textbook selection or the personnel budget) or in the extent of authority they transfer to the school (advisory or binding), but the transaction is widely understood to be a one-way move of authority, opportunity, and resources from the central office to the schools.

Chapter Two of this volume describes Lawler's model for high-involvement management in the private sector. According to this model, information, rewards, knowledge, and power, which are traditionally concentrated at the top of the organization, are moved to their lowest levels. Extensive delegation of these four resources is intended to promote active participation at all levels of the organization.

This rationale echoes the view of those who advocate school-based management. Since most people think primarily about SBM as decentralizing only power, the three additional factors identified by Lawler enable us to think about the reform in more complex, realistic, and useful ways.

However, there are two assumptions embedded in this model that may limit its applicability in schools. First, applying the high-involvement model to education starts with the assumption that the organization of foremost concern is the school district rather than the school. Many involved in school reform believe that the school site is the primary organization and that the school district is secondary, functioning as a support for school-site efforts. In fact, some reformers focus their efforts exclusively on the schools (Sizer, 1992), virtually ignoring the district as an organization with goals of its own.

Second, this model assumes that the central office is the source of all information, power, knowledge, and rewards, and that school-site councils and staffs are beholden to district officials for all that they have or exercise. In fact, many of the school district's resources already are to be found in the schools.

Although Mohrman suggests that participants at the bottom of an organization can influence its policies and practices, it is not clear how such influence occurs. The empirical literature on teachers' roles in SBM is still quite limited, but recent case studies suggest that a new approach to employee involvement is emerging, one that differs in several important ways from the approach represented in a top-down model. First, schools are not regarded simply as components of the larger organization, but organizations in their own right. While the district organization is understood to exercise legitimate influence on their work, schools are not seen to exist for the sake of the district.

Second, people in the schools have their own sources of power, knowledge, rewards, and information, independent of those bestowed by the central office. The district may delegate to school sites the formal power to select a curriculum, but teachers already hold the power to determine the fate of such a curriculum in their classrooms (Cuban, 1990). The district may provide schools with information about systemwide goals or test results, but the schools, themselves, already possess information derived from school-based planning and portfolio assessments of students' work. The district may offer knowledge in the form of in-service workshops, but teachers have their own knowledge, based on pedagogical expertise, that can be used to inform the system. Finally, the district may dispense the extrinsic rewards of pay and promotion, but the schools are where teachers seek the more valued intrinsic rewards of successful work with students and colleagues (Johnson, 1990).

Third, there is evidence in districts that have seriously embarked on SBM that the emerging relationship between the schools and the central office is a dynamic one of mutual influence, that the practice of each depends on the practice of the other. Adjustment and accommodation are ongoing, much like the mutual adaptation described by analysts who characterized the process of policy implementation in the 1970s (Elmore and McLaughlin, 1988).

Therefore, an elaborated model for SBM would depict both the school and district as separate, though related, organizations; would recognize a two-way exchange of knowledge, power, information and rewards; and would anticipate that there will be ongoing, mutual influence between the district and the school.

Figure 5.1.

Two-Way Mutual Influence Model.

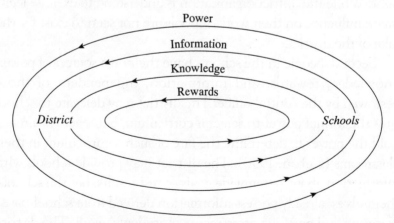

When the four factors are incorporated into a Two-Way Mutual Influence Model (see Figure 5.1), it becomes clear that the potential interactions between the schools and the district are, indeed, complex. In the following sections, we describe and discuss strategies for decentralizing each of the four key factors, within the context of the two-way model.

Strategies for Decentralizing Power

By far the most extensive discussion in the literature on SBM centers on power and whether or how those in the schools, particularly teachers, have it. A few local districts delegate both the formal authority and the budgetary means to effect change in the organization, staffing, and program of the school. Others grant school-site councils only modest authority to think about change and insufficient funds to carry out their plans. The following examples concentrate on those that delegate both power and financial discretion to the schools.

Miami–Dade County's plan for school-based management and shared decision making allocates substantial funds to over 160 schools. "Financial discretion is substantial, as much as $1 million per school. Site-based management of nearly all salary accounts affords schools the flexibility to add and delete positions, including teachers, administrators, classroom aides, and community aides, according to school-determined needs" (Phillips, Kerchner, King, and Koppich, 1992, p. 21.) Schools may petition districtwide committees, composed of teachers and administrators, for waivers to labor contracts, school board rules, or state regulations.

Similarly, Cresswell (1993) studied reform in Greece, New York, and found "a fairly rapid movement toward site-based management and enhanced decision making roles for teachers and other staff in both budget and operational decision making within school buildings." He cited a "dramatic example" that power had been decentralized when the district turned over "all planning and staffing for a new building" to a committee of teachers and parents (p.2).

Kerchner (1992) also documented opportunities for participants at 131 school sites in Louisville, Kentucky, to exercise considerable authority under a program of participative management. Language included in the teachers' contract provides for participation in the program when two-thirds of the employees at the school site have approved it. In designing changes for their schools, councils can request waivers of contract provisions, except in matters of employee discipline and evaluation, personnel files, transfers, lay-offs or recalls, grievances, or compensation (p. 7). Notably, only twelve waivers have been voted by school faculties, most of them in middle schools where faculty chose to add a period to the school day (p. 12). Although the district does not prohibit the schools from dealing with any particular topics, the powers exercised by the councils tend to be more limited than in Miami-Dade. Kerchner observed that, although there were few rules regulating what a school might do, there were self-imposed, "implicit limits." For example, he found teachers approaching "the job of dividing scarce resources very gingerly . . . at first, uncomfortable with decisions that favor one teacher over another." Moreover, "both teachers and administrators wanted to leave personnel rating and assignment decisions in the principal's hands, although some respondents saw this reluctance as temporary" (p. 18).

Hill and Bonan reported that in 1990–91, the central office in Columbus, Ohio, was to "allocate all district funds that exceed minimum state standards to the six communities of schools using a weighted formula that is sensitive to differential local needs and demands. These resources represent a common fund to be used by all schools in the community to fund their reform activities." Leaders of the community of schools would then allocate those funds "based on (1) the activities and programs proposed by the schools in their reform plans and (2) the needs of other schools within the community." Similarly, the district would allocate resources for student services to each community of schools. A school could then "broker resources with other schools in that community of schools, for example, exchanging a school nurse for a counselor, or a mathematics expert for a reading teacher" (1991, p. 78).

Under school-site management in Edmonton, Alberta, schools have discretion over 75 percent of the district's operating budget and control "such day-to-day school operations as budgeting, central office services, and personnel" (Hill and Bonan, 1991, p. 81). They decide when to hire substitutes and do so themselves. In addition, fifteen schools participating in a pilot project can purchase services from the central office or buy them from private providers.

"The bulk of the district's operating budget" is also transferred to the schools in Prince William County, Virginia, but it is the principal rather than a site council who has the authority to draw up staffing patterns, hire employees, purchase supplies, structure the organization of the school, and implement educational innovations. The district office specifies that administrators, teachers, parents, and students must be involved in each school's shared decision-making effort and that all members but administrators must be elected by their peers. The major responsibility of the schools is to draw up an annual school plan, which must incorporate both districtwide and school-site goals. The district then grants waivers on the basis of these plans (Hill and Bonan, 1991, pp. 90–91).

The teachers' contract in Rochester, New York, calls for all schools to participate in school-based planning (Koppich, 1992). Teachers hold the majority of positions on school-based planning teams, which are chaired by principals and include administrators, parents, and students in the high schools. Koppich explains that "each school team negotiates with the district to set targets for student performance and to secure the resources necessary to achieve the school's targets." Although school-based planning teams can decide "anything that directly or indirectly relates to instruction and student performance" (p. 24) and can request waivers from restrictive rules and regulations, budgetary authority is yet to be phased in.

In Chicago, local school councils (LSCs) composed of six parents, two community members, two teachers, and the principal, exercise broad responsibilities for budget, staffing, and program under the Chicago School Reform Act (Moore, 1990). They hire their principals and develop school improvement plans, which must conform to systemwide educational reform goals. Unlike virtually all other SBM plans in the United States, teachers are in the decided minority on LSCs. Those who drafted this legislation deliberately did not vest greater authority in teachers and principals. Moore explains: "School-based management strategies that shift decision-making primarily to teachers and principals are unlikely to lead to major improvements in the quality of services to students at risk and in their performance. Under these circumstances, most schools are likely to make very modest improvements in service quality, since the extent of change is constrained by frames of reference that shape beliefs about what is possible, existing organizational routines, and political bargains" (1990, p. 193). In addition to their two votes on the LSCs, Chicago teachers advise the principal and council through their school-based professional personnel advisory committees.

In each of these districts, there are substantial shifts of power from the central office to the school site. However, important differences exist among the strategies used, the degree to which schools are bound by district guidelines, the range of decisions the schools are empowered to make, the extent of budgetary authority they may exercise, and the number of schools participating.

Hill and Bonan, reflecting on this variation, observe: "Many key issues remain unresolved: Must site-managed schools control their own budgets and have the freedom to select new staff members who fit into the school's academic program and social climate? May a site-managed school create its own curriculum, or should it be guided and constrained by goals and principles of instruction set elsewhere? May a school community, including staff and parents, define the grounds on which performance shall be evaluated, or must it continue to be judged by central authorities on standard performance measures?" (1991, pp. 6–7).

There are also important differences in the relative power of principals, parents, and teachers on the councils. Most districts that have instituted SBM through collective bargaining provide teachers with majority representation. By contrast, Chicago's reform legislation assigns parents and community members the largest number of seats, while in Prince William County, where SBM was introduced and promoted by the superintendent, principals have the final say.

White studied the matter of teachers' representation in her 1992 study of three small districts (Kalispell, Montana; Poway, California; and Winona, Minnesota) with at least five years' experience with decentralized decision making. Ninety percent of the teachers interviewed said that staff had "a lot of involvement in school budget decisions" and 92 percent said that teachers had a "lot of involvement in school curriculum decisions" (pp. 71–72). White concluded that "school-based curriculum development has enabled teachers to recommend new courses, to redesign report cards, to make scheduling changes, to select in-service workshops, and to participate in textbook selection" (p. 73). Teachers held the majority of positions on school-site councils as well as district and school-site budget, curriculum, and hiring committees. White (1992) concluded that decentralization plans that "emphasize teacher involvement rather than community involvement may have a greater capacity for allowing teachers increased input as well as influence" (p. 80).

Teachers' responses to their minority roles on LSCs in Chicago are more mixed. An initial survey of elementary teachers, sponsored by the Consortium on Chicago School Research (1991) after one year of reform found that "about 60 percent agreed that their school is getting better and that they are more optimistic about improvement since reform began. More than half said they felt better about working in their school. . . . While it is fair to say that 'on balance' teachers are pro-reform, it is also fair to assume that in many school communities cooperation among teachers around reform has yet to develop. Prior to school reform, many feared that the radical change in school governance would result in negative consequences. For the most part, these have not occurred" (p. 3). Also, an "over-whelming majority (over 75 percent)" of Chicago teachers surveyed said that the professional personnel advisory committees repre-sented their views and over 60 percent said these committees had "increased their involvement in policy decisions" (p. 5).

There are, therefore, various approaches to decentralizing power within school districts. Some increase teachers' access to decision making; others simply transfer authority from central office admin-istrators to school-site administrators.

There has been little attention to the role of the principal under SBM, even though it seems clear that the principal can be central in championing or thwarting the reform, encouraging teachers to take initiative or quashing the enthusiasm of those who try to lead. While studies repeatedly emphasize the importance of the princi-pal in school change (Fullan, 1991; Fullan and Hargreaves, 1991; Levin, 1991), local programs to decentralize schooling are often characterized as efforts to professionalize teaching and are champi-oned by teacher unions. By contrast, those SBM plans that devolve power to the school and place it in the hands of the principal are not likely to empower teachers.

Murphy, Evertson, and Radnofsky (1991) interviewed fourteen teachers with diverse roles and found them split about whether, under school reform, principals should be eliminated or given more power. Elmore's (1991b) account of District 4 in New York City reveals that principals there have been replaced by teaching pro-gram directors. By contrast, Louis and Smith (1991) found princi-pals central in defining the vision and values of effective schools. Principals in Louisville are expected to make SBM work. Kerchner (1992) explains, "Failure on the part of an administrator to under-stand the direction in which the school district is moving places his or her tenure at risk" (p. 17). The principal is to play a new role: "Principals are expected to develop but not to announce the vision and mission of the school, and they're expected by their staffs to orchestrate the implementation of the mission" (p. 18). Notably, however, the principal's power is constrained: "There is an asymmetry in who gets to vote for reform: the district and union have officially adopted participative management as policy, and the teachers in individual buildings vote themselves in—but individual principals have no vote" (p. 29).

Similarly, principals struggle to define their new roles under SBM in Bellevue, Washington, where local documents ambiguously refer to them as "the key players and the equal partners in decision making" (Malen, 1992, p. 39). In Chicago, where the stakes are high because principals are hired and fired by local school councils, one of their primary obligations is to make SBM work. Policy makers in Pittsburgh have sought to address the ambiguity of the principal's role by introducing a "levels of involvement" scale, which specifies seven different roles for teachers to assume in decision making (Kerchner, 1992, p. 19).

Principals in several districts have actively challenged the teachers' right to assume new responsibilities. Cincinnati principals have resisted shared decision making at the school site. King explains: "They are equally concerned about what the teachers have gained as well as what they perceived themselves to have lost" (1993, pp. 22–23). The administrators' union in Rochester "vocally denounces" the district's reform efforts, complaining that the union never participated in designing the change (Koppich, 1992, pp. 29–30). Recently, though, 85 percent of Chicago principals reported that, under school reform, they have cooperative relationships with their professional personnel advisory committees, which are composed of teachers (Consortium on Chicago School Research, 1992).

Whether or not teachers acquire new power from the central office or from their principals, accounts of school-site restructuring efforts suggest that they already hold and exercise power of their own, power that has not been delegated by the central office, power that principals have not necessarily encouraged them to exercise, power that they sometimes do not even recognize they hold. Shedd and Bacharach (1991) argue persuasively that teachers already are involved in the management of their schools through their instructional responsibilities (p. 33). Lichtenstein, McLaughlin, and Knudsen (1991) interviewed Los Angeles and San Francisco teachers in the Urban Math Collaborative and found them empowered by their "professionally relevant knowledge," even though many were working in traditionally organized schools. The authors argue that "current decentralizing reforms misconstrue the essential spirit of empowerment when they delegate to teachers authority they may not seek or define empowerment in narrow bureaucratic terms" (p. 19).

Similarly, Davis and Sanders (1992) documented that teachers involved in site-based decision making in sixteen Denver-area schools focused on different goals from those set forth by project officials. They found that: "teachers focused on the student learning process to the exclusion of measurable outcomes; that the teachers were successful in bringing about significant changes in instruction and organization of schools and classrooms; and that the changes implemented had little direct logical or empirical relationship to the types of goals envisioned at the state and national policy levels" (pp. 7–8).

Boles' 1991 study of a restructuring project in Brookline, Massachusetts, illustrates teachers' power to exercise collegial influence and to make far-reaching changes in their work with surprisingly little support from the system. By contrast, Potter's 1990 study of one high school faculty's decision not to join the Coalition of Essential Schools illustrates teachers' power to refuse opportunities to participate in school reform that have been advanced by school officials.

Therefore, although certain new powers are delegated under SBM, teachers already have the power to decide whether to implement new programs, whether to spend time in new forums of governance, whether to assume new roles of leadership, and whether to confront their colleagues with new expectations. Successful SBM depends not only on the district decentralizing authority to the schools and principals sharing power with teachers, but also on teachers exercising influence at the school sites and, through those efforts, making SBM work for the district.

Strategies for Decentralizing Knowledge

Two kinds of knowledge become prominent for teachers under SBM. The first, which grows out of participants' new responsibilities at the school site, includes knowledge about such things as how to organize meetings, how to reach consensus, or how to develop budgets. The second, which informs the instructional and programmatic changes of the schools, includes knowledge about teaching, learning, and curriculum. Where school districts have paid attention to the need for new knowledge under SBM, it has been primarily by providing the first kind of training to school-site councils. In the few districts that have taken seriously the need to expand teachers' knowledge about instruction, that effort seems to be less top-down in character and to draw upon the knowledge that teachers and principals already possess.

There are repeated accounts in the literature about the difficulties of making school-site councils work. Chapman (1990, p. 240) reports that SBM in Victoria, Australia, faltered during implementation because school councils needed more than power: "Although the devolution effort accomplished part of its objective to share decision-making more broadly, it is clear that the implementation of the plan suffered from a gross neglect of the need for retraining and in-service activities designed to foster the learning of the new attitudes and roles that were fundamental to the new style of decision-making and management that was mandated." Similarly, White found that the need for training was one of three major constraints on teachers' participation in decision making. Teachers who had been involved in school-based decisions about budgeting reported that their participation was limited because they "had not been trained specifically in participation in school budget decisions" (1992, p. 73).

Some districts plan for such training, although it seems that there is never enough. The Chicago School Reform Act provides for assistance to LSCs, and supporters of this plan contend that "training and assistance must be available over a period of years for local school councils and school staff, from both independent organizations and from the central administration, and schools must have a choice in deciding who to turn to for this help. Further, their ability to choose must be guaranteed by their control over resources to purchase services" (Moore, 1990, p. 23).

Recent research about teachers' roles in shared decision making indicates that short-term interventions are not enough, since teachers must change deep attitudes about their appropriate roles outside the classroom and must learn to think in new, less constricted ways about what is possible (Cambone, Weiss, and Wyeth, 1992).

Some analysts contend that teachers' lack of skills to conduct business on the councils is far less problematic than their limited views about instruction. Elmore (1991b) observes that the "practices associated with teaching for understanding require subject matter knowledge and pedagogical skills well beyond that currently possessed by the majority of teachers" (p. 11). Cohen (1990) documents one teacher's difficulty learning to teach a new mathematics curriculum. Moore (1990) explains that those who planned the reform legislation in Chicago assumed teachers' knowledge base to be "very modest" (p. 193).

In response, a number of districts have introduced plans by which district offices offer a broad range of training and consulting services to the schools. Teachers in Edmonton may purchase services from the central office or hire independent consultants (Hill and Bonan, 1991, p. 18). On the basis of his work with Accelerated Schools, Levin recommends that "personnel from the central office in the various service areas would work directly with the steering committee of a school or specific task forces at the school site" to identify and narrow the problem, "help set out the inquiry process," and "provide the specific technical services needed for addressing curriculum, instructional strategies, staff development, implementation, and evaluation" (1991, p. 21).

Implicit in such proposals is the belief that central-office staff have knowledge that teachers lack. Sometimes this is so, but often it is not. Teachers in many schools contribute rich insight and experience to collective efforts to improve instruction at the school site. For example, Boles (1990) describes how two elementary-school teachers in Brookline, Massachusetts, collaborated with full-time graduate interns from nearby Wheelock College to create mixed-age, team-taught classes; a new hands-on science curriculum; in-class provision of special education services; and released time for faculty to assume new responsibilities in research, curriculum development, and the supervision of student teachers.

Similarly, Miller and O'Shea (1992) report about an elementary school in Gorham, Maine, where teachers have been "engaged in an ongoing process of reflection for almost five years. . . . [The school's] restructuring effort is distinguished by its focus on 'what children know and how they know it' and by its expectations that teachers who conduct systematic and collaborative inquiry in their classrooms will invent new ways to organize instruction and to assess performance. The school makes an explicit connection between the intellectual engagement of teachers and the engagement of the students they teach" (p. 197). Unfortunately, teachers' isolating working conditions and persistent norms of privacy (Little, 1990) often discourage them from sharing the knowledge they have with others.

Several districts have recognized the need to draw upon the knowledge of teachers. For example, Miami-Dade established the Dade Academy for the Teaching Arts, which provides nine-week programs for cohorts of twenty teachers, "planned and operated exclusively by teachers for teachers" (Fernandez, 1990, p. 234; see also Provenzo, 1989). In Louisville, Gheens Academy, a kind of professional laboratory, is the centerpiece of reform (Kohli, 1989; Kerchner, 1992). It involves both teachers and administrators in an effort to "*invent* excellent schools rather than simply to identify and teach promising practices" (Kerchner, 1992, p. 14). Kerchner reports that the Gheens Academy provides both centralized and decentralized opportunities for staff development: "In some initiatives, such as participative management, program funds are almost totally decentralized and lodged at school sites. For other initiatives, such as an initiative on changing student assessment, funds and program operations are carried out centrally" (p. 16).

There is considerable evidence that teachers' commitment to restructuring is enhanced by opportunities for continued learning about subject matter and pedagogy, particularly when staff development is embedded in practice. Teachers involved in Project SHAPE in Toledo collaborated with university faculty in creating curriculum materials and implementing instructional strategies that help to motivate students and accelerate student achievement (Kretovics, Farber, and Armaline, 1991; Gallagher and Lanier, 1992). Louis and Smith (1991) documented the "importance of continuing experimentation and skill development to [professional] engagement among teachers in 3 public, non-selective, lower SES high schools that were actively engaged in reform" (p. 21).

Although there is yet very little research about the role of new knowledge in SBM, initial accounts suggest that teachers involved in the process need a complex understanding of both decentralized school governance and instructional reform. However, it does not appear that the only strategy for increasing teachers' knowledge lies in top-down schemes to move curriculum and instruction experts from the central office to the schools. Rather, more promising approaches, such as the Dade Academy of the Teaching Arts and the Gheens Academy, are joint efforts that draw upon the knowledge of teachers, administrators, and outside experts. They are models of ongoing staff development in which teachers enrich the system with their acquired practical wisdom while drawing on new sources of understanding provided by the district.

Strategies for Decentralizing Information

Lawler (1991) explains that information must be decentralized in high-involvement organizations so that "individuals and work areas" have what they need "to coordinate, manage, and evaluate their own performance. . . . Great care should be taken to ensure that each individual understands the overall operation of the organization and has the kind of financial, planning, and market information that will allow him or her to understand how the business is doing" (pp. 199–200).

In business, employees need information about the company's goals and performance to work productively. In education, however, it is less clear whether teachers should attend primarily to information about the school or the district organization. In part, this reflects a tension that exists in SBM about what to do when the interests of the school and the district are at odds.

In some districts, the constraints on school-site practice are stringent and there is little variation from school to school. In that instance, school-site participants need information about the district's priorities and about their students' performance relative to the district's standards. However, in other districts, such as Chicago, schools are encouraged to develop distinctive practices to meet their students' needs, with only general attention to the district's goals. In that case, school-site participants need more locally derived information about student outcomes.

Evidence from the literature suggests that, to achieve an appropriate balance between school-site autonomy and districtwide goals—what Murphy (1989, p. 810) calls "integrated decentralization"—the organization's information system must also be two-way, with data from the schools informing districtwide policies and data from the district informing school-site practices. Districts are only beginning to recognize the logic of mutually reinforcing information systems.

In Prince William County, Virginia, the individual school is to become "a self-directed, responsible, and educationally accountable entity within the parameters established by the school board and the division superintendent, and where decisions are economical, efficient, and equitably facilitate learning" (Hill and Bonan, 1991, p. 90). The central office there evaluates students' academic progress using "multiple indicators, the most important of which is standardized test scores" (p. 92). Such centralized assessment calls into question the district's stated commitment to "self-directed" schools.

By contrast, a wider array of information is collected by Edmonton administrators, who use "sophisticated, detailed opinion surveys [of principals, teachers, staff, parents, and students] to evaluate and assess how well its schools are performing" (Hill and Bonan, 1991, p. 83). The central office analyzes these data "school by school and administrator by administrator for indications of potential problem areas in schools and in the district at large" (p. 82). In Columbus, each school has ready access to "information on some 40 variables, including attendance, enrollment in certain academic courses, dropouts, and mobility. . . . These data [compiled by the district office] are disaggregated by race, sex, and socioeconomic status." The schools then use the data in developing school plans and evaluating the success of SBM; the central office uses them "in evaluating the schools' performance" (p. 79).

As these examples suggest, information about the operation and outcomes of SBM can be used both formatively and summatively. To the extent that schools are expected to meet districtwide goals, they need information about their performance relative to those goals. If, on the other hand, schools are accountable primarily to their students and parents, as with Central Park East School in New York City (Elmore, 1991a), then they need information about the extent to which they are meeting their clients' needs. If SBM is intended to promote competition among schools, as in a market-based choice plan, then participants at the school site must have information about their performance relative to other schools.

McKenzie (1990) observes that "local decision making is likely to be assisted when schools are able to view their own operations from the broader perspective offered by comparable data from other schools" (p. 184). He argues further that "the challenge is to provide schools with the incentive and the analytical means to use readily available information in a more systematic and focused manner" (p. 189). Similarly, Levin (1991) urges that information be provided to schools "in order to enhance their decision-making capacity." He envisions a centralized system doing this: "To a large degree, this type of service will become the responsibility of the school district, since such information capabilities benefit from centralization and economies of scale" (p. 15).

Case studies suggest that, although most districts can provide schools with data from standardized tests, they are only beginning to give them additional information needed to develop school-based plans and to assess their progress. Phillips, Kerchner, King, and Koppich (1992) report that in Miami-Dade, schools now have "on-line access for viewing updated allocations and making changes. Teachers can see a display of fringe benefits next to each salaried position and the updated total of unallocated funds" (p. 21). Kerchner reports that a computerized system in Louisville, "through which schools report attendance and communicate with the central office, has a data base of grant possibilities that are open to proposals from teachers and schools, along with names of district resources to help write and process applications" (1992, p. 17). Such examples are rare in the case accounts, but they suggest how those in schools might benefit from greater access to districtwide information.

It is important to emphasize that the information system of a decentralized school district must also include data about the combined goals of the organization, generated by those in the schools.

For example, many districts require schools to prepare school-based plans. Current accounts suggest that administrators usually review those plans to monitor compliance with districtwide goals rather than to inform the system about promising practices emerging at the sites.

Information about students' performance on standardized tests is reported, for the most part, by central offices as an accountability measure. Superintendent Richard Wallace of Pittsburgh uses frequent tests to influence teaching practices since "what gets tested gets taught" (Kerchner, 1992, p. 7). Teachers often view this emphasis on test results critically, in part because it disregards the much more complex information they gather daily about their students' performance. However, the introduction of systematic portfolio assessment in districts such as Pittsburgh, San Diego, and Rochester may introduce new balance into this historically top-down information system as the review of students' work moves up from the classroom, to the schools, and, ultimately, to the district. District officials necessarily will rely on teachers to provide them with more complex and meaningful judgments about the curriculum, pedagogy, and student performance. If seriously implemented, portfolio assessment systems will fundamentally change the path of information about the performance of students and the efficacy of the curriculum.

Strategies for Decentralizing Rewards

Translating Lawler's principles of high-involvement management to public education becomes most difficult in the area of rewards. In the private sector, it is understood that high performance leads to greater profits, but funding in public education is rarely increased in response to success. Schools that perform admirably one year may face devastating budget cuts the next. In some instances, this is accidental; in others it is a deliberate penalty for creativity and success, as in a Seattle elementary school where eliminating pull-out programs led to staff reductions (Moody, 1988). Further, efforts to introduce performance-based rewards for teachers and schools are impeded by inadequate assessment systems that fail to adjust for uneven patterns of students' development and high rates of student mobility. A basic tenet of extrinsic reward systems—that the employee see the relationship between pay and performance—has not yet been met in education.

Very few districts engaged in SBM have decentralized financial rewards. Teachers continue to be paid on a standardized salary scale and districts continue to allocate funds on a per-pupil basis, sometimes, as in Columbus, adjusting those allocations on the basis of need. Although policy makers often like the idea of rewarding successful schools with more resources, budget constraints would oblige them then to allocate less to schools that are failing, an untenable approach to school improvement. Although competitive merit pay plans survive in a few places, they tend to differentiate little among teachers and schools. For example, teachers in Granville County, North Carolina, can win a 4 percent salary bonus on the basis of individual and school performance. However, "a full 90 percent of Granville County's teachers earn the entire 4 percent individual bonus. And 10 of the district's 12 schools earned their 2 percent schoolwide bonus last year" (Gursky, 1992, p. 16).

Several districts actively involved in decentralizing school management continue to develop districtwide career ladders and peer-appraisal systems, plans that are consistent with Odden and Conley's (1992) recommendations that reward systems be skill based. For example, both Cincinnati and Rochester identify lead teachers who assume special responsibilities and earn extra pay, although, notably, neither of these is a school-based effort (King, 1993; Koppich, 1992).

Teachers who reach the advanced levels of the Career Ladder Program in Toledo qualify for extra responsibilities at higher pay and can receive funding for projects that reflect their own interests and competencies as well as the district's needs (Gallagher and

Lanier, 1992). Greece, New York, has developed "a system of points to represent the relative value of district-sponsored professional development activities [including participation on districtwide committees]. The points could then be translated into extra compensation of various sorts" (p. 20). Again, this is a districtwide rather than a school-based plan. A few districts have introduced incentives for schools to capture the savings realized by using energy more efficiently or reducing the number of substitute teachers hired, but there is little evidence that districts involved in SBM are moving toward school-based rewards for teachers, even though reformers recommend such plans.

It is clear from research about teachers' work that an effective reward system must include opportunities for achieving both intrinsic and extrinsic rewards. There is substantial evidence that, although teachers are concerned about pay, they are primarily motivated in their work by the prospect of achieving success with students or enjoying collaborative work with peers (Lortie, 1979; Johnson, 1990).

Firestone studied two reward systems—merit pay and job enlargement. Teachers in both programs said that the reforms "changed both how they taught and how they felt about their work." In the merit-pay district, "enthusiasm for teaching declined, and instruction was standardized," while in the job-enlargement district "teachers became more enthusiastic about their work, and instruction became more diversified" (Firestone, 1991, p. 274). Firestone found that job enlargement "created three conditions that increased intrinsic rewards: more time for preparation, better curriculum, and increased training" (p. 277). Such intrinsic rewards are achieved in the schools rather than at the central office. If a school district seeks to develop a reward system with real incentives for teachers, it must augment opportunities for teachers to succeed in their schools.

Conclusion

Although most SBM plans focus on decentralizing power, the other elements identified by Lawler—information, knowledge, and rewards—are important components of any plan to involve teachers in the reform of schooling. Further, although reformers have conceptualized most SBM programs as moving authority from the top to the bottom of the system, we see a different, more promising relationship emerging between schools and the district. It is a two-way relationship of mutual influence that achieves a workable balance between autonomy and regulation, one that promotes invention and community at the school level while ensuring equity and efficiency at the district level.

There are, as yet, no fully working models of such systems, although many districts are moving toward them, devising new strategies as they go. This two-way relationship of mutual influences requires far more complex arrangements for integrating the efforts of teachers, principals, and district-level administrators than the conventional bureaucracy provides. Shedd and Bacharach observe that "the problems now besetting America's systems of public education require more discretion *and* more control, more flexibility *and* more direction, more room for professional judgment *and* more ways of ensuring accountability" (1991, p. 5).

People long accustomed to narrow roles and clearly defined responsibilities must expand their purview and cope with considerable ambiguity. The transition necessarily will take time, money, determination, creativity, and good will. If such resources are available, SBM can meaningfully engage teachers in the challenge of improving schools. If they are lacking, it seems likely that central administrators will reassert control, teachers will retreat to their classrooms, and school-based management will be declared a failure.

References

Boles, K. C. (1990). *School restructuring: A case study in teacher empowerment.* Cambridge, MA; Harvard University, National Center for Educational Leadership.

Boles, K. C. (1991). *School restructuring by teachers; A study of the teaching project at the Edward Devotion School.* Unpublished doctoral thesis. Harvard University, Cambridge, MA.

Cambone, J., Weiss, C. H., and Wyeth, A. (1992). *We're not programmed for this: An exploration of the variance between the ways teachers think and the concept of shared decision making in high schools.* Cambridge, MA; Harvard University, National Center for Educational Leadership.

Carnegie Forum on Education and the Economy (1986). *A nation prepared: Teachers for the 21st century.* New York: Carnegie Forum on Education and the Economy.

Chapman, J. (1990). School-based decision-making and management: Implications for school personnel. In J. Chapman (Ed.), *School-based decision-making and management* (pp. 221–244). New York: Falmer Press.

Cohen, D. K. (1990). A revolution in one classroom: The case of Mrs. Oublier. *Educational Evaluation and Policy Analysis, 12,* 311–329.

Consortium on Chicago School Research. (1991). *Charting reform: The teachers' turn.* Chicago: Consortium on Chicago School Research.

Consortium on Chicago School Research. (1992). *Charting reform: The principals' perspective.* Chicago: Consortium on Chicago School Research.

Cresswell, A. M. (1993). Greece Central School District: Stepping back from the brink. In C. T. Kerchner and J. E. Koppich (Eds.), *A union of professionals: Labor relations and educational reform* (pp. 79–97). New York: Teachers College Press.

Cuban, L. (1990). Reforming again, again, and again. *Educational Researcher, 19*(1), 3–13.

Davis, A., and Sanders, N. (1992, April). *Local decisions and national goals: The irony of restructuring.* Paper presented at the annual meeting of the American Educational Research Association, San Francisco, CA.

Elmore, R. F. (1991a). *Teaching, learning, and organization; School restructuring and the recurring dilemmas of reform.* New Brunswick, NJ; Rutgers University, Center for Policy Research in Education.

Elmore, R. F. (1991b). *Community School District 4, New York City: A case of choice.* New Brunswick, NJ; Rutgers University, Center for Policy Research in Education.

Elmore, R. F., and McLaughlin, M. W. (1988). *Steady work.* Santa Monica, CA: RAND Corporation.

Fernandez, J. A. (1990). Dade County Public Schools' blueprint for restructured schools. In W. H. Clune and J. F. Witte (Eds.), *Choice and control in*

American education. Volume 2. The practice of choice, decentralization and school restructuring (pp. 223–250). New York: Falmer Press.

Firestone, W. A. (1991). Merit pay and job enlargement as reforms: Incentives, implementation, and teacher response. *Educational Evaluation and Policy Analysis, 13,* 269–288.

Fullan, F. G. (1991). *The new meaning of educational change.* New York: Teachers College Press.

Fullan, M. G., and Hargreaves, A. (1991). *What's worth fighting for? Working together for your school.* Toronto, Canada: The Ontario Public School Teachers' Federation.

Gallagher, J., and Lanier, P. (1992). *Toledo: Peer review and beyond.* Claremont, CA: Claremont Graduate School, Claremont Project VISION.

Gursky, D. (1992). Against all odds. *Education Week, 11*(22), 1.

Hill, P. T., and Bonan, J. (1991). *Decentralization and accountability in public education.* Santa Monica: RAND Corporation.

Johnson, S. M. (1990). *Teachers at work: Achieving success in our schools.* New York: Basic Books.

Johnson, S. M. (1991). *Teachers, working contexts and educational productivity* (Working paper No. 14). Los Angeles; University of Southern California, Center for Research in Education Finance.

Kerchner, C. T. (1992). *Louisville: Professional development drives a decade of school reform.* Claremont, CA: Claremont Graduate School, Claremont Project VISION.

King, B. (1993). Cincinnati: Betting on an unfinished season. In C. T. Kerchner and J. E. Koppich (Eds.), *A union of professionals: Labor relations and educational reform* (pp. 61–78). New York: Teachers College Press.

Kohli, W. (1989). Restructuring a school system: The Jefferson County Public Schools. In J. M. Rosow, R. Zager, J. Casner-Lotto, and Associates (Eds.), *Allies in educational reform: How teachers, unions, and administrators can join forces for better schools* (pp. 206–224). San Francisco: Jossey-Bass.

Koppich, J. E. (1992). Rochester: The rocky road to reform. In C. T. Kerchner and J. E. Koppich (Eds.), *A union of professionals: Labor relations and educational reform* (pp. 136–157). New York: Teachers College Press.

Kretovics, J., Farber, K., and Armaline, W. (1991). Reform from the bottom-up: Empowering teachers to transform schools. *Phi Delta Kappan, 73,* 295–299.

Lawler, E. E. (1991). *High-involvement management; Participative strategies for improving organizational performance.* San Francisco; Jossey-Bass.

Levin, H. M. (1991). *Building school capacity for effective teacher empowerment: Applications to elementary schools with at-risk students.* New Brunswick, NJ; Rutgers University, Consortium for Policy Research in Education.

Lichtenstein, G., McLaughlin, M., and Knudsen, J. (1991). *Teacher empowerment and professional knowledge.* New Brunswick, NJ; Rutgers University, Consortium for Policy Research in Education.

Little, J. W. (1990). The persistence of privacy; Autonomy and initiative in teachers' professional relationships. *Teachers College Record, 91,* 509–536.

Lortie, D. C. (1979). *Schoolteacher: A sociological study.* Chicago: University of Chicago Press.

Louis, K. S., and Smith, B. (1991). *Breaking the iron law of social class: The renewal of teachers' professional status and engagement.* Madison: University of Wisconsin, National Center on Effective Secondary Schools.

Malen, B. (1992). *Bellevue: Renewal and school decision making.* Claremont, CA: Claremont Graduate School, Claremont Project VISION.

Malen, B., Ogawa, R. T., and Kranz, J. (1991). What do we know about school-based management? A case study of the literature—A call for research. In W. H. Clune and J. F. Witte (Eds.), *Choice and control in American education, volume 2: The practice of choice, decentralization and school restructuring* (pp. 289–342). New York: Falmer Press.

McKenzie, P. N. (1990). Information needs for decision-making at the school level. In J. Chapman (Ed.), *School-based decision-making and management* (pp. 183–197). New York: Falmer Press.

Miller, L., and O'Shea, C. (1992). Learning to lead: Portraits of practice. In A. Lieberman (Ed.), *The changing contexts of teaching: Ninety-first yearbook of the National Society for the Study of Education—Part I* (pp. 197–211). Chicago: University of Chicago Press.

Moody, F. (1988, May 11). High marks for Montlake. *Seattle Weekly,* pp. 30–39.

Moore, D. R. (1990). *Chicago school reform: The nature and origin of basic assumptions.* Chicago: Designs for Change.

Murphy, J., Evertson, C. M., and Radnofsky, M. L. (1991). Restructuring schools: Fourteen elementary and secondary teachers' perspectives on reform. *The Elementary School Journal, 92,* 135–148.

Murphy, J. T. (1989). The paradox of decentralizing schools: Lessons from business, government, and the Catholic church. *Phi Delta Kappan, 70,* 808–812.

National Education Association. (1991). *Site-based decisionmaking: The 1990 NEA census of local associations.* Washington, DC; NEA.

Odden, A. R., and Conley, S. (1992). Restructuring teacher compensation systems. In A. R. Odden (Ed.), *Rethinking school finance: An agenda for the 1990s* (pp. 41–96). San Francisco: Jossey-Bass.

Phillips, L., Kerchner, C. T., King, B., and Koppich, J. (1992). *Miami: After the hype.* Claremont, CA: Claremont Graduate School, Claremont Project VISION.

Potter, J. (1990). *Bayview High School: A case study of educational reform: The planning stage*. Unpublished qualifying paper. Harvard University, Cambridge, MA.

Provenzo, E. F. (1989). School-based management and shared-decision making in the Dade County Public Schools. In J. M. Rosow, R. Zager, J. Casner-Lotto, and Associates (Eds.), *Allies in educational reform: How teachers, unions, and administrators can join forces for better schools* (pp. 146–163). San Francisco: Jossey-Bass.

Shedd, J. B., and Bacharach, S. B. (1991). *Tangled hierarchies: Teachers as professionals and the management of schools*. San Francisco: Jossey-Bass.

Sizer, T. (1992). *Horace's school: Redesigning the American high school*. Boston: Houghton-Mifflin.

Smylie, M. (1992). *Glenview, Illinois: From contract to constitution*. Claremont, CA: Claremont Graduate School, Claremont Project VISION.

Smylie, M. A., and Tuermer, U. (1992). *Hammond, Indiana: The politics of involvement v. the politics of confrontation*. Claremont, CA: Claremont Graduate School, Claremont Project VISION.

Wehlage, G., Smith, G., and Lipman, P. (1992). Restructuring urban schools: The new futures experience. *American Educational Research Journal, 29,* 51–93.

White, P. A. (1992). Teacher empowerment under "ideal" school-site autonomy. *Educational Evaluation and Policy Analysis, 14,* 69–82.

Chapter Six

Education by Charter

Priscilla Wohlstetter

One approach to decentralizing school management that has the potential to be very dramatic is the charter school concept. Charter schools operate under a written agreement, or statement, of purpose, between a group of individuals and the charter-granting authority, usually a school district or the state. The charter is, in effect, a declaration of independence that enables schools to try to become more effective, free of the restrictions of many local or state regulations.

Both the schools and the charter-granting authority are held accountable by some mechanism for results and for fulfilling curricular expectations. But the means by which those results are achieved are left largely to the discretion of the individual school community. In some cases, the form of school governance is spelled out in the charter-authorizing legislation but, even in those cases, the schools operate with a large degree of independence. For this reason, the growing number of charter schools across the country may offer strategies for implementing school-based management.

Local, state, and federal policy makers are drawn to charter schools for reasons similar to those that make school-based management attractive. Freedom, it is thought, will allow teachers and administrators to deploy resources and tailor curriculum and instructional strategies to better educate students and improve school performance.

In 1992, the New American Schools Development Corporation, a business-backed nonprofit group organized at the behest of the Bush Administration, funded eleven design teams to create "break the mold" schools that are to contract with states to operate as charter schools. Legislation was first introduced in Congress in 1991 to provide federal monies to help establish charter schools in the states (Mulholland and Amsler, 1992), and then in 1994 under the Clinton Administration, Congress passed Goals 2000, which authorized the use of federal monies for charter schools.

At the state level, Minnesota's 1991 charter school measure authorized eight charter schools, and the nation's first charter school opened in September 1992. A charter school bill that became effective in California in January 1993 calls for the creation of 100 charter schools and includes a provision allowing a district to convert all its schools to charter status. To date, nine schools have been approved in California for charter status (Merl, 1993). Other states that have enacted charter school legislation include Colorado, Georgia, Massachusetts, Missouri, New Mexico, and Wisconsin. Lawmakers in at least six other states—Connecticut, Florida, Michigan, New Jersey, Pennsylvania, and Tennessee—also considered charter school proposals during recent legislative sessions (Kolderie, 1992; Olsen, 1992; Schmidt, 1993). At the local level, charter schools have appeared recently on district agendas in Chicago, Detroit, Philadelphia, Baltimore, and Milwaukee (Kolderie, 1992).

U. S. educators are not alone in their apparent fascination with charter schools, which can be seen as a potentially radical form of school-based management. The English Parliament's Education Reform Act of 1988 gave schools the opportunity to opt out of local control and to operate as so-called grant-maintained schools funded directly by the national government.[1] As of February 1994, 693 schools in England, including primary, middle, and secondary schools, had broken free of the local school authority, and another 41 had been approved for incorporation (Wohlstetter and Anderson, 1994).

This chapter examines charter schools as a vehicle that creates school-based management in new school organizations. Charter schools may be newly established or simply converted. Either way, they may offer strategies for transforming schools into high-involvement organizations.

As with our model for school-based management, people in charter schools need access to four resources if they are to use their independence to find ways to increase school performance: power, knowledge, information, and rewards. In what follows, charter schools in England and the United States are examined to highlight strategies for decentralizing resources in new school organizations.

An Overview of Charter Schools

Charter schools are a new category of public schools that offer free education for all their students. They differ from district-controlled schools in that they have a board of directors that is responsible for every aspect of the school's functioning. As noted in Table 6.1, which highlights charter school legislation in England, California, and Minnesota, charters may be granted by the local school board, the state or, as in England, the central government. Charter schools feature site-based management, since they are set up as autonomous organizations and managed by people at the school site.

Charter schools have some similarities to one of the most advanced forms of high-involvement organizations found in the private sector—the "new-design" plant (Lawler, 1986). These are plants that are built from the ground up to empower the workforce by providing them with power, information, knowledge and skills, and rewards for performance.

Many new-design plants have written management philosophy statements that express the values that are important to the plant and how the organization is to treat its employees. Comparable statements also are common with charter schools. For instance, to win approval for charter status, applicants typically must provide a description of the educational program, learning outcomes and how

Table 6.1.

Charter School Legislation: Comparing England, California, and Minnesota.

	England	California	Minnesota
Authorizing legislation	Education Reform Act of 1988	Charter Schools Act of 1992	Outcome-Based Schools Act of 1991
Number of charter schools allowed	No limit	100 schools statewide	8 schools statewide
Organizer	a) Resolution by governing body of a school; or b) Petition by at least 20 percent of parents at a school	Teachers, parents, or community members	One or more licensed teachers
Sponsor	At least 50 percent of parents at a school	a) 50 percent of teachers at a school; or b) 10 percent of teachers in a district	One or more licensed teachers

	Central government (Department for Education)	Local school board with approval of state board of education; right to appeal to county board of education	Local school board with approval of state board of education
Charter-granting authority	Central government (Department for Education)	Local school board with approval of state board of education; right to appeal to county board of education	Local school board with approval of state board of education
Length of charter	Not specified	5 years, renewable	3 years, renewable
School governance council	Size left up to school but must include 5 parents; 1 but not more than 2 teachers; and the principal, who serves ex-officio	No requirements; left up to school	Size and composition left up to school but licensed teachers must hold a majority
Stipulations of charter school contract	1. Members of school governing board 2. Management and administration of the school 3. Admissions policies 4. Provisions for pupils with special needs 5. New teacher induction plan	1. Description of educational program 2. Pupil outcomes 3. How pupil progress will be measured 4. School governance structure 5. Qualifications of school employees 6. Health and safety procedures	1. Description of educational program 2. Pupil outcomes 3. Management and administration of the school 4. Health and safety procedures 5. Admission policies 6. Methods of financial and program audits

Table 6.1.

Charter School Legislation: Comparing England, California, and Minnesota.

	England	California	Minnesota
Stipulations of charter school contract	6. In-service and professional development plan for all teachers	7. How racial and ethnic balance will be achieved 8. Admissions policies 9. Methods of financial and program audits 10. Procedures for suspending and expelling students 11. Attendance alternatives for pupils not attending charter school 12. Employee rights	7. Insurance coverage

they will be measured, classroom organization and instructional approach, and a plan for managing and administering the school. With new-design plants, the management statement often is used as a screening device to select employees compatible with the organization's philosophy; and over time, the statement has served as a check to ensure that as the plant matures, new developments are congruent with the original philosophy.

In the United States, the charter school concept first surfaced during the late 1980s when Ray Budde, an educational consultant in Massachusetts, wrote a report entitled *Education by Charter* (1988) that was subsequently popularized by Albert Shanker, president of the American Federation of Teachers, in his *New York Times* column, "Where We Stand" (July 10, 1988). Budde proposed the charter school idea as a way to empower teachers by creating new professional opportunities, such as the opportunity to be responsible for the learning program at the school site. Budde envisioned groups of teachers designing instructional programs, filing applications for charter school status, and being awarded the charters directly either from the local school board or from the state. Charter schools in the United States continue to be viewed as a vehicle for teacher professionalism. Both the California and Minnesota laws state specifically that a key purpose of charter schools is to "create new professional opportunities for teachers, including the opportunity to be responsible for the learning program at the school site."

In contrast to initiatives in the United States, England's policy was not designed specifically to expand professional opportunities for teachers, and this is reflected in the content of the law. As noted in Table 6.1, teachers have no vote as to whether their school applies for grant-maintained status; and once a school opts out, its governing board is obligated to have one but not more than two teachers (compared to five parent representatives).

According to Davies and Anderson (1992), the rationale for changing the education system in England related more to the need for greater flexibility and accountability in schools. Proponents believed that if schools were freed from bureaucratic control and allowed to manage themselves, alternative educational programs would surface to respond more effectively to student needs. This, in turn, would expand the range of public school options available to parents and students. Charter school laws in California and Minnesota also push to increase learning opportunities for students and encourage the use of innovative teaching methods. California's Charter Schools Act, intended partly to head off a voucher initiative that was on the ballot in 1993, is even more direct in promoting choice through charter schools. One of the act's stated purposes is to "provide parents and pupils with expanded *choices* in the types of educational opportunities that are available within the public school system."

Reformers both here and in England also were concerned about accountability. One form of accountability relates to the fact that charter schools operate like schools of choice or magnet schools: they are grounded in an educational marketplace philosophy. Charter schools must compete for students; if they cannot attract enough students (and tuition dollars), their existence may be jeopardized. Thus, one form of accountability is directed outside the professional hierarchy—the local school board and district superintendent—toward the community: parents may choose not to send their children to the school.

Another form of accountability rests with the party that grants the charter—that is, the funding authority. In the United States as in England, a key feature of all charter school reforms has been holding schools accountable for educational outcomes, not process. Charter schools, through their contracts, set forth outcomes or goals for students and the method by which student progress will be measured (see Table 6.1). California's Charter Schools Act states that the charter will not be renewed by the local school district or state if the school "does not demonstrate educational achievement at least equal to the average of all schools in the state with similar grade levels or if the school is not complying with terms of the charter." Minnesota's law, known as the outcome-based charter schools bill, also ties accountability to pupil performance, stating that a contract may be terminated or not renewed by the state if the school fails to meet the requirements for pupil performance contained in the contract.

Although schools set their own goals, charter schools must comply with curriculum policies set forth by state and local governments, much like schools that remain under district control. Grant-maintained schools in England are required to deliver the national curriculum and to use national tests to evaluate student learning. California and Minnesota, likewise, have statewide performance standards, and charter schools are held accountable for achieving these learner outcomes, in addition to any additional outcomes that may be in the contract. California also has a statewide student assessment system that charter schools must use. Further, charter schools both here and in England are subject to the same audits as district schools, including financial, program, and compliance audits. In these ways, charter schools are not much different from schools operated by the district.

In the United States, accountability to the funding authority is further strengthened by the fact that charter schools exist under a written agreement with a fixed term of three or five years. This has the effect of a sunset provision; it triggers an *automatic* review of the school before the agreement is renewed. Whereas a state department of education is very reluctant to shut down a local school district or take it over, the charter agreement may be revoked if the school does not achieve the conditions of its agreement by the end of the contract period. By contrast, grant-maintained schools in England are not set up on a fixed-term agreement. The schools continue to exist and be funded unless the secretary of state for education takes action to close an individual school.

Decentralization Strategies

The discussion now turns to strategies for decentralizing power, knowledge, information, and rewards in new school organizations. Research on new-design plants, a parallel phenomenon in the private sector, suggests they are revolutionary in the degree to which they move resources and decision-making powers to the lowest levels of the organization (Lawler, 1978, 1986).

Power

As with school-based management, charter schools typically establish their own governing bodies to handle the new policy-making and management responsibilities of the school site. These governing bodies are composed of some combination of administrators, teachers, parents, and community representatives, some appointed and others elected (see Table 6.1). Because it is a representative body, it may or may not create the feeling of an increase in management levels; that depends on the extent to which this group operates in a manner that empowers the staff or controls the staff.

As suggested earlier, the political motivations for charter schools in England and the United States were somewhat different; as a result, the forms of decentralization adopted seek to empower different groups (see Wohlstetter and McCurdy, 1991). Consider the decision to initiate a change to charter status. In the United States, where the reform is linked to teacher professionalism, teachers have a great deal of influence, even veto power over whether the change occurs. In Minnesota, for example, only licensed teachers can ask a local school board to authorize a charter, subject to approval by the state board of education. Once a charter is granted, the school's licensed teachers must be a majority of the members of the governing board. California's Charter Schools Act allows parents and community members as well as teachers to petition to start a charter school. But 50 percent of the teachers at the school or 10 percent of those in the district must approve before a request for charter status can be submitted to the district. Because of that, in practice, teachers will likely control the governing bodies of charter schools in California.

In England, reformers were more interested in strengthening lay control over schools and so the majority of people on the governing body, which is known as the board of governors, must be community representatives. This is similar to Chicago's local school councils under school-based management. In addition to community members who are invited to serve on the basis of their expertise, there are some elected members on the board of governors: five parents and one or two teachers.[2] Indicative of England's push for community control is the fact that a majority of a school's parents must approve the application for grant-maintained status before it is considered by the secretary of state for education. Table 6.1 compares the organizers and sponsors of charter schools in England, California, and Minnesota.

Reformers in England intended that the board adopt a strategic, policy-making role and leave the tactical management of the school to the senior staff. The principal, who serves ex officio on the governing board, runs the school on a day-to-day basis and is largely responsible for administration of the school, including the use of buildings and monitoring school performance. The governing body of a grant-maintained school is equivalent to the board of trustees of a private school, while the principal acts as school headmaster. This is in contrast to many site-managed schools in the United States, where the division of responsibility between the school's governing board and principal is often ambiguous and provides a real challenge.

In the United States, there is less division between governing and management responsibilities. As noted in Chapter Three, the tendency in the United States is to endow site councils with the duties of both a governing board and the principal. Minnesota's charter school law states that the role of the governing board is "to decide matters related to the operation of the school," including hiring and firing staff, contracting for services, budgeting, curriculum, and operating procedures. In England these are defined as day-to-day management responsibilities under the jurisdiction of the principal. California's charter school measure allows each school to define its own governance structure, which presumably could feature the principal as school manager, as in England, or the site council in a management role.

Charter school reforms in the United States and England vest school sites with considerable control in the areas of budget and personnel. On a management continuum ranging from centralized district control to decentralized management with school-site discretion, charter schools are at the decentralized end in terms of the amount of discretion sites have over budget and personnel. By contrast, most school-based management projects fall somewhere in the middle of the continuum.

In terms of budget, charter schools receive lump-sum allocations from the charter-granting authority—England's Department for Education and local school boards in the United States. The school is allowed to determine how to budget and expend those monies without intervention by funding authorities. Notwithstanding this autonomy, charter schools are subject to financial audits just as district schools are. Across the three charter programs, the bulk of the money is allocated based on some measure of per-pupil expenditure. In addition, charter schools receive their share of categorical funds based on the numbers of, for example, compensatory education and special education students enrolled.

In England, an often-cited reason for opting out and becoming grant-maintained is that it increases the resources available to the school. For example, grant-maintained schools receive their share of the district's expenditures on centrally provided services, which is on average about 15 percent of direct costs for grant-maintained schools. Consequently, every time a school opts out, the budget of the local school district is reduced to reflect the shift of money directly to the school. By contrast, charter school laws in the United States usually do not offer extra money for administrative costs or start-up costs.[3]

Financial incentives available to grant-maintained schools in England also include two seed grants that can be used during the transitional period—the time from approval to incorporation—and immediately thereafter. The first seed grant, called the transitional grant, is made available to the new governing body of a school immediately after approval and is used to prepare for grant-maintained status. Schools typically use transitional grants to purchase computer and communication systems, and to recruit and select staff to be employed after incorporation or to begin employment, if they are administrative staff whose work is directly related to the school's preparation for grant-maintained status.

The second seed grant is known as special purpose grant (restructuring); the board of governors of newly approved or incorporated grant-maintained schools can apply for this grant. It is available to support staff restructuring during the school's early period of grant-maintained status. Often the grant is used to finance lump-sum payments to staff who are laid off or retire early, where it can be demonstrated that management restructuring has resulted in certain staff positions being excess to future needs.

In the area of personnel, charter schools have the flexibility to determine how many staff are needed and at what level of salary. In both the England and the United States, charter schools are permitted to opt out of labor contracts. Whereas traditional schools receive a fixed number of staff according to the contract's student-teacher ratio, charter schools have the flexibility to set pay and conditions for teachers and administrators. England's Department for Education is encouraging schools to experiment with performance-based pay. In California charter schools are allowed to decide if they want to hire teachers who are *not* licensed by the state, as is the practice in private schools.

In contrast to new-design plants in the private sector, where the trend is to eliminate management levels, England's grant-maintained schools tend to expand management staff at the school site. Nearly all grant-maintained schools have appointed a staff person to handle the increase in financial and administrative responsibilities at the school site. Previously such matters were handled within the principal's office, usually by an administrative assistant. Grant-maintained schools typically create a completely new position at the vice-principal level, called bursar-administrator, and the person hired is frequently from outside the world of education. The bursar-administrator then becomes a member of the school's senior management team and brings to the team knowledge about all the noneducational facets of the school. The role usually encompasses at least some aspects of financial management, personnel management (particularly administrative staff), contracts, leasing, sites and buildings, capital development, marketing and fundraising. By contrast, many new-design plants tend to be very lightly staffed in support personnel. Functions like budgeting are as much as possible decentralized to work teams (Lawler, 1986).

Approaches other than creating a new position also have been adopted by grant-maintained schools. In some schools, particularly primary schools, the position of administrative assistant to the principal has been upgraded to take on financial administration, or one of the vice-principals has been moved into this position. Primary schools usually find the cost of employing a bursar-administrator as part of the senior management team prohibitively expensive, and so such responsibilities have been shared among existing teaching and nonteaching staff. However, unlike work teams in the private sector that are organized on a product or area basis, there is little evidence that charter schools are restructuring staff into teams and empowering them with budgeting or personnel authority to improve student performance.

In conclusion, charter school status vests schools with considerable discretion in the areas of budget and personnel. It is important to note, however, that the devolution of power, at least in

England, was not immediate but gradual. Parliament's Education Reform Act of 1988, in addition to authorizing grant-maintained schools, mandated that all schools move to site-based management, or what is known in England as Local Management of Schools (LMS). LMS schools remain part of the district but are given responsibility, for important aspects of resource management. This means that all grant-maintained schools first gain experience with school-based management before becoming completely independent.

The effect has been that school staff and governing board members have taken on additional financial and administrative responsibilities over a period of time, thereby allowing them to develop the appropriate skills and to gain experience. At the same time, district offices under LMS are downsizing and retooling for their new, more service-oriented roles. In this way, the move to grant-maintained status has been a natural progression from LMS, and staff and board members have felt more confident about taking the step to total self-management.

In sum, this developmental approach (as opposed to an immediate radical change) has supported and encouraged management changes at the school and district levels that are required for effective site-based management. In the United States, the progression from school-based management to charter status was not built into the reforms. Consequently, as schools gain experience with site decision making and begin to formulate plans that require deviation from district practices, they must continue to rely on waiver processes. There is usually not a planned progression to increased authority.

Knowledge

Lawler argues that for individuals in an organization to exercise power, they must have managerial knowledge, including administrative and financial skills, interpersonal skills for group work, and technical skills. In new-design plants, training also is viewed as a way to develop consensus around desirable organizational goals and to develop the kind of coordination and cooperation needed to begin operations.

In school districts, the central office typically coordinates and organizes professional development activities whether or not schools request services. The training, moreover, tends to be one-shot and may not be related to the needs of the school. Charter schools decide for themselves what training should be offered, who should provide it, and how much should be spent on it.

Grant-maintained schools are required to lay out their plan for the induction and in-service training of teachers in their application for grant-maintained status. They receive a special-purpose grant for professional development, and they are also allowed to use their general funds. Echoing findings from research in the United States on schools and private companies, principals of grant-maintained schools report that the most beneficial training takes place at the school site, rather than when educators are sent off-site: "Not only is it more cost effective, but also there is a greater feeling of practical relevance when it is done at the place of work" (Barker, 1992, p. 59).

Although grant-maintained schools recognize the need to train governors in their new responsibilities, considerably fewer resources have been expended with that group. As one principal commented: "Thankfully, the advent of LMS has prompted many LEAs [local educational agencies or school districts] to train governors and this will certainly help them take on full responsibility under grant-maintained status." He added, however, that "some governor training for grant-maintained status is likely to be necessary and should be budgeted for" (Barker, 1992, p. 59).

A few grant-maintained schools have attempted joint governor-staff training to strengthen relations between the two groups. However, evidence to date suggests that if training is not properly organized it may worsen relations, with factions appearing that subsequently can interfere with both the day-to-day operations of the school and long-range planning (Davies and Anderson, 1992). New-design plants, which typically place a heavy emphasis on training, have used cross-role training to reinforce the design of the organization and to encourage necessary behavioral changes (Mohrman and Cummings, 1989). For instance, in a new-plant startup at a pharmaceutical company, all managers, supervisors, and union leaders were trained together before the plant opened, to underscore the type of cooperation needed to bring the plant on line. Once the plant opened, general skills training occurred in the total group, while intact work teams were trained together in specialized skills relating to their function.

Schools in England have created various decision-making structures to administer professional development. One strategy used by many grant-maintained schools is to establish a new position of "professional tutor" at the school site. One principal reports that the professional tutor, as set up in her school, is responsible for creating a whole-school staff development policy, including preparing the bid for the special-purpose grant for training; establishing a system to assist both teaching and support staff with their personal development; and ensuring that the school's development activities are directed toward the achievement of school goals (Morris, 1992). Another strategy is for the school to appoint a staff development committee. At one grant-maintained high school in England, such a committee includes the vice-principal responsible for curriculum, a senior teacher with responsibility for new teachers, representatives from the heads of academic departments, and a classroom teacher representative (Perks, 1992).

Thus far, grant-maintained schools have bought professional development services from several sources. In some instances, schools in England have bought from central district offices—either the one they formerly were under or another that has developed an expertise in a particular training area. Another source for professional development is the Grant-Maintained Schools' Centre, an organization set up with government funding to provide assistance to schools that are opting out of local district authority.

In the United States, the content and delivery of professional development services have changed only slightly with the adoption of school-based management (SBM). Although many districts offer at least some initial management training for SBM council members, training for teachers in SBM schools continues to focus on knowledge about teaching, learning, and curriculum, and such efforts are not usually linked to SBM. As in England, local authorities in the United States have not yet addressed the need to retrain the central office in how to be "helpers, not tellers." Further, most SBM schools do not have the option to purchase services from providers outside the district. With a captive audience for their services, districts in the United States have not paid much attention to developing new training opportunities for people in the central office or at individual school sites.

Information

In order for schools to create an educational plan, including goals for students and staff, to monitor progress, and to handle the business of operating a school, people at the site must have information. One category of information relates to teaching and learning.

Between the United States and England there are distinctly different views about who should receive information about student performance. In England, where grant-maintained schools were designed at least partly to improve accountability by schools to their clients, disseminating information to parents is the major focus. In fact, parents are the primary audience for district-controlled schools as well, since all schools in England are schools of choice. The Department of Education and Science (1992a, 1992b) requires schools to provide an annual report to parents that includes specific types of school performance data in a particular format that allows for comparisons across schools.

By contrast, in the United States charter school legislation focuses on the flow of information from the school to the charter-granting authority. As noted in Table 6.1, contracts let under Minnesota's Outcome-Based Schools Act specify outcomes pupils are to achieve within the three-year contract period; at the end of the period, information about pupil performance must be submitted to the charter-granting authority for the contract to be renewed. Similar provisions are contained in California's charter school legislation, which authorizes contracts for five-year periods.

Student performance data have many benefits. Such information is necessary for creating educational goals and for monitoring school performance so that implementation can be modified enroute to improve outcomes. Next year's teachers want to know what students know and can do, and so student-specific data also are important. From parents and students—the clients—the people managing schools will want to know if they are satisfied: Do students feel engaged? Is homework useful? Charter schools, like schools of choice or magnet schools, must compete for students and tuition dollars. Information about the extent to which clients are satisfied helps to ensure schools are developing in ways that comport with their clients' visions. In addition, such information is helpful in communicating the character of the school and its performance record to parents of prospective students. Despite all these benefits to student performance data, grant-maintained schools have not spent much time developing systems that provide educators at the site ready access to this information.

Aside from information related to teaching and learning, schools need administrative and financial data to manage the site. Such business data have been the focus of information systems in England. As mentioned earlier, schools are eligible to receive a transitional grant once they have been approved for grant-maintained status. Governing boards have used these grant monies to purchase computer equipment, including both hardware and software required for administrative purposes and for accounting/payroll systems (Davies and Anderson, 1992). Sometimes schools in England contract with a payroll company or a school district for special business services, such as payroll. Grant-maintained schools generally prefer the latter, if the facility is available at a competitive price, since central offices specialize in payrolls for schools.

There is no formal or informal network among grant-maintained schools that shares information. Information systems are site specific. Consequently, if grant-maintained schools are interested in how their operating costs fit in with district schools or how they compare to other grant-maintained schools of like character, such information is not readily available. Efforts, however, are made to network personal computers at the site, to make data readily accessible to school faculty and to promote information sharing and communication.

To assist grant-maintained schools, the Grant-Maintained Schools' Centre (GMSC) offers a transitional service that more than 60 percent of them have used. This service assists schools in adapting and setting up administrative and financial systems at the school site, such as which data elements to include in management information systems and which services might be contracted out. GMSC also has a role in disseminating information, via newsletters and occasional papers, that is of general interest to grant-maintained schools.

Site-managed schools, unlike England's grant-maintained schools, still remain part of the district organization and part of its information network. Thus, there continues to be a strong emphasis on how information is shared vertically between individual site-managed schools and the district office, and whether schools are adhering to regulatory policies. Resources for developing information networks in SBM districts tend to be focused on building the capabilities of central offices to monitor school compliance, and not on providing information to schools to help them monitor their own performance or building local capacity to promote information sharing across schools.

Rewards

In both England and the United States, legislation governing charter schools allows individual schools the flexibility to opt out of the salary and promotion arrangements set forth in the union contract and to create their own compensation systems. Evidence to date suggests little realization of that potential.

In Minnesota, charter schools may be established as either nonprofit organizations or cooperatives. In the first instance, teachers are employed by the governing board of the school and have the rights available in the state to organize and bargain collectively. However, teachers at the school would not be represented by the union (since the school is autonomous); instead they could act as their own separate bargaining unit (Kolderie, 1992). In sum, teachers at charter schools could remain union members, but the union would not bargain for them. In the second case, when a charter school is established as a cooperative by a group of teachers, the teachers would be *members* of the cooperative but not *employees*. Hence, argues Kolderie, "If the teachers were not employees and there were no employer there would be no bargaining . . . the 'employee' and 'professional' models could be combined" (1992, pp. 4–5).

In California charter schools, teachers are considered employees of the school, and the law gives individual schools the power to decide whether or not they want to remain part of the district's collective bargaining unit or to establish themselves outside the district's agreements.

In England, where teachers' salaries are set nationally, grant-maintained schools since 1992 have been able to create the pay and conditions of their own teachers, but to date there has been little change. As practiced, such decisions typically are under the jurisdiction of the governing board, which decides not only how many staff will be employed but also at what salary level. Deem and Davies, writing an "insider account" of a secondary school that had opted out, offered several predictions regarding compensation: "First, GM [grant-maintained] schools will almost certainly have staff on different conditions of service to those in LEA [district] schools; in some cases . . . these will be substantially better than those offered by many LEAs. Second, in some schools staff will no longer be on national pay rates" (1991, p. 169).

Davies and Anderson, after conducting a comprehensive, in-depth analysis of grant-maintained schools in England, point out the suitability of performance-based pay to decentralized management: "The concept of treating people as individuals and empowering them to have more control over their working lives also begs the question of rewarding staff. If there are flexible budgets in terms of choice of resource expenditure is it desirable to reward every teacher on the same salary despite the different contributions they make? Performance related pay may be the way to achieve and reward excellence in schools" (1992, p. 129).

Based on their own observations, along with advice from principals at grant-maintained schools, Davies and Anderson (1992, pp. 91, 129) recommend that schools devise reward systems that:

- Include both teachers and administrators.
- Acknowledge skills and competencies over and above those described in a job description (for example, individual involvement in management issues).
- Are based on output, so that a principal who increases her output by 25 percent would receive a 25 percent salary increase.
- Measure performance by specific targets.

The success of using pay for business performance to motivate and enhance employee performance has been borne out by research in nonschool organizations in the private sector in such programs as gain sharing. Odden and Conley (1992) offer suggestions for how to adapt the principles of performance-based pay to schools. Currently, Kentucky is in the process of developing templates for a pay system that would reward educators on direct indicators of performance, including the knowledge and skills they possess and school productivity. In the United States, where charter schools are focused on achieving particular outcomes, reward systems that link pay to performance, as judged by the extent to which outcomes are achieved, seem especially fitting. However, at this point, such systems are not in place in most charter schools or SBM schools.

Conclusion

While charter school reforms in the United States have only recently been launched, England's experience with grant-maintained schools provides a number of procedural and policy strategies that seem to be applicable to school-based management. One implementation issue, for example, is how to account for the overhead paid for by the district office, when a school begins operating under school-based management. In England, grant-maintained schools are credited with a revenue increase of about 15 percent to cover overhead. They also receive a transitional grant that can be used to plan and prepare for their new status. Another grant, known as a special-purpose grant, can be used to purchase equipment, such as computer and communications systems, and to recruit and select staff. A third type of grant supports in-service training for teachers. The grants and the stipend to cover overhead indicate an awareness that charter school status is not achieved simply when a request for status change is approved. Rather, it is a process of change and learning.

The English innovation of requiring all schools seeking to become grant-maintained to first operate under an idea similar to school-based management, known there as Local Management of

Schools, also may be instructive. Once again, the scheme demonstrates an awareness that the transition to independence takes time and adaptation.

Another idea that could well benefit schools seeking to operate under school-based management, is the idea of hiring someone from outside the circle of educators to act as an administrative assistant or even as a general manager for the school. This person could handle accounting and other administrative jobs but would not become involved in educational decisions. This frees the principal, as well as the teachers who serve on the school's governing body, to concentrate their energies on curriculum and instruction. Many grant-maintained schools also establish another new position: professional tutor. This person functions as a kind of lead teacher, responsible for designing the school's staff-development strategy. This gives individual schools the capacity to contract for and design the training most appropriate to the needs of their organization.

Despite those innovations, on the whole, charter schools are not yet advanced enough to provide many lessons for school-based management. At least in England, however, they have taken a much more aggressive posture with respect to moving power, information, knowledge, and skills into the school. They have also established an accountability system. On the other hand, at least in England, there has been little attention to the role of the teacher.

Charter schools clearly have the potential to be guiding lights, especially since many state laws allow them to be created from the ground up. It remains to be seen, however, whether transferring these resources into the school will result in the staff becoming involved in improving school outcomes. If the structure of charter schools, like that of traditional schools, remains largely unchanged and hierarchical, with a principal in charge and teachers working in isolation in their classrooms, teacher talents will not be fully tapped and the instructional model will not change. Thus, so far, the potential of charter schools remains unrealized. This suggests that if charter schools are to lead to involvement of teachers, mechanisms must be established to involve teachers not only in the technical areas of schooling but also in issues of governance and management.

Endnotes

1. In addition to grant-maintained schools, the Education Reform Act of 1988 authorized a host of other reforms, including a national curriculum, national testing for students, open enrollment, and school-based management. For a completely readable description of interpretation of the act, see S. Maclure, *Education Re-formed: A Guide to the Education Reform Act* (2nd edition), London: Hodder & Stoughton, 1989.

2. The community representatives selected to serve on the board of governors are known as "first governors" and are nominated by the governing board of the school that existed before the school opted out. The number of first governors must be sufficient to form a majority of the whole governing board; that is, more than the combined total of the elected parents, teachers, and the principal, who serves ex officio.

3. The only exception is New Mexico's Charter Schools Act of 1993, which provides planning grants of $5,000 for up to ten schools interested in developing charters.

References

Barker, K. (1992). Managing finance in a grant-maintained school. In B. Davies and L. Anderson (Eds.), *Opting for self-management: The early experience of grant-maintained schools.* (pp. 56–72). London: Routledge.

Budde, R. (1988). *Education by charter: Restructuring school districts.* Andover, MA: The Regional Laboratory for Educational Improvement of the Northeast and Islands.

Davies, B., and Anderson, L. (1992). *Opting for self-management: The early experience of grant-maintained schools.* London: Routledge.

Deem, R., and Davies, M. (1991). Opting out of local authority control—Using the Education Reform Act to defend the comprehensive ideal: A case study in educational policy implementation. *International Studies in Sociology of Education, 1,* 153–172.

Department of Education and Science. (1992a). Reporting pupils' achievements to parents. (Circular No. 5/92). London: HMSO.

Department of Education and Science. (1992b). The parent's charter: Publication of information about school performance in 1992. (Circular No. 7/92). London: HMSO.

Kolderie, T. (1992). The charter schools idea. Available from Center for Policy Studies, 59 West Fourth Street, Saint Paul, MN 55102.

Lawler, E. E. (1978). The new plant revolution. *Organizational Dynamics, 6*(3), 2–12.

Lawler, E. E. (1986). *High-involvement management.* San Francisco: Jossey-Bass.

Lawler, E. E. (1992). *The ultimate advantage: Creating the high-involvement organization.* San Francisco: Jossey-Bass.

Merl, J. (1993, February 12). State gives charters to 9 schools. *The Los Angeles Times,* p. A3, A34–35.

Mohrman, S. A., and Cummings, T. G. (1989). *Self-designing organizations: Learning how to create high performance.* Reading, MA: Addison-Wesley.

Morris, J. (1992). Managing staff development in a grant-maintained school. In B. Davies and L. Anderson (Eds.), *Opting for self-management: The early experience of grant-maintained schools* (pp. 93–103). London: Routledge.

Mulholland, L., and Amsler, M. (1992). *The search for choice in public education: The emergence of charter schools.* San Francisco: Far West Laboratory for Educational Research and Development.

Odden, A. R., and Conley, S. (1992). Restructuring teacher compensation systems. In A. R. Odden (Ed.), *Rethinking school finance: An agenda for the 1990s* (pp. 41–96). San Francisco: Jossey-Bass.

Olsen, L. (1992, September 30). California is second state to allow charter schools. *Education Week,* pp. 1, 23.

Perks, R. (1992). Managing a school and developing a grant-maintained school. In B. Davies and L. Anderson (Eds.), *Opting for self-management: The early experience of grant-maintained schools* (pp. 42–55). London: Routledge.

Schmidt, P. (1993, January 20). GA's Miller proposes raising compulsory age to 18. *Education Week,* p. 16.

Shanker, A. (1988, July 10). Where we stand—Convention plots new course, a charter for change. *The New York Times,* p. 7, section 4.

Wohlstetter, P., and Anderson, L. (1994). What can U. S. charter schools learn from England's grant-maintained schools? *Phi Delta Kappan, 75,* 486–491.

Wohlstetter, P., and McCurdy, K. (1991). The link between school decentralization and school politics. *Urban Education, 25,* 391–414.

Chapter Seven

Establishing the Conditions for High Performance

Priscilla Wohlstetter

Susan Albers Mohrman

In this chapter we consolidate findings from the previous six chapters, with a twofold purpose: first, to examine where school-based management (SBM) fits into an overall model of high performance for schools; and second, to propose ideas for how schools can expand the boundaries of SBM beyond the transfer of power to include the other elements necessary for achieving and sustaining high performance. This chapter, like the rest of the book, uses Lawler's high-involvement model.

Underlying the concept of school-based management is the redistribution of decision-making authority from the central district office to individual schools. The hope is that with this shift in authority, schools will have the power and tools to make decisions that will lead to improved school performance. The mechanism for bringing this capacity to bear on school-level decisions is most often a school-site council that consists of some combination of the principal, teachers, students, parents, and the community. However, if school-based management is to affect the outcomes of schools, including student learning, more than a simple shift in governance is required.

In addition to the power to make decisions, schools need the wherewithal to make good decisions. The resources that provide the underpinnings for this include access to extensive information to make well-informed decisions and to develop school plans that take into account goals, performance, trends, and various aspects of the school organization including resource constraints and concerns from the community.

Knowledge and skills are also needed. People in SBM schools need to learn how to plan and deliver curriculum using new and innovative approaches. They also need to have the skills necessary to participate effectively in group decision-making processes and management functions that are essential to this form of governance.

The high-involvement framework also stresses performance-based rewards. This is the motivation piece, and it includes intrinsic as well as extrinsic elements. The manner in which rewards are distributed has to fit with the way the work is designed. The ultimate goals of high-involvement management and of school-based management are similar: to improve performance by giving those closest to the production process, or to teaching, influence over and a personal stake in how well the organization functions. To accomplish these goals, school personnel need to be rewarded for the way they perform and what they contribute to the organization's success.

If defined merely as a devolution of authority, SBM may not have a place in the creation of high-performing schools. Defined broadly, however, SBM may be a requirement for creating the conditions that have been shown to contribute to the success of high-performing schools. These conditions are illustrated in the four models reviewed in Chapter Four. For example, schools using these models give teachers more influence over the school program. They expand the number of stakeholders involved in managing the school to include groups that traditionally have been excluded, such as parents and members of the business community. The focus on goals is an aspect of high-performing schools that is facilitated by engaging different constituencies in shared decision making. In addition, most of these schools are given control over at least a portion of the budget, enabling them to concentrate resources on high-priority issues. They often devote some of their discretionary resources to staff development projects that further curricular or process goals. Another high priority of these schools is keeping constituents informed, in particular about school goals and student performance. Thus, built into the four models of high-performing schools are many of the elements of high-involvement and school-based management.

Creating these conditions and learning how to work effectively within them take time. This is not surprising. Mohrman, in Chapter Two, makes the point that studies of private-sector high-involvement organizations found that companies that have been at it the longest have experienced the most significant impact on organizational outcomes. An initial impact of the new approach is improvement in the internal conditions of the organization, including communication and decision making. Measurable outcome changes take longer to emerge.

In the longer term, SBM can enable schools to redesign curriculum and instruction. Through staff-development activities school-level educators can gain new knowledge to supplement what they observe in classrooms about what works with their own students. As Johnson and Boles pointed out in Chapter Five, SBM often gives teachers the opportunity to expand their influence in many areas, including curriculum development. This positive outcome of teacher empowerment has been seen in Accelerated Schools, for example, where teachers are more likely to make radical changes in their classrooms once they are freed from top-down constraints on their work (King, 1993). To the extent that SBM focuses the attention of school-level actors on improvement and provides them with resources to try to transform their inspirations into reality, it should be a key element of school reform.

Where does SBM fit into the model of a high-performing school? It creates the conditions where school-site participants can bring about changes in performance. SBM, by itself, will not improve the process of teaching and learning. Nor will it necessarily change the way educators organize themselves and apply resources to accomplish their goals. This depends on what school-site members *do* with the power that is devolved. The other three resources—information, knowledge and skills, and rewards—are required to create the capacity and the motivation to make the kinds of fundamental changes in how educators go about their tasks that are implied in "teaching for understanding" and other strands of education reform.

As intuitive as it might seem that school-site participants would use their new authority to improve education, the link between SBM and high performance remains uncorroborated. Indeed, as Ogawa and White point out in Chapter Three, even though approximately one-third of the nation's school districts have SBM programs, there remains scant evidence in the research literature that conditions in schools, let alone student performance, have improved. Johnson and Boles (Chapter Five) are more optimistic, based on recent indications from districts that have used SBM longer. Nevertheless, there are some worrisome signs. For example, some districts that at one time introduced SBM have recentralized (Brown, 1992). Perhaps the most notable such shift was in Dade County, Florida, which had been a SBM pioneer: layers of bureaucracy were added back to the district office when the superintendent who championed SBM moved on to another city.

On the other hand, as Johnson and Boles point out, there are positive trends in some schools and districts. Furthermore, they note that school reform cannot occur without buy-in from teachers. Teachers are the agents of instruction, and unless they change the way they enact their roles, teaching and learning will not change. All four models of high-performing schools, described in Chapter Four, rely on local will to create a more effective school. The question is how to implement SBM in a way that leads school-level actors to focus on teaching and learning.

Barriers to Improvement

The high-involvement management model requires mechanisms that decentralize power, information, knowledge and skills, and rewards. Schools often fall short of that ideal, in ways that may limit the commitment and involvement, as well as the capabilities, of site personnel to effect improvement.

Power

SBM schools cannot always exercise power over the factors necessary to improve teaching and learning. Some councils may have authority over only a very small portion of the budget, for example, because the majority is constrained by labor contracts and grant requirements. In other cases, councils may have been granted sufficient power, but in practice they may not exercise it. Thus, instead of being self-governing, SBM schools may use their authority to make decisions that only marginally affect teaching and learning. Frequently, these decisions focus on the day-to-day operations of the campus: where the copy machine should be located, when lunches should be scheduled, what to do about students wandering the halls, and so forth. These issues affect the quality of work life and the climate of the school, but they will not change classrooms to more fully engage students. They also do not put into question the philosophy of teaching and learning, and as a consequence, school stakeholders are not engaged in serious dialogues about missions, values, and strategies.

The fact that schools do not have unlimited authority is not in and of itself a barrier to improving schools. Even the most extreme form of site-based control—charter schools—are constrained by charters that may require adherence to state or national law, for example. On the other hand, there may be what Ogawa and White refer to as a "web of constraints" that creates a sense of impotence and skepticism. When it constrains a school's ability to apply resources to deliver educational services or to adapt teaching and learning to its student body, this web can be stifling.

Just as worrisome is the ambiguity around the role of the council. Many councils have become caught up in day-to-day managing, not governing—a distinction that seems to be more effectively defined in charter schools. Multistakeholder groups ought to be dealing more with issues of policy and direction. Preoccupation with the school's daily operations may deflect energies away from core educational concerns and contribute to the burnout that seems to plague some SBM efforts.

Information

Even those SBM schools that do focus on important decisions often lack information essential to their improvement efforts. SBM schools need to be able to draw on student, budget, policy, testing, and other information that has historically been collected by and held at the district office. Further, the information needs to be distributed in a useful form to those who are actually engaged in decision-making. In addition, there needs to be an upward flow of ideas and information from schools to the district, so district operations take the needs of schools into account.

Districts may not have the information systems to provide schools with timely information. In many cases, the districts themselves do not have trend data or even aggregate yearly data broken down into categories useful for management and educational decisions. Most districts also do not have a goal-based performance feedback and accountability system. Furthermore, schools do not have a heritage of such data-based decision making.

Knowledge and Skills

At the school level, SBM participants are often inadequately trained for their new roles. School systems have historically spent far less on training than private-sector businesses (Bradley, 1993). The problem is compounded in SBM schools where scant training dollars must fund in-service needs pertaining to the new approaches to teaching and learning and training related to the new responsibilities entailed in SBM and school restructuring. In some cases, only a few campus personnel are trained directly, and they are expected to become trainers for the rest of the staff. That, too, is a drain on time and energies.

Another problem for many SBM schools is that the district retains control over professional development activities: when they will occur, what they will cover, and where they will be held. Consequently, schools are put in the position of being able only to respond to the district's training opportunities, not to initiate their own. Many SBM schools have little authority or resources to design their own opportunities, to select the service providers, and to have the training delivered at their own site at a time that is convenient and appropriate to the school's schedule.

Rewards

Several of the authors of this volume have made the point that few rewards are linked to the practice of SBM and generally schools have little control over the allocation of those that do exist. The district office typically controls remuneration through systems that attach increased value (pay) based on surrogate indicators of ability such as experience or formal education (Odden and Conley, 1992). Often pay schemes for teachers, administrators, and other staff are locked in by union contracts. Furthermore, such contracts also may specify ratios and require that schools employ certain classifications of teachers regardless of the work design the school is employing. With a few—but increasing—number of exceptions, several of which were mentioned in Chapter Five, there is no extrinsic incentive for performance.

Lessons About What Works

• *To improve the design of SBM, the balance of power between central administration and individual schools needs to be clearly defined with real decision-making authority devolved to schools.*

SBM entails new roles for both the central office and the schools. Typically, the main focus of school-based management has been decentralizing power. The process traditionally is seen as an equation where schools gain decision-making authority in one or several areas (budget, curriculum, or personnel, for example) and often the power to seek waivers from district or state policies. On the other side of the equation is the district office, which is perceived to lose power as a result of the schools' new authority. This idea of a zero-sum game can put the schools and the district office in adversarial roles.

Building on the mutual influence model described in Chapter Five, an improvement on the current situation would be to rethink the idea of SBM as one of shared power. This is compatible with trends in corporations to take a value-added perspective on what activities and decisions to put in corporate and what to place in operational units (Galbraith, 1994). Instead of questions of gaining or losing power, the focus is on what decisions should be locally determined and what decisions should remain centralized for reasons of organizational effectiveness.

As Wohlstetter pointed out in Chapter Six, charter schools are usually outside the district context and, within the specified bounds of the charter, are self-determining and self-governing. As such, they would occupy one end of a SBM continuum. At the other end would be schools that have very little self-determination, including, unfortunately, many operating today in traditional districts. SBM schools ideally would rest somewhere in the middle. Linked together, the district and the school would complement each other. The district would adopt a stance of offering valuable services to schools. Schools would have influence over the agendas of district services, and the district would influence schools where there is a need for uniformity of policy, common direction, or economies of scale.

• *School-based management should employ a variety of mechanisms for different purposes and appropriately involve many people and different stakeholder groups in managing and improving the school.*

When a school adopts decentralized management, one of the first steps during implementation is to create a council or decision-making body for the school. The membership of the council varies from school to school. As was pointed out in Chapters Three and Four, the composition often depends on the political history of the SBM reform: did it arise as a strategy bargained by the union, or was it the result of community action to exercise more local control of schools? Thus, the issue of SBM is often viewed as a governance issue: which group is being given legitimacy to govern the school?

This view of SBM is problematic for several reasons. First, as Ogawa and White pointed out (Chapter Three), it is often unclear what this transfer of power means in organization terms. If the multistakeholder council is doing the job of the principal, then is it a management group? This view tends to lead to a situation where the council is making decisions the principal used to make, and often results in a paralyzing power struggle between the principal and the council. If the council is viewed as a local miniboard, then it should be dealing primarily with policy and direction and only minimally involved in the daily management of the school. Is the council viewed as an improvement group? In this case then it should be focusing on innovation and new directions, and less on day-to-day management. The point is that there are many possible interpretations when power is transferred: different participants have different expectations and conflict is inevitable.

A second problem with the focus on the council is that a small group of people feel great pressure to perform all the different roles: principal, miniboard, and improvement group. For instance, unless the SBM council is extremely good at involving its various constituencies, it can become a "principal surrogate"—a collective that is doing the job of the principal. Just as important, this role puts a huge time and energy burden on council members, many of whom are classroom teachers or have other full-time jobs in the community. This can be a primary source of burnout, as teachers try to add managerial duties to their teaching responsibilities.

Third, the focus on the council can result in a limited view of what school-based management is and a limited approach to improving the capabilities of the school. If the intent of SBM is to decentralize decision making to improve the schools' ability to deliver educational services that effectively meet students' needs, then it stands to reason that more than council members need to participate. Indeed, many SBM schools have a constellation of councils and subcouncils for different purposes.

The models of high performance discussed in Chapter Four also tend to advocate diffusing power within the school. It is common for these schools to involve a wide variety of stakeholders in decision making, including parents, students, and business or community leaders, in addition to teachers. Subcommittees to the SBM council are often set up to examine and work on a specific area of interest, and function similarly to legislative subcommittees. Some of the restructured schools used teams or minischools (houses or schools within schools) that give a group of teachers responsibility for a larger piece of the process or a defined population of students. The diffusion of involvement lessens the burden on any one group, and can spread commitment and help prevent burnout.

Charter schools in England, described in Chapter Six, address the first two problems by separating governance and management responsibilities from teaching duties. The principal, who serves as an ex-officio member of the school's governing board, is responsible for the day-to-day operation of the school and its administration. The governing board, on the other hand, is the equivalent of the board of trustees at a private school, and sets policy and direction for the school.

Some private-sector organizations deploy a large variety of mechanisms to involve various stakeholders in decision making. For example, customers may get involved in influencing the direction of an organization by participating on advisory councils or task teams charged with exploring new directions, and by constant polling to determine customers' levels of satisfaction and sources of discontent. Technical contributors (the equivalent of teachers) would serve on task teams to explore new processes for doing work and to pilot new approaches. Work teams (often cross-functional) would be set up to conduct a piece of the business or a set of integrated processes, such as serving a segment of customers or producing a piece of the product. These teams would manage themselves and determine how to apply their resources to accomplish the task, and then be held accountable for outcomes. Multistakeholder advisory groups or policy-making groups would address broader issues of strategy. Managers (principals in education) would serve as organizational leaders, helping to manage change and integrating and managing the performance of the organization. The managers also would ensure that the involvement mechanisms produced broad participation, so that concerns of all stakeholders were addressed and people were involved appropriately in the management and improvement of the organization. What constitutes appropriate involvement would be determined by which perspectives were needed for which purposes, the energies and interests of people, and what application of people's time makes the most sense given the large numbers of tasks that have to be accomplished in the organization.

Given that the purposes of education are not well established and that different stakeholders have different preferences, school organizations cannot avoid dealing with the issue of governance. On the other hand, this preoccupation with control will not in and of itself make education better, no matter what stakeholders hold the majority or minority on the council, and no matter what mandate the council has. Schools will improve only if they establish appropriate forums for participation, and continually involve people in many activities of self-management and improvement.

• SBM *requires extensive development for school-level and district administrators to help them carry out their new roles. This will include classic training and development approaches as well as a host of on-the-job development activities.*

Experience in the private sector has found that organization-wide development provides a foundation for widespread organizational involvement (Lawler, 1986). In schools, this means that entire faculties will require opportunities to deepen or broaden professional knowledge. Deeper pedagogical skills, for example, might include expanding the repertoire of teaching techniques and understanding when best to apply each. Broader skills might include interdisciplinary teaching capabilities, but they also might include gaining knowledge about and skills for dealing with the multiple cultures that are in classrooms, or counseling skills to deal with troubled students.

All SBM participants also will need involvement skills and an understanding of the organization and how it is managed. Management knowledge and skills might include budgeting and scheduling, either an understanding of how they are done in order to be an informed participant, or an ability to do these skills, perhaps at the level of a school-within-a-school.

Such training helps all SBM participants contribute to the organization in many ways, to be informed participants in decisions, and to be knowledgeable about needed improvements. Besides the obvious benefit of improving the knowledge and skills of school staff, training creates a common language and provides a foundation on which to develop a common understanding of what the school is striving to accomplish. Further, it can be used to introduce inno-vations and new approaches.

In the private sector, some development occurs in workshops and courses, but increasingly team skills, organizational improve-ment techniques, and even job skills are developed on the job. This is done in several ways. Facilitators and trainers come into the workplace for meetings and projects to conduct training while the work is being done. A second on-the-job approach is for co-workers to train one another. Another trend involves visits to other sites and conferences where people are exposed to and sometimes immersed in alternative approaches.

These approaches are also being used in many high-performing schools. The high-performance models, described in Chapter Four, include varied training opportunities for multiple stakeholders. The schools adopting these approaches are remarkable in two ways. First, they focus resources on a wide variety of in-service offerings. Sec-ond, they often look outside traditional educational circles, such as to local companies, for sources of in-service opportunities. This is also true of some SBM schools that use staff development to sup-port new approaches to instruction as well as new approaches to managing the school. Johnson and Boles (Chapter Five) described a number of schools that are using innovative approaches to help teachers share knowledge and take charge of their own learnings. Many of the new approaches to instruction require that the school itself become a learning community (Cohen, McLaughlin, and Tal-bert, 1993).

A lesson learned by almost all organizations making the transi-tion to high involvement is the difficulty that managers experience in adopting new styles of relating to employees, and that staff groups experience in adopting a new service role vis-à-vis operating units (Mohrman and Cummings, 1989). Their development is made more difficult because of a sense of loss of influence and power base, but also because there are not many models available for their new roles. Schools embarking on SBM may find that principals, district administrators, and staff support groups will need every bit as much development assistance as the school-level personnel who are newly empowered to take part in school management.

- *To improve the design of SBM, schools must have access to information about the school and its performance. There also should be opportunities for sharing information and learnings across schools and within schools.*

Traditional bureaucratic organizations collect information at the top of the organization for purposes of hierarchical control and decision making. That information flows out and down to the various managerial and organizational levels on a need-to-know basis. By contrast, high-involvement operating units tend to have direct access to data on performance. Information provides the basis for outcome-oriented decision making. Good outcome data also enable performance units to be held accountable for results, rather than controlled by inputs and scrutinized hierarchically for uniform processes.

In schools, the information available is usually much narrower in scope and is often collected to ensure compliance with district, state, and federal policies. Individual schools are rarely held accountable for performance because they lack information about goals, measurements of goal attainment, trend data to measure progress, and benchmark data to know how well the school is doing compared to similar schools. Without such performance data, self-regulation and improvement are difficult because the school and its stakeholders cannot assess how well they are doing, either on an absolute or a relative scale. Accountability for results is also impossible. Developing an information system that provides the infrastructure for an accountability system is essential if SBM is to fulfill its potential.

The multidirectional flow of ideas is equally important (Lawler, 1986). Both formal and informal networks can be created to facilitate information sharing within and among schools. As Johnson and Boles pointed out in Chapter Five, such networks can foster innovative practices and significant learning among teachers. Creating opportunities for teachers to interact with and learn from one another should be a high priority for SBM schools.

Mechanisms for communication among a district's schools are difficult to create, because schools often are reluctant to compare themselves with others. As a result, benchmarking data are difficult to develop or attain, and diffusion of ideas occurs with difficulty if at all. The district can create mechanisms to help diffuse ideas and anxieties, such as monthly principal meetings and teacher networks or discussions during districtwide training sessions. Some high-involvement corporations have established regular visitation across sites, so that people become aware of new approaches being used elsewhere. Establishing ongoing multidirectional communication is necessary if the district is to prevent the isolation of new practices within individual schools or single classrooms.

• *SBM is more likely to lead to instructional improvement if school-level participants are rewarded for increased school performance.*

In high-involvement organizations in the private sector, rewards are often used to motivate people to achieve organizational goals and to improve organizational performance. These rewards align people's outcomes with the organization's desired outcomes, and can serve to motivate higher levels of performance (Lawler, 1981). Individual merit pay has not been particularly successful as a motivational tool, but approaches that reward people in a team or business for the performance of that unit, such as gain sharing or other team incentive systems, have shown significant impact (Lawler, 1992). The goal is to encourage the members of these units to continue striving to improve performance. Since organizations in the private sector are engaged in producing profits, sharing gains with employees is a logical approach.

Another compensation practice that is used in high-involvement companies is skill- or competency-based pay. This approach increases pay as employees acquire and demonstrate proficiency in skills and methods that the organization values. This differs from the pay structure that is common in schools, because the competencies that are rewarded are tied to the organization's work design and the processes they use. The employee not only has to demonstrate that education and training have occurred satisfactorily, but also that new skills can be applied on the job with good results. Thus, if an organization has decided to move to computer design methodologies, designers may get salary increases if they master this approach and use it successfully on the job to increase the quality and efficiency of designs. This allows an organization to pay for the competencies it values, namely those required to carry out its performance strategy.

Schools do not deal in profits and so the concept of gains is difficult to transfer to school settings. Even instructional improvements that can be quantified do not generate additional revenues for schools or districts. "Revenues" are unrelated to performance for schools, except in the case of charter schools or magnet schools, where attracting students translates into operating dollars and staff positions. For these reasons, the concept of pay for performance is impossible to translate directly from the private sector to public school settings. Hand in hand with this practical difficulty goes the assumption, deeply embedded in the educational establishment, that people who are involved in education are not motivated financially but instead derive satisfaction from intrinsic factors such as having students succeed.

There are of course many reasons why educational institutions have shied away from pay for performance, including the strong power of teacher unions and associations that resist pay differentials based on qualitative distinctions between teachers or distinctions that are affected by factors beyond the teacher's control, such as student ability and socioeconomic status. Other limiting factors include the lack of consensus about the important goals and outcomes of schooling, and a lack of confidence in existing measuring systems. Without these variables in place, school performance is difficult to define and assess. Thus, schools are left to develop reward programs that are not money-based, including many creative approaches to recognition and celebration of success.

This is a critical issue, for even in schools doing a good job of transferring power, establishing mechanisms for disseminating information, and developing skills and knowledge, one question still cries out for an answer: What will motivate the masses of educators to undergo the imposing demands and pain of transition? As SBM councils and other involvement groups start to identify desirable new approaches that require changes in teacher behavior and in the way schools are organized for teaching and learning, they are being faced with the reality that the reward system of the organization may not fit with the new approaches. In fact, the system may promote continuing old practices, particularly if teachers experience few consequences for not becoming part of the new direction and if the major personal consequence for innovating is more work.

The concept of making outcomes contingent on performance is a critical part of the accountability system of organizations. As was pointed out in Chapter Five, some districts are experimenting with different approaches, generally at the group level. These group approaches will fit in well with the nature of schooling as collaborative learning among teachers, teaching teams, and schools-within-schools become more common.

Rewarding the whole faculty is a common practice in schools adhering to the high-performance models described in Chapter Four, in recognition of the fact that improving the schools is a collective endeavor. In some cases it is the school, and not the individuals in it, that receive rewards. Although the merits of this approach can be debated, because it may lead to a situation where there are "have" and "have-not" schools, it does demonstrate that different approaches to the incentive issue are possible.

While it is clear that a system of rewards based purely on external, financial rewards will never be possible or desirable in schools, the alignment of the reward system with the new performance demands on schools and changing approaches to instruction is important. Further, our analysis suggests that decentralizing management without accountability for outcomes and incentives for performance may be like launching a boat without a rudder. Little attention will be paid to the destination: performance goals and school improvement.

Conclusion

Given the multiple factors that influence high performance in schools, a change in governance, while required, is not sufficient. School improvement will result when the school is empowered to introduce changes and make decisions that enhance its capacity to deliver better services to students. But the other conditions for effective involvement and high performance also need to be in place: information, knowledge and skills, and rewards. Once these resources become available, the focus at the school site can shift from implementation to the goal of SBM: school improvement.

An important argument that underpins this chapter is education's underdeveloped accountability system; we believe this is a major factor impeding the effectiveness of SBM. Part of the problem is an absence of goal consensus. Another factor is the failure of educational systems to collect and track information pertinent to making tradeoffs about resource use, and to methods of teaching, learning, and governance. All four of the high-performance models described in Chapter Four include, to some extent, the need for school-level participants to agree on what they are trying to accomplish. Many SBM districts and schools now are in the process of setting goals and creating systems for disseminating information and measuring performance. When these pieces are in place and accountability is introduced, it is far more likely that SBM will lead schools to focus on educational outcomes.

In conclusion, we believe that the high-involvement approach to management offers a useful framework for examining the way decentralized management is being implemented in schools. The model is geared to the same objectives as SBM: to engage school-level actors more broadly in how they educate children and ultimately in improving organizational performance. In SBM schools, the focus of the reform to date has been on the transfer of power. The high-involvement framework suggests the importance of rethinking this focus by expanding the boundaries of SBM beyond governance to include the three other elements that research on productivity in the private sector has shown to be linked to high performance—information, knowledge and skills, and rewards.

References

Bradley, A. (1993, March 24). Basic training: Strengthening professional development to improve schools, support student learning. *Education Week*, pp. 4, 15–18.

Brown, D. (1992). The recentralization of school districts. *Educational Policy*, 6, 289–297.

Cohen, D. K., McLaughlin, M. W., and Talbert, J. E. (1993). *Teaching for understanding: Challenges for policy and practice.* San Francisco: Jossey-Bass.

Galbraith, J. (1994). *Competing with flexible lateral organizations* (2nd ed.). Reading, MA: Addison-Wesley.

King, B. (1993). Cincinnati: Betting on an unfinished season. In C. T. Kerchner and J. E. Koppich (Eds.), *A union of professionals: Labor relations and educational reform* (pp. 61–78). New York: Teachers College Press.

Lawler, E. E. (1981). *Pay and organization development.* Reading, MA: Addison-Wesley.

Lawler, E. E. (1986). *High-involvement management.* San Francisco: Jossey-Bass.

Lawler, E. E. (1992). *The ultimate advantage: Creating the high-involvement organization.* San Francisco: Jossey-Bass.

Mohrman, S. A., and Cummings, T. G. (1989). *Self-designing organizations: Learning how to create high performance.* Reading, MA: Addison-Wesley.

Odden, A. R., and Conley, S. (1992). Restructuring teacher compensation systems. In A. Odden (Ed.), *Rethinking school finance: An agenda for the 1990s* (pp. 41–96). San Francisco: Jossey-Bass.

Part Two

Creating High Performance

Chapter Eight

Making the Transition to High-Performance Management

Susan Albers Mohrman

During the 1970s and 1980s, rapid and fundamental changes in the environments of organizations in many different sectors of the economy led to extensive programs of organizational change. Global competition, deregulation, and the emergence of a well-informed and demanding consumer population have resulted in greatly increased pressure for organizational performance. Simultaneous pressures for reduced costs and enhanced quality and speed have pushed organizations to examine their guiding assumptions and longstanding patterns of organizational behavior and to implement wide-reaching change. Rapid advances in information technology have enabled new forms of work and its coordination. Although change has in many cases been painstakingly slow and difficult, there have been enough case studies of successful and unsuccessful organizational transition to provide a knowledge base about the processes of large-scale organizational change.

One type of large-scale change that is common in the private sector is the transition from central, hierarchical control and bureaucratic functioning to more participative modes. A closely related phenomenon in the field of education is school-based management (SBM). The objective of these high-involvement approaches is to increase the commitment of employees to organizational success, to give them the tools they need to improve performance, and to change the control orientation from hierarchical to more lateral self-management (Lawler, 1992; Walton, 1985). High-involvement management involves a change in the distribution of four resources in the organization: information, knowledge and skills, power, and rewards. These resources, which have traditionally been disproportionately placed at the top of the organization, are moved downward and throughout the organization. This chapter will examine the learnings about large-scale organizational change. The intent is not to present an exhaustive review of the change literature, but rather to extrapolate from it three ways of conceptualizing change that seem particularly appropriate to the transition into SBM.

Large-Scale Change: Its Nature and Genesis

Large-scale change is "a lasting change in the character of an organization that significantly alters its performance" (Mohrman, Mohrman, Ledford, Cummings, and Lawler, 1989, p. 2). Change in character implies fundamental change in the key aspects of the organizational system—for example, in the way it relates to its environment, in the transformation processes and structures that the organization uses to produce its outputs, and in the nature of the outputs themselves. In the shift to high-involvement management, the organization may become more closely linked to its customers; it may introduce new processes for sharing information, making decisions, and rewarding performance; it may create new participative structures, redesign work, and flatten the hierarchy; and it may define higher performance standards or qualitatively different performance outcomes. One outcome that is intended to be significantly enhanced by the change to high-involvement management is employee commitment. The cumulative impact may be an organization whose character has fundamentally changed, and that has attained new kinds and levels of performance.

Large-scale change has two characteristics that make it distinct from the small adjustments and minor changes that occur continually in the life of all organizations. It is *pervasive* and it is *deep*. Pervasive change alters a large number of the organization's subsystems. Because the change process involves multiple, simultaneous focuses, its design and management are themselves significant tasks. Deep change affects the most fundamental aspects of the organization: the beliefs, assumptions, and values that guide behavior. As a result, the change process must build in approaches that allow organizational participants to develop new shared ways of understanding their world.

The change to high-involvement management is both pervasive and deep. In order to spread power, information, knowledge and skills, and rewards downward and throughout the organization, almost all facets of the organization have to change. Many organizations learned the hard way that high involvement does not result from one-pronged change such as setting up participation structures. For these structures to enhance employee involvement in improving organizational performance, many other aspects of the organization have to change, so that there is a hospitable context for the participative structures (Ledford, Lawler, and Mohrman, 1988).

Systems have to be created to provide employees with the information they need to make effective decisions. Employees and managers have to learn new skills and gain new knowledge to enable them to work effectively in groups, apply technical knowledge, and use effective decision-making and problem-solving algorithms. Involvement may change the psychological contract (the level of effort employees feel they owe the organization in return for the outcomes they receive), and thus the reward system may need to be altered. Work may need to be redesigned to allow teams to interactively manage their work processes, and to provide more discretion and autonomy to the line worker.

In addition to requiring change in almost all subsystems, the transition to high-involvement management entails major shifts in beliefs, values, and assumptions. It is deep change. For example, changing the role of middle managers from control to facilitation and coaching entails fundamental change in how they understand the management process. Employees must begin to assume responsibility for shaping their own context: they have to shift from thinking that management is responsible for the things that make it hard to do their work to taking personal responsibility for being part of the solution. High-involvement management entails fundamental value shifts about issues of control and self-management.

Change of this magnitude does not happen as a natural evolutionary process. It generally happens in response to major environmental shifts that profoundly alter the organizational capabilities required for success (Nadler, Gerstein, and Shaw, 1992; Lawrence, 1989). Many of the firms that were on the *Fortune* list of the 500 largest firms in the United States ten years ago no longer exist—dramatic testimony to the fact that large-scale change is far from an automatic response in a changing environment.

Translating environmental change into large-scale organizational change is a multistep process. It involves accurately registering the changes, forming an organizational strategy for adapting to the new requirements, developing a new design for the work processes and structures of the organization, and implementing, assessing, and refining the design. If this sequence is interrupted at any point, the organization will fail to make the necessary changes in its performance capabilities. This chain of change can be interrupted for many reasons: because the organization does not recognize the need for one or more of the steps, because it lacks the resources to go through the change sequence, or because key stakeholder groups are not involved in the process and are able to undermine the change dynamics.

Large-scale change cannot simply be "adopted," and thus the change-adoption literature does not provide a great deal of help in understanding it. This literature has been focused on how an organization can adopt innovations that have been developed and found to be effective elsewhere; it sees the change process largely as a question of making the adoption decision process and overcoming resistance. The literature about high-involvement management makes plentiful reference to organizations where one or more units have successfully redesigned themselves for high involvement and high performance but confronted roadblocks when attempting to diffuse the new approaches to other organizational units. One explanation is that managers in other units see and do not like the changes that this transition would require in the way they perform their roles, that the new approaches challenge how they think the organization should be run, and that they consequently resist the change.

This explanation seems to fit many situations, but it does not explain the cases where managers decide to emulate the successful changes and fail in the implementation process. In these cases the adopting organizations focused on the change as a series of discrete changes (for example, introducing work teams or a new incentive scheme), and were unable to see the intricate web of changed practices, structures, and behaviors that are required to support the new way of performing (Mohrman and Cummings, 1989). They fail to approach the change process as a dynamic process of gradual redesign and learning.

The Dynamics of Large-Scale Change

Organizational transition has been described in several frameworks, each of which looks at the phenomenon through a particular set of lenses and consequently focuses on different aspects and dynamics. Three frameworks are described in this section: the stage dynamics of transformation, change as redesign, and change as a contextually embedded phenomenon. Each of these frameworks is important, as all of these aspects and dynamics operate simultaneously during a large-scale change process.

Dynamics of Transformation

This framework focuses on the stages that an organization goes through in transforming itself. It is based on the work of Tichy and Devanna (1986), who applied a psychologically based stage model of individual change, originally developed by Bridges (1980), to the phenomenon of large-scale organizational change. This framework posits that successful renewal has to begin with an understanding of the need for change that enables an individual to leave behind old patterns of behavior and embark on a transition. Thus, change starts with an ending: a disengagement from the status quo. The transition process includes a period of exploring what is possible and developing a vision of the future, followed by implementing changes that result in a new way of functioning.

This framework is quite similar to Lewin's (1951) dynamic framework of change, which talked about three stages: unfreezing the old patterns by noticing the gap between what is aspired to and what is currently occurring; changing; and refreezing, or institutionalizing the changes so that they are not discarded. Most current dynamic models of organizational change do not evoke the "refreezing" image, primarily because the magnitude of environmental change today requires ongoing self-renewal.

Tichy and Devanna identified three stages of organizational transition:

Stage 1.   Recognizing the need for change
Stage 2.   Creating a new vision
Stage 3.   Implementing and institutionalizing change

The first stage entails both the process of registering the environmental factors that are requiring the organization to go through the threatening and painful process of self-renewal, and the process of letting go of the old way of functioning. The latter is particularly difficult because in most cases the established ways of functioning have been the foundation of past personal and organizational success.

At this stage, it is important for the leaders of change to allow people to challenge the need for change. All participants must work through the defensive reactions to the thought that their own behavior may have to change to be part of the solution, while they are processing the information that the current way of doing business is not adequate to meet the needs of the future. In high-involvement management transitions, for example, many of the most successful managers in the old order were those who had fine-tuned the art of control; being asked to change styles not only brings into question their own sense of self-worth but it also challenges their deeply held beliefs about what leads to high performance. In SBM transitions, principals who have been good administrators may be faced with learning new skills and finding new ways to deal with the faculty. Principals may find the former too threatening and the latter time-consuming and inefficient.

It is at this stage of change that the phenomenon of resistance to change is most acute, and it is here that organizational members are tempted to collude in their own demise by individually and collectively denying the data that point out the need for change and by focusing on past success as a rationale. Because the process of letting go is threatening and psychologically painful, change proponents will often be frustrated during this stage by the amount of negativism within the organization, and will be tempted to cut short the dialogue that is necessary to achieve a collective sense of the desirability of change.

The second stage entails the formation of a model or vision of how things can be different and better. It involves processes of imaging how the organization needs to perform to address its environmental requirements, identifying the gaps between where it needs to be and where it is, and defining the changes in practice, process, and structure that will be required. This stage involves organizational participants in forming a positive end-state goal and fleshing out a common image of the changes that will be required. Managers and their employees might together create a scenario of their department as a more autonomous unit, and how all of their roles might change as a result. The high-performance models described in Chapter Four recommend that local participants develop a shared vision of the school. It is here that positive change energy begins to emerge.

The third stage entails the hard work of implementing the changes and trying to get them to become an ongoing part of the new way of doing business. During this stage, the change management challenge is not only to design and carry out a complex set of implementation activities, but also to deal with the political, technical, and cultural resistances that will continue to serve as an undertow to the change process until a new status quo is achieved (Tichy and Devanna, 1986).

Getting changes to stick is the most difficult part of large-scale transitions (Kanter, Stein, and Jick, 1992), in large part because changes become stable only when the critical mass of organizational systems, processes, and structures have been changed to redefine the status quo. Up to that point, the predominance of behavior is still shaped by elements that were designed to support the old way of functioning. Organizational members can point to aspects of the way the organization is operating that "prove" that management is not serious about decentralizing: "District office employees are still telling us what to do," they may say; or "the board turned down our waiver request"; "the transportation department won't change the bus schedule"; and so forth. This is a precarious time, for the frail consensus around the new order can evaporate quickly if leadership changes or organizational attention otherwise slips away from the focus on the desired end-state.

This psychologically based stage theory of the dynamics of change is particularly useful in understanding how deep change occurs. Changes in belief structures, values, and assumptions involve letting go of old frameworks of understanding and replacing them with new ones. At any point in time, different individuals in the organization will be at different stages of transition or resistance. In high-involvement management transitions, for example, some organizational members will quickly sign on to the new vision of doing business. In schools some groups of teachers will quickly take advantage of the introduction of SBM to propose and take responsibility for implementing new approaches to teaching. Others will be pulled in that direction by emerging systems and structures that place immediate demands on them for a new response. For example, they may be faced with a new curriculum that requires team planning and delivery. Part of the challenge of managing organizational change is to devise change processes and interventions that address the inevitable multiple simultaneous dynamics—inevitable because personal change occurs at different speeds. Some groups will be actively redesigning parts of the system while others are still coming to grips with the need for change.

Dealing with the personal differences in how people respond to change is a particular challenge in schools. Teachers have historically managed their isolated classrooms, and they are at different starting places with respect to teaching philosophy and methodology. The transition to SBM, added to other educational reforms that are introduced, will require much more change for some than for others. Resulting within-faculty rifts can mean that conflict management is an integral part of managing the dynamics of change.

Large-Scale Change as Self-Design: A Learning Perspective

There is increasing recognition in the organizational literature that organizational design is variable and that the fit between the design of the organization, the technology of the work that is done, and the organization's strategy is a key to high performance (Galbraith, Lawler, and Associates, 1993; Nadler, Gerstein, and Shaw, 1992).

The frameworks that are presented in this section underpin a focus on organizational change that treats the organization as an artifact that can be consciously designed and whose design determines its outcomes. Three models are pertinent: the notion of the organization as a system; the design model of the main subsystems that constitute the organization; and the dynamic model of redesign that is the essence of large-scale change.

The Organization as a System

The open systems perspective on organizations posits that they are designed to achieve certain purposes in particular environments (Cummings, 1980; Katz and Kahn, 1978). The environment provides both the resources required for the organization to perform, and the demand for its outputs (see Figure 8.1). The organization thrives to the extent that it relates effectively to its environment: gaining necessary inputs and providing desired outputs in a manner that optimally applies resources to outcomes. The open systems perspective stresses not only the internal design of the elements that constitute the organization but also the design of its often blurry interface with environmental elements.

Figure 8.1.

The Organization as an Open System.

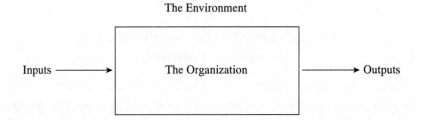

The environment is, of course, multifaceted, and most organizations have to relate simultaneously to multiple environmental forces that create sometimes conflicting pressures. Minimally, organizations must meet requirements from the consumers of their products and services, the governments that regulate their activities, and the labor markets that supply employees. In addition, they may need to respond to their boards, their shareholders, or in the case of public agencies, the public that votes to provide resources. As expectations held by these various environmental forces change, so must the organization's performance.

This perspective is the basis for earlier assertions that fundamental organizational change is usually triggered by fundamental environmental change. The open systems perspective would go so far as to say that if fundamental change is occurring in the environment, an organization that is not able to fundamentally transform itself will be unable to meet the performance demands of the environment and will eventually lose its ability to secure resources. Such organizations will die, unless artificially propped up by infusions of resources.

The Model of Organizational Design

The design model presented in Figure 8.2 has been adapted from Galbraith (1977), and is one of a number of models that pick out key elements or subsystems of an organizational system that can be purposefully designed. It is increasingly being understood that the way these organizational features are configured determines the performance capabilities of the organization, and can consequently provide a competitive advantage or disadvantage. Organizations can, in effect, be "architected" for more effective mission accomplishment (Nadler, Gerstein, and Shaw, 1992). This design model identifies strategies and tasks that are implied by the organizational mission and goals as key inputs into the organizational transformation process.

Figure 8.2.

Organization Design Components.

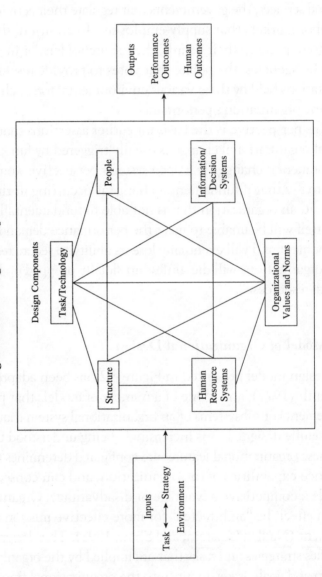

Source: Susan Albers Mohrman and Thomas G. Cummings, *Self-Designing Organizations: Learning How to Create High-Performance* (pp. 37, 39). © 1989 by Addison-Wesley Publishing Company, Inc. *Reprinted by permission of the publisher.*

For a large-scale change process to occur, the organization has not only to accurately identify environmental changes, but also translate them into an organizational strategy for performing optimally in the changed environment. Many organizations in the private sector are facing increasingly competitive conditions leading to price erosion and to the necessity to be more responsive to diverse customer requirements. Faced with the necessity to deliver a more complex set of products and services with fewer resources, many have developed an organizational strategy that reduces the costs associated with top-down control and that improves performance by more directly involving employees in more aspects of the business and by empowering them to make changes required for successful performance. This general organizational strategy is referred to as high-involvement management in this book, following Lawler's terminology (1986). Others have referred to similar approaches as high-commitment (Walton, 1985) or "empowerment" (Block, 1990) approaches.

The main box of the systems design model in Figure 8.2 displays what has been referred to as the architecture of the organization (Nadler, Gerstein, and Shaw, 1992): the configuration of elements that determine how the organization performs in taking inputs and transforming them into outputs and outcomes. Each of these can be described using illustrations from high-involvement management.

Task/Technology/Work Design. Tasks are the patterns of activities that organizations carry out to transform raw materials into products or services and to address the requirements of their environment. Technologies are the tools and methods that enable tasks to be effectively performed. The search for better methods is an integral part of organizational improvement. Involving organizational members in discovering and learning new methods is part of high-involvement management.

Work design is the way individuals and groups are configured to perform tasks and employ technologies. In high-involvement management, work is designed to give individuals and groups maximum control over the technologies, resources, and activities they use so that they control the factors necessary for effective performance. Work teams are frequently created to perform a whole task or service, replacing individual work designs that may have artificially segmented tasks that are in fact closely related. For example, a group of teachers might have access to certain time, space, and material resources with which to educate a particular set of students. These teachers may be held collectively accountable for applying those resources to most effectively deliver instructional resources to those students rather than each being held individually accountable for their own class.

People. The people are the individual employees of the organization. They can be understood in terms of their demographic characteristics, skills, experiences, expectations, values, and attitudes. In high-involvement management, an effort is made to hire and develop individuals with a broad array of knowledge and skills, who can contribute flexibly to organizational success. In addition, it is important that they expect to influence the organization and to take responsibility for and be empowered to work for continual improvement of performance. They must also expect to continually update their own skills as technologies advance and organizational requirements change.

Information/Decision Systems. These are the activities aimed at processing information and making decisions, including communication, goal-setting, and feedback and measurement processes. High-involvement management is characterized by widespread sharing of organizational and performance information, decentralized and participative decision-making and goal-setting processes, and the use of feedback and measurement to support continuous organizational improvement. Accountability for results is made possible by these processes.

Human Resource Systems. These include the systems for selecting and hiring, training and development, and appraising and rewarding performance. They are the practices that integrate people into the organization, specify the relationship between the individual and the organization, and define accountability. High-involvement management is characterized by participatory selection and hiring processes that involve the applicant and potential coworkers in determining fit with the organization and, if applicable, with the team. Extensive continuous investment in training and development provides a knowledge and skills foundation for effective decentralized decision making and performance improvement. Appraisal systems emphasize aligning the job expectations and appraisal criteria with organizational performance outcomes; employees are rewarded for their scope of contribution and for organizational, team, and, where appropriate, individual performance. Likewise, developmental activity or reassignment may be required if performance is not adequate.

Structure. Structure is the grouping of task activities into organizational units and the coordinating mechanisms among those groups, including hierarchy, councils and other coordinating units, task forces, and specialized integrating and support roles. High-involvement management emphasizes control by lateral influence between performers and a concomitant decrease in the day-to-day control function of the hierarchy. Employees are involved in coordination of work and in making decisions that affect the organization as a whole. As much as possible, all functions required for high performance are moved into the performing unit itself rather than placing key support functions in specialized external units. Accountable performing units are self-regulating within the constraints of the broad direction, goals, and resource constraints of the organization.

Organizational Values and Norms. These are the shared meanings among organizational members about what is important and how members should behave. They are expressions of the organizational culture that have arisen historically, largely because of the way the organization has been designed. Changes in shared meanings can be achieved partly through interactive processes for jointly determining organizational direction and norms of performance.

In large part, however, culture derives from the other design elements that shape the way people go about doing the work of the organization. It changes only when new processes and structures for doing work result in new behaviors and altered expectations and understandings. For example, the cultural value of hierarchical control changes only when new decision-making practices establish new patterns of control. In some schools, for example, the culture may be for teachers to retreat to their classrooms and expect the administration to do something about the conditions in the school that make it difficult to teach. This cannot be changed by simply declaring a new culture. The culture will slowly change as teachers increasingly become involved in deciding how to deal with the conditions and are held accountable for improvement in outcomes.

The systems model is completed by picturing the outputs of the organization in terms of its performance goals and the outcomes that accrue to its members. Feedback from the environment about how those outputs are accepted constitutes an ongoing input. High-involvement approaches to management include methods for making all employees aware of trends in absolute performance and performance relative to other organizations, and of environmental reactions to those outcomes, such as market success and customer satisfaction.

The concept of fit is embedded in the systems view of the organization. According to this principle, an organization can optimize its performance only if the various design elements fit and mutually reinforce each other. Furthermore, the constellation of design features (the overall architecture of the firm) should enable the organization to address the environmental demands being placed on it and to carry out the strategy that has been developed to fit those demands (Nadler, Gerstein, and Shaw, 1992; Nadler and Tushman, 1988). When various aspects of the design do not fit with one another, energy is drained because they are working at cross purposes. For example, establishing participative decision forums without altering the information that is shared and the skills that are developed is an inefficient use of organizational resources and leads to bad decisions that may consume even more organizational resources. Untrained SBM councils can consume a tremendous amount of time and energy inefficiently and ineffectively.

The fact that effective large-scale change requires change in a large number of system elements poses challenges for its management through time. In the interim, the organization will have made some changes that may even appear to work against performance because of the tension between the changes and the other features that remain from the status quo (see Figure 8.3).

A Process of Gradual Transition

For example, schools may be given responsibility for decisions in a certain domain before relevant staff groups have been relieved of accountability for that same domain and before the members of the staff group have learned a new way to influence and support the organization. This tension results in frustrations and cynicism that contribute to resistance to change. The discrepancies have to be openly addressed and confronted. Ironically, these tensions will lead people to want to slow down the change, when actually speeding up the change would be the quickest route to reduce the tension. The pace of change is limited by the need to deal with the dynamics of resistance and by the time and other resources required to complete the necessary steps in the change process.

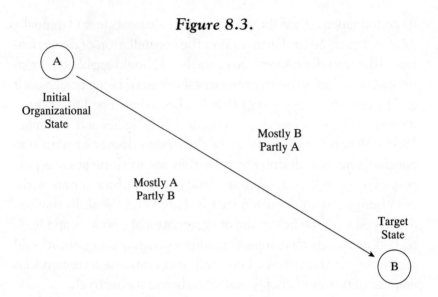

Figure 8.3.

On the other hand, resisters can always outlast the champions of change. Therefore it is important to maintain the momentum of change and to actively work to create a critical mass of contributors to change rather than wait for everyone to get on board. This way intent is demonstrated, and the organization changes around the resisters.

The next section provides a conceptual roadmap for complex organizational redesign, one that recognizes that such change is iterative and involves learning through time.

Self-Designing Organizations

Large-scale change requires extensive organizational learning. Organizational learning occurs when more effective ways of understanding the mission and means of the organization become embodied in its processes and structures. For organizational learning to occur, individual learning is necessary—but not sufficient.

Figure 8.4 illustrates the iterative cycle of learning and design that constitutes large-scale change. The premise of the model is that each organization must go through its own learning and redesign processes. An organization cannot simply copy design solutions that have been found to work elsewhere. The change process illustrated in the model is referred to as the self-design model. It was derived from in-depth case studies of fundamental change in organizations, and is explicated in greater detail elsewhere (Mohrman and Cummings, 1989). It is an idealized model in that it abstracts from the messiness of actual change processes and pulls out the fundamental steps that seemed necessary to move the process forward. It might best be considered a functional roadmap for large-scale change.

Figure 8.4.

The Self-Design Strategy.

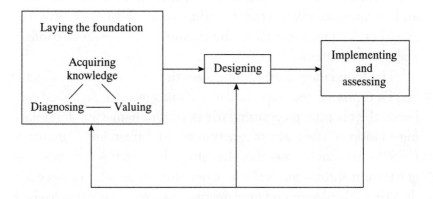

Source: Susan Albers Mohrman and Thomas G. Cummings, Self-Designing Organizations: Learning How to Create High-Performance (pp. 37, 49). © 1989 by Addison-Wesley Publishing Company, Inc. Reprinted by permission of the publisher.

This model graphically posits that the most important phase of change is laying the foundation. The foundation consists of determining the values toward which the organization will be redesigned, acquiring learning and awareness about organizational design principles and alternatives, and diagnosing the current organization to gain awareness of the gap between the way the organization currently functions and how it needs to function to successfully achieve its values, given its environmental and technical requirements. This stage results in the identification of criteria to guide the design and implementation stages.

Shared meaning regarding the criteria for change is essential for collective redesign. Skipping this stage results in different participants enacting their different understandings and being at cross purposes. In a school setting, some participants may see SBM as a way to empower teachers and disempower administrators. Others may emphasize educational outcomes. Still others may see SBM as a way to respond more fully to the needs of the community. A shared understanding would probably be an integrated perspective that includes elements of teacher involvement, educational outcomes, and community involvement. Failure to establish such an integrated understanding early in the change process leads to conflict and disillusionment.

The foundation stage encompasses the first two stages of Tichy and Devanna's three-stage model of transformation, described earlier in the chapter: recognizing the need for change and formulating a vision of a new way of functioning. Mohrman and Cummings (1989) state that in cases that they studied where this first stage was given short shrift—for example, where the organization proceeded directly to the design and implementation step—organizations had to recycle to the beginning and lay a foundation.

The tendency is to skip this stage. Organizations may be implementing the change because of a corporate or district edict. Organizational leaders learn of a new program or design that has helped another organization improve its performance and decide to adopt a similar change. Such a mechanical decision to implement is a mistake for two reasons: First, what works in one setting does not necessarily fit another setting. Second, when the foundation is not laid, the change takes on no meaning for organizational members, reducing the likelihood of successful implementation.

A frequent error in large-scale change is not to adequately identify the values that underlie the transition. As organizations try to transition to a high-involvement model, for example, they frequently emphasize humanistic or ideological values such as involvement, growth and development, or democratic functioning as a justification for embarking on this complex change process. They lose sight of the performance requirements of the organization, and assume that organizational performance will flow from the implementation of changes that result in humanistic or ideological gains. In fact, one study has shown that the positive employee outcomes are *less* likely to result when the change is justified for reasons of humanism or democracy. Humanistic and democratic gains are more likely to result when the organizational performance values are clearly specified. Then individuals can collectively derive success from being part of the process of improving performance, and they can understand environmental performance imperatives that require them to live through the demanding and ideologically conflictual change process (Lawler, Ledford, and Mohrman, 1989).

The second stage of self-design involves changes in the design elements of the organization. This is frequently done by representative participatory design teams, often with different teams redesigning different subsystems. For example, in the change to high involvement, it is not unusual for one team to be examining the work processes that are used and then to focus on the work design and structures of the organization, while another team is looking at information systems design or at the training and development or rewards systems. Coordination between the various design processes is critical.

At this stage, it becomes painfully apparent if an adequate foundation has not been laid, for various change efforts in the organization will be designing changes that do not complement one another. The organization will have to recycle into a stage of clarifying values and identifying criteria. The design piece of large-scale change is much easier if there are agreement and understanding of the criteria for successful change.

The third box of the self-design model portrays another component of the change that frequently receives short shrift, and that is critical to success: careful design of the implementation process, including the support that will be needed for organizational units and members to implement the change. However, it is unlikely that the organization will be able to completely define the change or the implementation process in advance. It will have to learn as it goes. Consequently, part of the implementation is the short-term and long-term assessment process.

Assessment of change is designed to surface implementation and design problems, and it results in tailoring and reworking designs through time as the organization learns what is required to make the new approaches work and to achieve its valued outcomes. Through periodic assessments of the SBM council, for example, principals may learn that their "participative" style is actually manipulative; parents may learn that they are not viewed as representing the views of their community; and teachers may learn that much of their time is spent fighting for the interests of their department rather than considering the total program. As a result, the council might be reconfigured, new two-way communication approaches may be established, or cross-department groups of teachers may be established as subcommittees to explore more integrated approaches to education.

This iterative process is an action-learning cycle (Lewin, 1951) in which diagnostic and environmental data guide the design of changes. An ongoing data collection and feedback process during implementation helps the organization learn which approaches are effective and ineffective. Successful action learning requires the development of norms that support the surfacing of problems and collective efforts at resolving them, and the willingness to cycle back and redesign.

This process is referred to as self-design because it assumes that the design must be tailored by organizational members to fit the particular environment faced by the organization and the strategy and goals that it formulates. Furthermore, Mohrman and Cummings point out that large-scale change is a series of nested designs that are put in place at different levels in the organization. Systemwide redesign activities (establishing broad strategic direction and operating principles; redesigning systems and processes that are organizationwide, such as budgeting or resource allocation processes; and establishing an overarching vision) create a framework within which organizational subunits redesign themselves. Organizational subunits design themselves to fit within the overarching umbrella, but are given a great deal of leeway to determine their own design. For example, budget and accounting processes may be organizationwide, and the allocation of resources across operating units may be done at the corporate level. However, the allocation of budget and application of resources within each unit is decided by the operating units. Thus, cross-role and multistakeholder groups re-create the design process in units throughout the organization. One key challenge in the self-design process is to establish a learning process so that units can learn from each other, so the organization does not have to sustain the cost of each unit rediscovering the wheel as if no learning had occurred in the organization. Another is to coordinate change sufficiently so that changes in different parts and subsystems do not work at cross purposes, but to allow diversity of designs so that local owners of the new design are not unnecessarily constrained. This fine line is especially important in the transition to high-involvement management because the underlying assumption and intent are that employees can be empowered to make changes to the design of their unit that will enhance performance.

The tension between more inclusive (for example, corporate or district) and less inclusive (for example, department, unit, school, team) levels of the organizational system during large-scale change is ongoing and cannot be avoided. How this tension is resolved constitutes the essence of the organizational learning process. It either limits or encourages the establishment of variation between units that constitutes one aspect of learning; it either promotes or discourages the diffusion and dissemination of local learning to other organization units, which is another aspect of learning (Ledford and Mohrman, 1993). Rolling out uniform new designs to all organizational units is an inappropriate way to produce organizational learning; so is the opposite extreme of completely localized change. Local design within the context of rich information-sharing networks and a broad corporate or district direction is most likely to yield organization learning.

The self-design process is pictured as an ongoing, iterative cycle. In today's environment, most management theorists are betting that the demand for change and improvement will not let up. Organizational designs are consequently truly temporary; they will be continually altered as the environment changes and the organization learns. A new role for management in this changing world is to ensure that ongoing organizational learning and periodic redesign occur (Senge, 1990; Mohrman and Cummings, 1989).

The Dynamic Context of Large-Scale Change

The case has already been made that organizations are open systems that exist in an environment that makes demands on them and provides the resources necessary for them to continue to exist. Consequently, the ability of the organization to continue to secure those resources depends upon it understanding itself in this context and developing a strategy for survival. This perspective stems from systems theory, which originally arose to understand the ability of a biological entity to survive in its environment.

Contextualism refers to a school of social science research that is concerned with understanding events and phenomena in their setting. According to this perspective, how change unfolds in the system of focus depends on what is going on in its context (Pettigrew, 1985). Thus, the manipulable dynamics of the change process are only one determinant of success. Contextual (or environmental) occurrences interact with and shape the change process as well.

This contextualist perspective leads to a historical perspective on the dynamics of change. We cannot understand why change takes hold or does not, assumes one form or another, unless we also keep in mind the contextual issues that are occurring simultaneously. For example, a premature end to an employee-involvement process may occur because of the retirement of a president or superintendent whose successor does not understand or support the new direction. Economic recession may result in withdrawal of resources needed to support the change process or preoccupation with daily operations in a way the deflects attention from the change process and results in organizational cynicism or resistance.

As an example, Pettigrew credits the election of Margaret Thatcher with having enormous impact on the process of change in at least one English firm because of the impact on unions and their increased resistance to being partners in change. The rapid changes in communications technology contributed to the decision in the United States to deregulate the telephone industry. These two contextual factors (technological change and deregulation) are credited with providing the impetus for massive organizational redesign in the telecommunications industry.

The context of schools will certainly affect the unfolding of SBM and school reform. The politics of the board, continuity of leadership, funding sources and levels, and legislative actions all can constrain the strategies a school can deploy. Changes in the community may require new approaches that are not preferred by school educators. New technological capabilities may make possible new ways to think about teaching other than an eight-hour day with six classes. Because the context will not stay still, the task of SBM is to develop a flexible set of approaches that can anticipate and adapt to contextual changes.

Thus, a full understanding of the change process, as well as a broad perspective on the planning of change, would take into account three components (Pettigrew, 1985): content, process, and context. Those guiding the change process would do well to take into account the impact of contextual events and trends.

Summary

This chapter has argued that large-scale change differs from change adoption in that it is concerned with change that is pervasive, systemic, and deep. Deep change alters the way people understand the organization and the assumptions they make. Large-scale change alters the character of the organization and its performance.

Understanding and guiding large-scale change require the simultaneous employment of three different frameworks. One focuses on the dynamics of transformation. It posits three stages that begin with the realization of the need for change and proceed through envisioning the future state to implementing and institutionalizing the change. Managers at the helm of large-scale organizational transformations must create the opportunities and momentum for the organization to move through these stages.

The self-design framework focuses on the redesign of the organizational system, and depicts the change process as an iterative process of learning and redesign. This learning and redesign process must be consciously shaped and managed. Contextualism stresses the importance of understanding both the content and process of change within the context in which it is embedded, and of understanding the independent influence exerted by contextual forces and the interaction of change dynamics with contextual occurrences. These contextual elements are part of the environment within which the change occurs and to which the organization must adapt.

References

Block, P. (1990). *The empowered manager: Positive political skills at work.* San Francisco: Jossey-Bass.

Bridges, W. (1980). *Transitions: Making sense of life's changes.* Reading, MA: Addison-Wesley.

Cummings, T. B. (1980). *Systems theory for organization development.* Chichester, England: Wiley.

Galbraith, J. R. (1977). *Organization design.* Reading, MA: Addison-Wesley.

Galbraith, J. R., Lawler, E. E., and Associates. (1993). *Organizing for the Future: The New Logic for Managing Complex Organizations.* San Francisco: Jossey-Bass.

Kanter, R. M., Stein, B. A., and Jick, T. D. (1992). *The challenge of organizational change.* New York: Free Press.

Katz, D., and Kahn, R. L. (1978). *The social-psychology of organizations.* (2nd ed.). New York: Wiley.

Lawler, E. E. (1986). *High-involvement management.* San Francisco: Jossey-Bass.

Lawler, E. E. (1992). *The ultimate advantage: Creating the high-involvement organization.* San Francisco: Jossey-Bass.

Lawler, E. E., Ledford, G. E., and Mohrman, S. A. (1989). *Employee involvement in America: A study of contemporary practice.* Houston: American Productivity and Quality Center.

Lawrence, P. R. (1989). Why organizations change. In A. M. Mohrman and Associates (Eds.), *Large-scale organizational change.* San Francisco: Jossey-Bass.

Ledford, G. E., Lawler, E. E., and Mohrman, S. A. (1988). The quality circle and its variations. In J. P. Campbell, R. J. Campbell, and Associates (Eds.), *Productivity in organizations: New perspectives from industrial and organizational psychology.* San Francisco: Jossey-Bass.

Ledford, G. E., and Mohrman, S. A. (1993). Self-design for high-involvement: A large-scale organizational change. *Human Relations, 46,* 143–175.

Lewin, K. (1951). *Field theory in the social sciences.* New York: Harper and Row.

Mohrman, A. M., Mohrman, S. A., Ledford, G. E., Cummings, G. F., and Lawler, E. E. (1989). *Large-scale organizational change.* San Francisco: Jossey-Bass.

Mohrman, S. A., and Cummings, T. G. (1989). *Self-designing organizations: Learning how to create high performance.* Reading, MA: Addison-Wesley.

Nadler, D. A., Gerstein, M. S., and Shaw, R. B. (1992). *Organizational architecture: Designs for changing organizations.* San Francisco: Jossey-Bass.

Nadler, D. A., and Tushman, M. (1988). *Strategic organization design.* Glenview, IL.: Scott, Foresman.

Pettigrew, A. M. (1985). Contextualist research: A natural way to link theory and practice. In E. E. Lawler and Associates (Eds.), *Doing research that is useful for theory and practice.* San Francisco: Jossey-Bass.

Senge, P. (1990). *The fifth discipline: The art and practice of the learning organiza-tion*. New York. Doubleday.

Tichy, N. M., and Devanna, M. A. (1986). *The transformational leader*. New York: Wiley.

Walton, R. E. (1985). From control to commitment in the workplace. *Harvard Business Review, 63*(2), 76–84.

Chapter Nine

Change in Schools:
Lessons from the Literature

David D. Marsh

Wohlstetter and Odden (1992) reviewed the use of school-based management (SBM) and found that it is "everywhere" yet "nowhere." It is everywhere in the sense that active efforts to implement it are afoot across the nation. But it is nowhere because, from the perspective of the conceptual framework they use, it has rarely been adequately implemented. Other authors confirm both the extensive interest (Clune and White, 1988) and the limited actual implementation (Clune and White, 1988; Malen and Ogawa, 1988; Wohlstetter and Buffett, 1992).

As Mohrman has described in Chapter Eight, school-based management must be set in the context of large-scale system redesign. In this context, SBM is part of a systemic change and not an isolated product, program, or practice. Lawler (1986) and Mohrman, Lawler, and Mohrman (1992) propose a conceptual framework for examining SBM using four elements of participation described in Chapter Two of this book:

1. Power to make decisions that influence organizational practices, policies, and directions.
2. Knowledge: both technical knowledge to do the job or provide the service, and managerial knowledge on decentralized management.
3. Information about the performance of the organization, including revenues, expenditures, and unit performance.

4. Rewards that are based on the performance of the organization and the contributions of individuals.

These four elements of participation provide the operational definition of school-based management in this chapter.

This chapter explores how strategies drawn from the local change literature could enhance the implementation of SBM on a broader scale. The focus is on SBM not because of its brilliant track record in education—others have correctly argued that, to date, SBM has been tried only in limited ways and with only limited success (Wohlstetter and Odden, 1992)—but because it is increasingly seen as a major focus for policy attention about how best to proceed with the comprehensive restructuring of America's schools.

The literature on the local change process in education will be used to suggest strategies for implementation. For this purpose, the literature has several important characteristics. First, it has a long history of theoretical and empirical research that has used a multidisciplinary perspective. Second, it has tangible and useful findings, such as a set of literature reviews and action-oriented propositional knowledge that can inform (in this case) what could be done to enhance school-based management. Finally, its focus has evolved to fit the various waves of reform in education; however, for the more recent waves, the change literature has a strong conceptual perspective and relevant clinical insights, yet with a less-developed empirical base. The current literature is potentially very useful to the problem of implementing a new framework for school-based management.

The chapter is grounded in several assumptions. The first is that schools ought to focus on higher-order thinking, conceptual understanding, and powerful communication for all students, which allow them to perform at high levels, by international standards, and to be ready to enter the information society of the twenty-first century. To reach this goal, a fundamental redesign of the system of schooling will be needed. Such a fundamental redesign requires, as

Mohrman discussed in the previous chapter, new connections between policy, practice, and redesign process that are complex and ongoing. This fundamental redesign must grow out of dramatic new approaches to teaching, assessment, and learning. In turn, schools will need to become the locus for planning and implementation for these major reforms. Finally, school-based management can play a very key role in achieving these outcomes.

The Literature on the Local Change Process in Education

There has been a dramatic shift in the focus of the local change literature, as educational reform in American schools has evolved over the last twenty years. In the 1970s, the focus of reform was on implementing innovations that were thought to be effective. The local change literature identified stages of the change process, roles for key players, and factors that enhanced implementation of these innovations. From a contemporary perspective, however, these innovations were too isolated, and the change process focused too exclusively on the adoption process and on factors internal to the school. They ignored the policy context and the value of useful outside resources, and made inaccurate assumptions about teacher commitment and engagement (see McLaughlin, 1990).

The next wave of reform, as Cuban (1990) and Murphy (1990) have characterized it, focused on making the existing system work better in traditional terms—standardized pupil achievement. Spurred by the 1983 national report, A Nation at Risk, this wave of reform emphasized more years of traditional subjects, higher standards, a longer school year and school day, and increased evaluation of teachers. Odden and Marsh (1988), Murphy (1990), and Odden (1991) summarize findings about the change process related to this wave of reform: implementation was more rapid than expected, and featured top-down strategies that provided direction, coordination, pressure, and assistance but did not transform the nature of schooling and created minimal improvement in student performance.

In the mid- to late 1980s, the focus of reform shifted to teacher professionalism and school-based management, often as ends in themselves. This wave of reform was launched in large urban districts such as Rochester, Toledo, Chicago, San Diego, Los Angeles, and Dade County, Florida. Typically, school-based management was emphasized with a focus on restructuring the teacher-administrator relationship and giving more authority to schools. Another emphasis was on teacher professionalism and school culture, which included how norms of collegiality, continuous improvement, common technical language, and experimentation could be enhanced. Valuable insights about the change process directly related to these reforms are provided in Chapter Five of this book and later in this chapter.

Odden (1991) and Fuhrman (1993) reported that, beginning in the late 1980s, the focus of reform was evolving toward powerful new views of classrooms, students, and outcomes. The point of departure for these reforms has been new perspectives on student learning: the importance of complex problem-solving, conceptual understanding, and powerful communication skills, which are linked to substantive understanding. While this emphasis is not new (it was first proposed in the late 1980s), it did receive new significance, a new schooling context, and new justification. For the first time, policy makers and practitioners were trying to create an educational system where all students learn to think, to solve complex problems, and to communicate at high international standards. It is insights from this era of reform that appear most useful in designing local change strategies related to school-based management.

The current local change literature in education can be summarized in terms of several complementary "lenses" that will focus strategies for implementing SBM in school settings. These five lenses are:

1. Linking policy and practice
2. Local change strategies—stages, factors, roles
3. Teacher professional culture and institutional norms
4. Change as a holistic journey
5. Changes in individuals—paradigms, attitudes, and practice

Collectively, the lenses provide insight about how to implement SBM as part of systemic reform.

Linking Policy and Practice

The systemic nature of change has been explored in the policy implementation literature (Smith and O'Day, 1990; Odden, 1991). This literature joins the macro- and microeducational systems and is focused on improving the technical core of schooling and student outcomes. Murphy (1990) and Odden (1991) draw several important conclusions about the linkages of policy and practice in fundamental reform. First, the educational system responds swiftly when there is a consensus for educational change on the part of policy makers, especially for developmental efforts that focus on new curriculum and instruction. Second, while the local school is the unit of organizational change, the local district, together with the state, is the unit of system change. Systems can identify the substantive direction in which local units (like schools) must move, while allowing sites to determine how specifically to move in those directions. Third, many local educators appeared to have the technical expertise to make the changes implied by state educational reform, when the reform focused primarily on new approaches to teaching and learning, and builds on pragmatic experience.

Finally, top-down initiation works for simpler reform, especially in implementing well-proven programs, where top-down adoption is followed by teacher involvement and sustained staff development. The implementation of SBM will be enhanced when pragmatic experience can be captured and used to shape policy. In turn, rapid concurrence with the reform may quickly follow development of these policies, especially if local leaders share that vision of reform and the local change process is characterized by teacher involvement and sustained staff development.

An important link between state policy and school-level change is the district office. Fullan (1991) has summarized a considerable body of research and offers several conclusions. "District staff are typically the ones to introduce new district programs. Even when the source of change is elsewhere in the system, a powerful determining factor is how central office administrators take to the change. If they take it seriously, the change stands a chance of being implemented" (p. 197). Second, "The leader's conceptual understanding of the dynamics of organization, the process of change and the people in his or her jurisdiction represent the most generative (or degenerative, if it is missing) source of ideas about what goes in a plan and what steps have to be taken when things go wrong" (p. 198). Finally, the central staff must provide specific implementation pressure and support (p. 198).

Huberman and Miles (1984), Firestone (1989), and others, have expanded the set of district functions that enhance successful reform. District leaders must do more than just "let go" to make SBM work; they must also build conceptual understanding of the organizational dynamics and create a new form of balance between pressure and support for the reform.

Local Change Strategies—Stages, Factors, Roles

The literature on local change strategies builds on the traditional idea that change typically goes through a set of stages: initiation, implementation, and institutionalization. For systemic reform that transforms classroom practice, an antecedent phase that builds teacher professional knowledge and expertise is important for the development of a professional site culture. The site culture can usher in the next phase of reforms and continue a collegial, exper-tise-driven, teacher-led curriculum change process (Marsh and Odden, 1991). For enhancing the implementation of SBM, four stages will be described: antecedent, initiation/adoption, imple-mentation, and institutionalization.

This lens also focuses on factors found to enhance initiation/adoption and implementation. Important factors and findings include:

1. Ambitious efforts were better.
2. High-quality, "proven effective" programs worked better.
3. Top-down initiation could work, especially with support and commitment from the central office and the support, commit-ment, and knowledge of site administrators.
4. Coordination of the change process is best accomplished by cross-role teams that included teacher participation in design-ing implementation.
5. Extensive, intensive, and ongoing training and classroom spe-cific assistance are required.
6. Extended teacher effort and teacher commitment followed rather than preceded implementation. (Odden, 1991, pp. 305–307).

A third part of the lens is the set of roles to be played by site admin-istrators, teachers, consultants, community members, and students. Fullan (1991) provides an extensive research summary for each role group. Teachers, for example, may be difficult to engage in SBM because in the past, they have gotten "the worst of all worlds—stu-dent benefit and procedural clarity [have been] low, and personal costs [have been] high" (p. 129). Moreover, in the past, innovations have been "rationally advocated from the point of view of what is rational to the promoter, not the teachers. Sometimes innovations are rationally sold on the basis of sound theory and principles, but they turn out not to be translatable into practice with the resources at the disposal of teachers. Or innovations may contain many good ideas and resources, but assume conditions different from those faced by teachers" (p. 130). In Chapter Five, Johnson and Boles point to the lack of authentic power or resources to carry out SBM management as a major constraint on its implementation in recent times.

Fullan (1991) also points to dilemmas in the principal's role, which may make full implementation difficult. These dilemmas include role overload and fragmentation, conservative tendencies associated with their recruitment, role constraints and psychic rewards, and system standardization. Principals are also middle managers and so face a classical organizational dilemma: "rapport with teachers is critical as is keeping supervisors happy" (p. 152).

Teacher Professional Culture and Institutional Norms

Another new theme in the local change process literature has been an examination of how teachers acquire knowledge and create a professional culture. Rosenholtz (1989) provided a fresh perspective on the teachers' workplace that included shared goals, teacher collaboration, teacher learning, teacher certainty, and teacher commitment: "Without learning opportunities, task autonomy and psychic rewards, teachers' sense of commitment seemed choked by a string of broken promises" (p. 209). It is clear in the local change literature that commitment typically follows, rather than precedes, action (McLaughlin, 1990; Fullan, 1993). Yet with a reform as politically loaded and complex as SBM, it will be difficult to provide learning opportunities, task autonomy, and psychic rewards of sufficient duration for commitment to be developed.

Little (1982, 1987) and Lieberman (1988) provide a rich perspective on the normative heart of teacher professional culture and how it can be nurtured. Important norms include continuous improvement, collegiality, risk taking, and experimentation. Yet

SBM will need strong norms across many schools when the litera-ture, at best, can point to how such norms can be developed in spe-cial and rare conditions still not fully understood by researchers or practitioners.

Lieberman and McLaughlin (1992) extend the professional cul-ture view with a synthesis of how teacher networks can enhance many aspects of a teacher's life. They report, "Teachers choose to become active in collegial networks because they afford occasion for professional development and colleagueship and reward partic-ipants with a renewed sense of purpose and efficacy. Networks offer a way for teachers to experience growth in their careers through deepened and expanded classroom expertise and new leadership roles" (p. 674).

Change as a Holistic Journey

More recently, the change literature has evolved into more holis-tic summaries of how the change process should be viewed. One aspect of this newer work is the writing of Goodlad and Sizer on how schooling can be viewed in more holistic terms. In this writ-ing, *holistic* refers to the need for a shared view of what students know and are able to do, and to how the many dimensions of schooling (including curriculum, instruction, assessment, and orga-nizational structures) need to be integrated and directed toward reaching the new student outcomes. These authors hint but rarely explicate how the change should take place. Another aspect of the newer work is found in the summaries about change and restruc-tured schools in Barth (1990), Cuban (1990), Sarason (1990), Schlechty (1990), Fullan and Miles (1992), and Fullan (1993).

Fullan echoes common themes in this literature on the change process. First, change is learning—loaded with uncertainty and complexity. Such transformational change cannot be directly man-dated because "what really matters for implementation success is in-depth understanding, and the development of skill and commitment to make them work" (1993, p. 23). Second, change is a journey, not a blueprint: it is loaded with uncertainty, is nonlinear, and sometimes even perverse. Consequently, under conditions of uncertainty, "learning, anxiety, difficulties, and fear of the unknown are *intrinsic* to all change processes, especially at the early stages. One can see why a risk-taking mentality and climate are so critical" (p. 25). The uncertainty comes from the external political climate and the administrator-teacher collaboration, but also from the call for high-stake performance by students and transformation of the learning environment in ways that are only partially understood, even by leaders in the reform.

Third, consequently, problems are seen as inevitable. However, as Fullan (1993) argues, "the good news is that you can't learn or be successful without them. . . . Change-related problems are often ignored, denied or treated as an occasion for blame and defense, instead of being treated as natural, expected and looked for . . . [and] providing the basis for understanding what has to be done in order to get what we want" (p. 26). SBM strategies will need external structures and facilitation as well as internal norms to meaningfully address problems that must be commonly acknowledged across role groups not often comfortable with open communication and cooperative action.

Fourth, the change process for SBM will be hungry for resources of many types—time, money, and personal energy. These resources must be available for the long haul and be stable, or the reform process at the local setting will be upset by the very policy structure and local key personnel most critical for its success. This lesson leads to the next, which is that reform must work at the individual and the collective level in dynamic synergism. Fullan (1993) reports that there are not one-sided solutions to isolation and groupthink, and emphasizes the need for the paradox of "creative tension between individual and group development" (p. 33). SBM represents a special challenge in this regard: it so easily becomes a justification for group action at the expense of individual initiative and perspective.

Fifth, change requires the power to manage it (cross-role groups that require legitimacy and the complexity of empowerment) and a systemic view of both components and culture. Yet all large-scale change is implemented locally and needs a perspective about how individuals learn and change, within the creative tension between individuals and organizations described above. These lessons portray change as an ongoing process of "getting it better" through a learning community.

Changes in Individuals—Paradigms, Attitudes, and Practice

A final lens focuses on the change process as a transition for individuals. Hall and Hord (1987) summarize the Concerns-based Adoption Model (CBAM) for planning and evaluating change. The model includes teachers' concerns about an innovation—seven stages that range from self, followed by task, and then consequence concerns. A second part of the CBAM model is the actual levels of use: eight levels that range from nonuse through mechanical and then routine use and refinement. The CBAM framework suggests that individuals will work through a set of stages of concern about their involvement in SBM.

Strategies for Enhancing School-Based Management

The literature on the local change process provides insights about how to enhance school-based management. These insights are discussed using Lawler and Mohrman's four elements (power, knowledge, information, and rewards) as the organizing framework and the operational definition.

Enhancing Power

- *Strategy 1: Changes in the locus of decision-making within SBM should be designed and implemented as part of a systemic reform—not as an innovation in and of itself. Conversely, avoid implementing SBM as an isolated innovation.*

Drawing on the research and thought about the new schooling outcomes, policy makers such as Smith and O'Day (1990) and Odden (1991) have proposed a new view of the technical core of schooling, and, using backward mapping, have proposed major redesign of the policy-practice linkages. SBM must be designed as part of a systemic reform, in part because previous efforts to implement it as an isolated innovation proved futile. Also, because if implemented in isolation, it loses its connection to the main purpose: enhancing high performance among students.

Previous approaches to SBM in education have emphasized issues of equity between decision-making partners; the importance of planning and a plan for school reform; SBM as a catalyst for schoolwide change; and the need to implement the created plan. From Lawler's perspective, these arrangements constitute the "parallel suggestions" model of SBM raised to a high level of hope that the suggestions would not just make incremental improvements but would change the school in fundamental and important ways.

Berman and Gjelten (1984) report that parallel process SBM succeeded more in elementary schools, where it was often seen as a process of change, than in secondary schools, where it was seen as a "program to be implemented" or as a funding source. For secondary schools, Marsh and Bowman (1989) report that SBM led to creating new school components that complemented rather than transformed schools, and focused on isolated sets of students rather than all students.

Levine and Eubanks (in press) point to six major obstacles in implementing previous versions of SBM:

1. Inadequate time, training, and technical assistance.
2. Difficulties of stimulating consideration and adaption of inconvenient changes.

3. Unresolved issues involving administrative leadership on the one hand and enhanced power among other participants on the other.

4. Constraints on teacher participation in decision making.

5. Reluctance of administrators at all levels to give up traditional prerogatives.

6. Restrictions imposed by school board, state, and federal regulations and contracts and agreements with teacher organizations.

Beneath these implementation problems, Levine and Eubanks warn us of deeper dangers concerning the implementation of SBM. The first is the confusion between teacher satisfaction and student performance. They report that "satisfaction may have been attained precisely through neglecting requirements for inconvenient institutional reform" (p. 20). Given this danger, and the complex relationship between role groups in the local setting, it is likely that systemwide focus on priority student outcomes, coupled with local flexibility on how to meet those outcomes, will be needed if teacher satisfaction is not to become the covert goal of SBM at the local level.

The second danger is that SBM approaches will be substituted for central responsibilities in comprehensive school reform (p. 20). The third danger is the confusion between SBM and the need to focus on instructional leadership, organization and implementation of instructional services, teacher development, and expectations and monitoring of student performance (Fullan, 1991).

Similarly, David (1990) studied eight of the most advanced SBM districts in the nation and found these efforts typically are intended to make differences in four aspects: curriculum and instruction, site decision making, new staff roles, and student assessment/school accountability. To date, she reports, only changes in the lives of adults were achieved. This conclusion confirms patterns found in Berman and Gjelten (1984), Levine and Eubanks (in press), and Fullan (1991).

Serious concern has also been raised about the vitality of the decision-making process itself within SBM councils (Berman and Gjelten, 1984; Malen and Ogawa, 1988). Malen and Ogawa report that "shared governance has done more than simply fail to alter traditional decision making relationships; it has actually worked to reaffirm them" (pp. 2–3). They go on to point out three sets of implementation problems with school-based councils. First, although the site councils were authorized policy makers, they functioned as ancillary advisers and pro forma endorsers. Second, teachers and parents were granted parity, but principals and professionals controlled the partnerships. Finally, relations on the council were hindered by the composition of its council, the relative power and role orientations of the principal, and the norms of propriety and civility between role groups.

Working to avoid the pitfalls of previous experience in SBM will be an important perspective on making the new approaches to SBM more effective. Fullan (1991, p. 203) concludes that "while the school is the unit of change, the concept remains one of the most misunderstood in the field of school improvement."

• *Strategy 2: Design and implement power arrangements within SBM based on a view of the new learning outcomes for students.*

It might seem to be begging the question to have a set of school outcomes and design components in mind as a prerequisite to designing the decision-making arrangements at a school. However, the track record for schools getting from decision-making processes (such as school-based councils) to schooling outcomes or teaching/learning components is so marginal that something else must be tried. Writers about policy implementation, the local change process, and the nature of needed reforms emphasize the need to plan backward from a view of what students will be learning (Elmore and Associates, 1990; Schlechty, 1990; Odden, 1991; Sizer, 1992).

Early experience with the implementation process for the new reforms in complex school organizations leads to several conclusions. First, decision making should be designed after the new view of schooling outcomes and key schooling components are clear, since they are built from this new view. The opposite orientation—building school-based decision making primarily in relation to the "top" of the district or school—leads to a vision-context paralysis.

Second, multiple decision-making structures at the school are needed—especially ones that build directly from student outcomes. The schooling redesign often involves early-on shifts in the organizational structure of the school; in turn, the new organizational unit represents a vital new decision-making arrangement at the school. This organizational redesign may create new organizational units between the individual teacher and the whole school, units that feature having day-to-day control over many aspects of a given student's life at the school.

These units may be a "house" (ten to fifteen teachers who provide education to approximately 400 secondary school students) or a "cluster" (typically a math, a science, an English and a social studies teacher who work with approximately 120 students over four class periods). A department would not count as one of these units because it typically is a support system, not a delivery of day-to-day instruction, and because it involves teaching related to only one small slice of a student's day. In Lawler's terms, departments are functional structures, which should give way to integrated service units as are described here.

These new organizational units have great potential as decision-making arrangements because they link planning, operation, and accountability for particular students in meaningful ways. Shanker (1990) emphasizes how these units need to work with students over several years to have the sustained impact needed for accountability.

Third, improved coordination among the various decision-making units is crucial and is often ignored. For example, coordination of houses with department, teaching team, and several schoolwide governance councils to enhance decision making will be needed. More generically, coordinating decision making that is primarily day-to-day with strategic decision making will need articulation. This linkage has not been done very well, according to the local change literature, but examples from the vision-oriented restructuring experiences of lead schools are very promising.

- *Strategy 3: Implementing new power arrangements within SBM will require new models of collaboration across schools and districts.*

New arrangements for power within SBM are not a matter of the centralizing or decentralizing decision making. Instead, decision making must be redesigned, based on new models of collaboration. Fullan (1991) summarizes four recent efforts where new forms of collaboration between school and district in support of new forms of SBM were implemented. In one study, Louis (1989) examined the degree of engagement (frequent interaction and communication, mutual coordination and influence, some shared goals and objectives) and degree of bureaucratization (the presence of extensive rules and regulations governing the relationship between school and district). The pattern of high engagement and low bureaucracy was the only clearly positive district context for the successful implementation of SBM. Louis summarizes this arrangement: "Essentially, the picture is one of co-management with coordination and joint planning enhanced through the development of consensus between staff members at all levels about desired goals for education" (p. 161).

The new decision-making partnership will need to focus in a new way on personnel issues. Rosenholtz (1989) reports that in districts that are on the move, leaders helped teachers improve and considered firing or counseling out as a last resort. Conversely, Fullan (1991) reports that "stuck districts, because of their internal isolationism, are less likely to take action against ineffective teachers" (p. 208). Overcoming isolationism is a function of knowledge and information; it will be discussed later in this chapter.

In summary, Fullan (1991) draws two broad conclusions about the change process linking decision making (within SBM) between the school and the district. First, sustained improvement requires serious restructuring of the school, the district, and their interrelationships. The role of students, teachers, principals, parents, and district staff are all affected, as is the structure, governance, and design of work and learning (p. 209). Second, equally important, but less obvious, is that schools cannot redesign themselves. The role of the district is crucial. Individual schools can become highly innovative for short periods of time without the district, but they cannot stay innovative without district action to establish the conditions for continuous and long improvement (p. 209).

• *Strategy 4: Implementing new power arrangements in SBM will require building a strong teacher professional culture.*

Little (1987), Lieberman (1988), Rosenholtz (1989), and Lieberman and McLaughlin (1992) propose that teacher culture is a major key to transforming schooling. In their view, the focus should be on discourse communities of teachers that "encourage teacher learning, but also serve as organizing tools to keep teachers working together, sharing, and learning from one another over time" (Lieberman and McLaughlin, 1992, p. 674). Consequently, less attention should be given to finalizing formal decision-making structures within schools until an authentic teacher culture and a student outcome focus have been established. This view shows decision making as following or interacting with—not necessarily leading—the creation of an vital teacher culture.

• *Strategy 5: Implementing new power arrangements within SBM will require viewing the change process as a journey, yet managing the change itself carefully.*

In the early literature on the local change process, change was conceptualized in terms of a set of linear stages, progressing from initiation through implementation to institutionalization. Interestingly for implementing SBM, Fullan (1991) portrays this structure as four boxes in linear sequence, ranging from initiation through implementation to continuation and finally to outcomes. The special dilemma for enhancing school-based decision making is that outcomes are to be considered only after full implementation and continuation (institutionalization) have been achieved. This linear structuring of the change process obviously is problematic for school-based management as it has been practiced to date.

Recently, authors in the change literature have shifted their perspective about the relationship of planning and doing. Fullan and Miles (1992) proposed that change should be viewed as a journey (as opposed to a blueprint), where the message "is not the traditional plan, but do then plan, do and plan some more" (p. 749). They report that even the development of a shared vision that is central to reform is better thought of as a journey in which people's sense of purpose is identified, considered, and continuously shaped and reshaped. This finding has two implications for decision making within SBM. The first, obviously, is that planning and doing will be intertwined in ways that take decision making well beyond a rational model of planning and then deciding. Second, it raises again the importance of a shared vision that must be a part of school-based decision making in ways that will be explored later in the chapter.

The view of change as a journey also points to the importance of coping strategies as ways to make decision-making structures more effective. Since change cannot be developed as a blueprint, no specific plan can last for very long, because it will either become outmoded due to changing external pressures, or because disagreement over priorities will rise within the organization (Louis and Miles, 1990). The style of coping strategy adopted by the school is very important to the success of SBM. Louis and Miles report that deep coping (the key to solving difficult problems of reform) is not a matter of muddling through, but requires reflection, data, and consideration of multiple points of view about problems before effective decisions can be made. Louis and Miles classified coping styles

ranging from relatively shallow ones (doing nothing at all, procras-
tinating, doing it the usual way, easing off, or increasing pressure)
to deeper ones (building personal capacity through training,
enhancing system capacity, comprehensive restaffing, or system
restructuring or redesign). They found that schools that were least
successful at change always use shallow coping styles. They also
report that the enemies of good coping are passivity, denial, avoid-
ance, conventionality, and fear of being too radical. Good coping
is active, assertive, inventive. It goes to the root of the problem.

Fullan and Miles report that coping appears more likely when
schools are "working on a clear, shared vision of where they're head-
ing, and when they create an active coping structure (for example,
a coordinating committee or steering group) that steadily and
actively tracks problems and monitors the results of coping efforts.
Such a structure benefits from empowerment, brings more resources
to bear on problems, and keeps the energy for change focused" (Fullan and Miles, 1992, p. 750). Successful participants in SBM will
have learned to link their shared vision to their deep coping strategies.

Successful SBM efforts will also embrace problems. Fullan and
Miles (1992) report that improvement is a "problem-rich process"
and that "change threatens existing interests and routines, height-
ens uncertainty and increases complexity" (p. 750). Schools that
have viable decision-making structures are ones that love problems
and seek to solve them.

Louis and Miles (1990) report schools typically bumped into
three or four major problems (and several minor ones) with reform
efforts: problems that range from poor coordination to staff polar-
ization, and from lack of needed skills to heart attacks suffered by
key figures. They see problems as arising naturally from the demands
of the change process itself, from the people involved, and from the
structures and procedures of schools and districts. The need for decision groups to embrace problems as the only viable way to create
meaningful solutions is an important finding. Fullan and Miles

(1992) report "too often, change related problems are ignored, denied, or treated as an occasion for blame and defense. Only by tracking problems can we understand what we need to do next to get what we want" (p. 750).

Enhancing Knowledge

In Mohrman, Lawler, and Mohrman (1992), knowledge includes the knowledge and skills "that enables employees to understand and contribute to organizational performance" (p. 1). It is important to consider knowledge and skills in the context of three aspects of work in school settings that are reported to be "critical in influencing the appropriateness of different involvement approaches: 1) the degree of interdependence; 2) the degree of complexity; and 3) the amount of uncertainty that has to be reduced. Education is arguably high on all these factors, although the organization designs and technology that are currently employed do not necessarily acknowledge that fact" (p. 7).

- *Strategy 1: Use knowledge informed by the new view of schooling and the diverse nature of students.*

The literature on local change process offers several important and useful perspectives about the interdependence, complexity, and uncertainty of school-based knowledge. Knowledge in school settings is uncertain for the usual reasons: political diversity about goals, lack of verifiable principles about teaching and learning, and the loose organizational structure. However, several new perspectives on knowledge uncertainty are extremely important to the current efforts in restructuring.

The first of these is the shift in student demographics, which has challenged researchers and practitioners to develop new knowledge about student engagement, learning, and student outcomes. These highly demanding outcomes are goals for all students, and new wisdom is needed about how to carry out each of the schooling components in the context of these new goals. Doubly troubling is the problem of integrating teaching, learning, organizational structure, curriculum, and assessment around these new goals; that integration is more demanding than is knowledge about individual components of the reform.

This knowledge can be developed several ways during the implementation process. An antecedent phase before beginning the reform across the school or district has helped individual teachers become aware of new approaches to curriculum and teaching. Marsh and Odden (1991) found that during the antecedent phase, teachers learned through contact with other teachers outside the school. These contacts were usually sustained (weeks of interaction, not hours) and featured common experiential learning, sharing of success and reflection on practice, and networks that supported teachers as they applied the knowledge in their own schools.

National and state task forces can effectively communicate this knowledge through reports that present an integrated vision of the new approach to schooling. Marsh and Crocker (1991) found that these reports educated local participants about the reform, provided credibility and validation of the ideas and the local leaders who supported them, and sustained local momentum during difficult times.

Fullan (1991) reports that districts could enhance this knowledge by having superintendents who "actively and systematically worked on the familiar ingredients for success: setting goal and expectations, selecting staff, supervising and supporting professional development, focusing on instruction and curriculum, ensuring consistency, and monitoring instructional programs" (p.209). Local knowledge of the reform was also enhanced through initial awareness training, sustained local assistance, and visits to lead schools.

Peer review processes involving quality indicators based on the new reforms also enhanced local knowledge of the reforms. Marsh and Crocker (1991) found that these reviews supported self-study (including reflection and critical review) of their reform efforts, provided feedback that enhanced local knowledge, and provided a common technical language that supported further growth of local knowledge.

- *Strategy 2: Use narrative and paradigmatic knowledge about schooling.*

Not only will new knowledge be needed, but also a new view of knowledge. We previously thought of knowledge in paradigmatic or propositional terms. Bruner (1990) provides a constructivist view of knowledge based more on narrative and craft insight than proposition or paradigms per se. The very curriculum centered on thinking and meaning that we intend for students is paralleled in the need for a thinking- and meaning-centered knowledge base for teachers and other school practitioners. The way school-based decision-making arrangements (either strategic or day-to-day) use this new view of knowledge itself, and the new integrated knowledge about schooling, will be closely related to the success of those decision-making structures.

For example, teachers using portfolio assessment of students' writing may capture what they have learned in stories that reflect their craft knowledge. Decisions to revise work arrangements and learning environments may then be based on complex stories rather than "hard knowledge." Decision structures that use outdated views of technical knowledge will most likely not be successful.

This new type of knowledge can be developed during the implementation process. Sparks (1983) found that teachers need to talk about their learning during workshops, and that reflective journals help teachers create personal insights and new meaning around professional activities. Teachers need to experience this type of knowledge generation in workshops and talk about its qualities. But most important, norms about the types of knowledge that can be appropriately used in SBM will be needed, and these can be discussed and practiced during the implementation of SBM.

- *Strategy 3: Implementation strategies must build both programmatic specificity and conceptual clarity as a knowledge base for SBM.*

McLaughlin and Marsh (1978) emphasize the importance of both programmatic specificity and conceptual clarity as ways of understanding SBM. Programmatic specificity often is reflected in detailed statements, typically in writing, that describe the intended change. This type of knowledge would typically be found among a few leaders early in the implementation process. Conceptual clarity about the overall reform is a type of knowledge that evolves over time and is the experience-based understanding that practitioners have of this change and its meaning both for them and for the school.

Similarly, Fullan and Miles (1992) point out that understanding change as a process of learning also puts ownership in perspective. In their view, "ownership of a reform cannot be achieved *in advance* of learning something new; a deep sense of ownership comes only through learning. In this sense, ownership is stronger in the middle of a successful change process than at the beginning and stronger still at the end. Ownership is both a process and a state" (p. 749). Consequently, both knowledge and ownership will evolve in complex ways in major change efforts.

Building programmatic specificity during the implementation process is a matter of clarity of expression about what SBM consists of and how it will work. Strategies for developing conceptual clarity among participants in SBM will be more difficult. Problems, for example, could be used to build conceptual clarity about SBM among participants as part of the implementation process. Change facilitators need to anticipate that participants will want to renegotiate their SBM arrangements as their understanding of it develops. In short, this knowledge cannot be "frontloaded" in the implementation process.

• *Strategy 4: Use networks and cross-role teams to build knowledge of both schooling and school change.*

It is likely that different role groups participating in decision making within SBM will need networks to other decision-making groups and with role-alike participants at other schools. Lieberman and McLaughlin (1992) point to a number of dilemmas that must be avoided in using networks. First, "networks typically are unencumbered by bureaucratic restrictions and are free of traditional form of inspection which creates excitement because there is no old political or social baggage to carry and teachers play a leading role in the venture" (p. 650). Unfortunately, this autonomy may create problems of quality, application, and stability for the network. There is also the danger that networks create such a sense of independence for teachers that the decision-making structure then is difficult to operate. They warn that it may be especially difficult to link to student successes or schooling experiences across the whole school.

Networks could aid implementation more effectively if they were managed by district-school cross-role teams. Odden (1991) reports that many studies have found cross-role teams to be important vehicles for managing the implementation process. Cross-role teams could provide the institutional focus that networks need without having teachers "submit" to administrative control. Cross-role teams link the local organization vertically and provide both the clinical expertise of teachers with the gatekeeping functions of administrators. Cross-role teams could also link teachers to each other in the local setting and help translate the knowledge gained from networks into organizational learning at the local site.

- *Strategy 5: School leaders need a deep understanding of the purposes and "connectedness" of schools.*

A related approach to building an effective decision-making structure within a school is to focus teachers at the school in a sustained discussion of desired student outcomes and schooling arrangements. Sizer (1992) provides an extensive and intriguing scenario in his book, *Horace's School*, where a leadership committee of teachers and administrators engage in discussion and reading that leads to a proposal for a dramatically refined school. This sense of in-depth discussion carried on in a sustained manner is an important way to build knowledge that will be vital to implementing school-based decision making.

Barth (1990) provides a similar view of members of the school community being a "community of scholars" and a "community of learners." Ad hoc strategies for engaging in discussion and reflection are provided in this exciting book. The challenge will be to help school-based decision-making groups engage in this type of deep reflection while also making more technical, managerial, and time-urgent decisions.

- *Strategy 6: Develop knowledge through an appropriate use of training.*
Traditional approaches to staff development offer (at their best) powerful models of training that enhance school-based decision making. Joyce and Showers (1988) provide an extensive synthesis of the staff development literature in a way that is relevant to training for school-based decision making. They point to four major outcomes of training: awareness, knowledge, skill application, and use of training in natural settings. They also point to five major components of the training process as including:

1. *Knowledge/theory.* This strategy provides school-based decision makers with an understanding of the overall theory and constructs some school-based decision-making principles.

2. *Modeling/demonstration.* This approach helps school-based decision makers understand simulated and actual examples of school-based decision making. Modeling typically should include both process and product modeling, which shows participants the process of engaging in decision making and typical results.

3. *Practice.* Participants would have a chance to practice relevant skills and cultural norms in a workshop setting. Multiple rounds of practice and discussion are important to the success of this training component.

4. *Feedback.* Both structured and unstructured feedback is needed, to help participants have a chance to talk about their feelings and perceptions of school-based decision making (unstructured feedback) and to examine their own practice against some criteria of excellence (structured feedback).

5. *Coaching for application.* Coaching includes assistance and observation by peers or experts on the use of decision-making strategies in their natural setting. Learning teams could observe each other and then have periodic discussions with experts in the decision-making process as well as with experts in the substance of school restructuring.

To build awareness-level understanding, only knowledge and modeling components of training are necessary. But to have extensive transfer of training into natural settings, all five components—especially coaching—are necessary. Without the coaching component, transfer is extremely weak. Successful coaching includes many of the elements found in the discussion of networks above. The implementation of SBM will need extensive training for local site participants and for related roles including students, parents, district leaders, and policy makers. Training should focus on teams, not individuals, and provide sustained assistance and coaching for on-site application.

• *Strategy 7: Provide multiple forms of assistance to enhance knowledge.*

Training alone will not be sufficient to implement SBM in educational settings. More comprehensive and integrated forms of assistance will be needed to build the knowledge and skill base. Huberman and Miles (1984) propose eight kinds of assistance:

1. Control, where the assister exerts pressure aimed at making the receiver do something.
2. Training, where the assister explicitly transmits information, developing receiver skill, and so on, usually in a structured way.
3. Solution giving, where the assister gives the receiver "answers," advice, or solutions to problems.

4. Resource adding, where the assister provides materials, money, time, or other resources needed by the receiver.

5. Advocacy, where the assister actively represents the interest of the receiver to some other audience (such as administrators or funders).

6. Facilitation, where the assister aids the receiver to achieve goals, giving at-the-elbow assistance with the process being used.

7. Inquiry, where the assister collects data from the receiver, or from the implementation situation more generally, and feeds it back in a "formative evaluation" to aid in the next steps.

8. Support, where the assister provides encouragement, reinforcement, or emotional support to the receiver.

SBM will be most effectively implemented when multiple forms of assistance are intertwined over the duration of the implementation process. Huberman and Miles found that control-style assistance actually needed to increase, as did support and inquiry in later stages of implementation.

Huberman and Miles provide several other lessons for the implementation of SBM, including:

1. SBM should be complex, well-designed, and demanding for practitioners to implement. Strong district support for SBM is critical.

2. Sustained assistance that integrates all of the types of assistance listed above will be needed over several years of implementation.

3. The latitude of what constitutes SBM should be kept no wider than moderate during the early implementation phase, and be closely linked to assistance.

4. Successful implementation typically includes reports from

practitioners that the early going is very rough; great care should be taken not to "downsize" SBM at that time. Moreover, a drop in participant morale should be anticipated in the short run.

These are important insights about the journey that is likely for participants undertaking complex forms of SBM.

Enhancing Information

Strategies for implementing SBM need to include specific ways that the availability and use of information can be decentralized and improved within the organization. In this context, the redesign of the information element will involve helping the organization become more outcome-driven. Moving from a rule- and input-driven organization to one focused on outcomes will be a major shift for most school districts, and the decentralization and improvement of the use of information must be set in this new organizational orientation.

Redesigning the availability and use of information in the organization must also be done in light of the new reforms themselves. For example, the organization will need to know about newly emphasized types of student outcomes, such as how students think and solve problems or how well they are prepared to participate meaningfully as citizens in a complex society. The organization will also need to know about teaching and learning that has new features, and how this teaching and learning are contributing to achieving these outcomes. Finally, the new organization will need not only to shift information from the top to the bottom, but also to connect the top and bottom through the redesigned use of this information.

The local change literature suggests four strategies for using information in these new ways.

• *Strategy 1: Focus on teacher-centered collaborative development of new information use.*

Experience with several teacher-centered collaborative efforts to develop decentralized and new uses of information in schools suggests strategies for how to implement the information element of SBM (see early efforts by Lauren Resnick in the New Standards Project, by Ann Brown in the University of California at Berkeley/schools collaborative, by Howard Gardner in Project Zero, and the Coalition of Essential Schools). Critical elements for successful use of new information are:

1. Sustained contact between researchers and teachers that builds on teachers' craft knowledge and classroom reality.
2. Use of networks of teachers across schools that have the characteristics of teacher networks described by Lieberman and McLaughlin above.
3. Collaborative invention of performance assessment and reflection strategies that reduce the seam between learning and assessment.
4. Planning backward from the new student outcomes.

• *Strategy 2: Strengthen the way information is shared and used within the school and district.*

Another strategy for enhancing information use within SBM is to alter how information is used in the relations between districts and schools. Fullan reports that districts with a strong and effective district presence in the schools "provided the site with a variety of school-specific performance data, discussed these data with the principals and set expectations for their use, and monitored, through recognized procedures, how and with what success the schools used the performance data" (LaRocque and Coleman, 1989, cited in Fullan, 1991, p. 205). The nature of the discussion should be collaborative rather than prescriptive. Sites then developed plans for improvement, although the process in developing and implementing the plans was monitored.

Conversely, in districts that were stuck, Rosenholtz (1989) reports that "with little helpful assistance, stuck superintendents symbolically communicated the norm of self-reliance and subsequently professional isolation" (cited in Fullan, 1991, p. 208). Establishing positive qualities in the interaction between the district and the site will be critical to implementing new arrangements for information within SBM.

• *Strategy 3: Launch an evolving systemic redesign of information use.*

Designing the way the information will be used will require a change process featuring a well-designed innovation, commitment from district and school leadership, cross-role teams to coordinate the implementation, and sustained assistance combined with pressure to enhance implementation and teacher effort to try the new use (Odden, 1991). The evolving system will also need to grow out of the experience of the teacher-centered collaborative efforts and the new dynamic patterns between district and school described above.

• *Strategy 4: Use information about the change process itself in new ways.*

The ways that information is used in the implementation process itself will strongly influence the use of information more generally in the organization. Many effective school leaders have used information about student performance as a way of portraying the current situation at the school as unacceptable. They have used this strategy to counter the common view in schools that current practice should be seen as adequate and that only the proposed changes need to be justified. Information about schooling is quite difficult to obtain, both for political and technical reasons. It is unlikely that most effective school-based decision-making groups will be able to gain access to meaningful information without extensive efforts to overcome these political and technical barriers.

Fullan and Miles (1992) emphasize the importance of information about implementation problems when they say, "Only by tracking problems can we understand what we need to do next to get what we want" (p. 750). They emphasize that problems must be taken seriously, that is, not attributed to "resistance" or to the ignorance or wrong-headedness of others. Strategies for obtaining deep understanding of problems will require information gaining and analysis strategies well beyond quantitative manipulation of conventional data.

Similarly, Fullan (1991) emphasizes that one of the main purposes of the process of implementation is to "exchange your reality of what should be through interaction with implementers and others concerned" (p. 105). The information needed for this exchange of reality must be subtle and qualitative, and is vital to the success of SBM. Fullan (1991) also emphasizes the need to get information about teachers' views regarding need, clarity, complexity, and the quality and practice of the innovation. This information would help avoid the dangers of "false clarity," where participants have a superficial understanding of the needed changes.

Enhancing Rewards

Focusing SBM decision making on achieving various student outcomes and the rewards for achieving them will be a difficult and major transformation of the school, as the literature on local change process shows. The literature, however, has a number of insights that would help this aspect of decision making become effective in school settings.

- *Strategy 1: Use a range of meaningful rewards.*
  The literature identifies a number of rewards that teachers find meaningful in school settings. Many are psychosocial in nature,

such as a sense of satisfaction of having helped individual students and having made a difference in their lives. Teachers also consider it a reward to be given extra time and materials useful to their teaching.

The point is that schools have typically not been driven primarily by financial incentives, although teachers have appreciated extra pay for attending staff development sessions or taking on leadership roles in schools. It must be pointed out, however, that these monetary incentives have been fairly modest. Lortie (1975) notes that all male teachers in his sample who were forty or older had a second job or a major hobby that attracted their time and energy; in other words, the locus of rewards was outside the school. These teachers tended not to think of teaching as a place where they could gain extra dollar incentives.

To help establish various rewards in a school setting, it will be important to use a range of rewards that include psychosocial as well as monetary ones, and to work with teachers to establish the credibility and cultural acceptance of these rewards. Attempts to lay rewards on schools from outside have been notoriously unsuccessful in the past.

- *Strategy 2: Focus on balancing teacher empowerment and accountability as a cultural, political, and technical issue.*

The problem is to establish both teacher empowerment and decision making while also establishing accountability for student outcomes in programs in the school setting. Teachers must play a key role in feeling empowered while also feeling accountable in schools. In the short run, strategies for enhancing rewards as part of decision making in SBM will need to try one of two strategies— either empowerment-dominated or accountability-dominated efforts.

In the absence of clear outcomes about schools (which many authors have described at length), school-based leaders are likely to shy away from an emphasis on student outcomes of any type, and instead rely on factors such as bureaucratic safety, response to external pressure, or approval of peer elites. Fullan (1991) points out that "in the absence of clearly defined output criteria, whatever is popular among leading professional peers is sometimes determining criteria" (p. 60). In some respects, this responsiveness to peer pressure is positive and important; however, the responsiveness increasingly must become linked to school outcomes. The design of rewards must include provision for the political stability of desired outcomes and a coherent design for SBM that aligns the incentives for site personnel.

Conclusion

In this chapter, the conceptualization of SBM is based on important work by Lawler and Mohrman and is defined as decentralizing power, knowledge, information, and rewards within systemic redesign of the educational system. Strategies drawn from the literature on local change process are proposed for enhancing the decentralization of those four components.

Three conclusions can be drawn from the analysis presented in the chapter. The first is that school-based management (SBM) in educational settings has not been successful to date, and that weak implementation processes were part of the problem. Too often, SBM was treated as an isolated innovation that was intended to improve curriculum and instruction, enhance site decision making, create new staff roles, and improve student assessment. However, its actual effects have been limited to changes in the lives of adults at the school, and even there, decision making has not been fundamentally revised. Its lack of effectiveness has been linked to weak implementation processes that included lack of time, inadequate participant training, and unresolved issues involving the links between the district and the school. Weak implementation was also found to result when participants confused satisfaction about the empowerment of adults with performance success for students.

The second conclusion is that SBM within systemic reform will require a robust implementation process. An antecedent phase of the change process must allow selected participants a chance to develop expertise and a professional culture that allows them to guide the initiation and implementation phases of the reform. Initiation must include careful design of SBM within systemic reform. For this, strong central-office support will be needed to create a reform that addresses issues of power and empowerment between the district and the site. A cross-role team must guide the implementation process, which itself will need resources and management.

Successful implementation will feature sustained assistance that balances training and control with inquiry and support for all participants, and links assistance with pressure to implement the reform and incentives for effort. Participants will also need to be networked with SBM efforts at other sites to share ideas and build a reflective professional culture. Care must be taken, however, that the networks are linked to the systemic reform effort at the local site; the danger is that the evolving professional culture will serve individual adult participants at the expense of the collective effort to reform the schooling experience for students.

The final conclusion is that successful implementation of SBM will require much more than decentralizing existing concepts of power, knowledge, information, and rewards within the existing organization. Instead, new forms of knowledge and information linked directly to student outcomes, such as conceptual understanding and critical thinking, will be needed. For this to happen, new assessment approaches (such as performance assessment) and models for teacher-centered information use must be developed. A cultural and political shift in schools toward an outcome focus for the organization and careful links between results and rewards must be developed.

References

Barth, R. S. (1990). *Improving schools from within.* San Francisco: Jossey-Bass.

Berman, P., and Gjelten, T. (1984). *Improving school improvement: A policy evaluation of the California school improvement program. Volume 2: Findings.* Berkeley, CA: Berman, Weiler Associates.

Bruner, J. S. (1990). *Acts of meaning.* Cambridge, MA: Harvard University Press.

Clune, W. H., and White, P. A. (1988). *School-based management: Institutional variation, implementation, and issues for further research.* New Brunswick, NJ: Eagleton Institute of Politics, Center for Policy Research in Education.

Cuban, L. (1990). Reforming, again, again, and again. *Educational Researcher, 19*(3), 3–13.

David, J. L. (1990). Restructuring in progress: Lessons from pioneering districts. In R. F. Elmore and Associates (Eds.), *Restructuring schools: The next generation of educational reform.* San Francisco: Jossey-Bass.

Elmore, R. F., and Associates. (1990). *Restructuring schools: The next generation of educational reform.* San Francisco: Jossey-Bass.

Firestone, W. (1989). Using reform: Conceptualizing district initiative. *Educational Evaluation and Policy Analysis, 11,* 151–164.

Fuhrman, S. H. (1993). *Designing coherent education policy: Improving the system.* San Francisco: Jossey-Bass.

Fullan, M. (1991). *The new meaning of educational change.* New York: Teachers College Press.

Fullan, M. (1993). *Change forces: Probing the depths of educational reforms.* New York: Falmer Press.

Fullan, M., and Miles, M. (1992). Getting reform right: What works and what doesn't. *Phi Delta Kappan, 73,* 745–752.

Goodlad, J. (1983). *A place called school.* New York: McGraw-Hill.

Hall, G., and Hord, S. (1987). *Change in schools: Facilitating the process.* Albany, NY: State University of New York Press.

Huberman, M., and Miles, M. (1984). *Innovation up close: How school improvement works.* New York: Plenum.

Joyce, B., and Showers, B. (1988). *Student achievement through staff development.* New York: Longman.

Lawler, E. E. (1986). *High-involvement management: Participative strategies for improving organizational performance.* San Francisco: Jossey-Bass.

Levine, D. and Eubanks, E. (In press). *Site-based management: Engine for reform or pipe-dream? Problems, pitfalls and prerequisites for success in site-based management.* Manuscript submitted for publication, 1989. Cited in M.

Fullan, *The New Meaning of Educational Change*. New York: Teachers College Press, 1991.

Lieberman, A. (Ed.) (1988). *Building a professional culture in schools*. New York: Teachers College Press.

Lieberman, A., and McLaughlin, M. (1992). Networks for educational change: Powerful and problematic. *Phi Delta Kappan, 77*, 673–677.

Little, J. W. (1982). Norms of collegiality and experimentation: workplace conditions of school success. *American Educational Research Journal, 19*, 325–340.

Little, J. W. (1987). Teachers as colleagues. In V. Richardson-Koehler (Ed.), *Educators' handbook: A research perspective*. New York: Longman.

Little, J. W., and others (1987). *Staff development in California: Public and personal investments, program patterns and policy choices*. San Francisco: Far West Laboratory for Educational Research and Development and Policy Analysis for California Education.

Lortie, D. (1975). *Schoolteacher: A sociological study*. Chicago: University of Chicago Press.

Louis, K. (1989). The role of the school district in school improvement. In M. Holmes, K. Leithwood, and D. Musella (Eds.), *Educational policy for effective schools* (pp. 145–67). Toronto: OISE Press.

Louis, K. S., and Miles, M. B. (1990). *Improving the urban high school: What works and why*. New York: Teachers College Press.

Malen, B., and Ogawa, R. (1988). Professional-patron influence on site-based governance councils: A confounding case study. *Educational Evaluation and Policy Analysis, 10*, 251–270.

Marsh, D. D., and Bowman, G. A. (1989). State initiated top-down versus bottom-up reform. *Educational Policy, 3*, 195–216.

Marsh, D., and Crocker, P. (1991). School restructuring: Implementing middle school reform. In A. Odden (Ed.), *Education policy implementation*. Albany, NY: State University of New York Press.

Marsh, D., and Odden, A. (1991). Implementation of the California mathematics and science curriculum frameworks. In A. Odden (Ed.), *Education policy implementation*. Albany, NY: State University of New York Press.

McLaughlin, M. W. (1990). The RAND change agent study: Retrospective. *Educational Researcher, 19*(9), 11–16.

McLaughlin, M., and Marsh, D. (1978). Staff development and school change. *Teachers College Record, 80*, 69–94.

Mohrman, S. A., Lawler, E. E., and Mohrman, A. M. (1992). Applying employee involvement in schools. *Educational Evaluation and Policy Analysis, 14*, 347–360.

Murphy, J. (1990). *The reform of American public education in the 1980s: Perspectives and cases.* Berkeley, CA: McCutchan.

National Commission on Excellence in Education. (1983). *A nation at risk.* Washington, DC: U. S. Government Printing Office.

Odden, A. (Ed.). (1991). *Education policy implementation.* Albany, NY: State University of New York Press.

Odden, A., and Marsh, D. (1988). How comprehensive state education reform can improve secondary schools. *Phi Delta Kappan, 69,* 593–598.

Rosenholtz, S. (1989). *Teachers' workplace: The social organization of schools.* New York: Longman.

Sarason, S. (1990). *The predictable failure of educational reform.* San Francisco: Jossey-Bass.

Schlechty, P. C. (1990). *Schools for the 21st century.* San Francisco: Jossey-Bass.

Shanker, A. (1990). Staff development and the restructured school. In B. Joyce (Ed.), *Changing school culture through staff development: 1990 yearbook of the Association for Supervision and Curriculum Development.* Alexandria, VA: Association for Supervision and Curriculum Development.

Sizer, T. R. (1992). *Horace's School: Redesigning the American high school.* Boston: Houghton Mifflin.

Smith, M., and O'Day, J. (1990). *Systemic Reform.* New Brunswick, NJ: Rutgers University, Center for Policy Research in Education.

Sparks, G. (1983). Synthesis of research on staff development for effective teaching. *Educational Leadership, 41*(2), 65–72.

Wohlstetter, P., and Buffett, T. (1992). Decentralizing dollars under school-based management: Have policies changed? *Educational Policy, 6*(1), 35–54.

Wohlstetter, P., and Odden, A. (1992). Rethinking school-based management policy and research. *Educational Administration Quarterly, 28,* 529–549.

Chapter Ten

Understanding and Managing the Change Process

Susan Albers Mohrman

Priscilla Wohlstetter

School-based management represents a large-scale change for school districts, involving far more than decision-making structures and processes. Furthermore, it is a part of an even more extensive transition that includes almost all aspects of public education—systemic reform. The change management challenges are overwhelming. This chapter draws on the learnings from change to high-involvement management in the private sector (described in Chapter Eight) and on the learnings from studies of change processes in schools (Chapter Nine). It presents principles about how to approach the large-scale transition to school-based management.

School-based management (SBM) is an effort to modify the governance structure of schools by moving authority into the local school. This has been referred to as the debureaucratization of schools, and is expected by its proponents to result not only in improvements in school performance but also in a democratization of control of schools that will align the school more closely with the preferences of its participants (Raywid, 1990). SBM has been conceptualized as an example of the dimension of the school reform movement that addresses the power balance between schools and their clients. The premise of this approach to reform, as reported by Elmore and Associates (1990), is that schools will be better able to produce results that are in line with their clients' preferences if they have a more direct link to their clientele and if they have a greater degree of control over their resources.

The goals of SBM are thus twofold: to increase the performance of schools and to more closely align their performance with the desires of the communities they serve. There are two other main streams in the school reform movement: knowledge-based changes in the core technology of schools, and changes in the occupational situation of the teaching profession (Elmore and Associates, 1990).

There has been some debate concerning whether these various approaches to reform are complementary or contradictory. This debate has centered largely on the issue of control. It has addressed the question of whether knowledge-based control (presumably with institutions of higher education taking a lead in the knowledge-generation process), professional control by teachers, and shared control with the community are compatible, and whether they dictate different organizational arrangements and different organizational outcomes.

The systemic reform movement combines all three of these reform strands in a holistic model of school reform (Fuhrman, 1993). In this framework, school-based management is one prong of a multipronged set of complementary reforms. It moves the authority into the schools to introduce powerful new curricular approaches, and relies on the development of a collaborative professional teacher culture. This conceptualization is shared by Marsh, who in Chapter Nine of this volume talks of school-based management as the "pathway to reform."

Mohrman and Wohlstetter have made the case several times that SBM implies a large-scale change in the character of the school as an organization, and that it can only be implemented in conjunction with a clear intent to use educational knowledge to improve school performance and to create a collaborative teacher culture so that the local school is capable of designing itself. Mohrman has compared the transition to school-based management with the transition to what in the private sector has been referred to as high-involvement management, a systemic and large-scale change in the organization to enable its participants to become more actively involved in improving the performance of the organization, including the work processes that are applied. This conceptualization of SBM leads to certain principles to guide the transition.

Principles of Change

The following principles of change management are compatible with the change frameworks described in Chapter Eight and with the school change literature overviewed in Chapter Nine. Since schools are organizations, it is not surprising that the principles of change would be similar in schools and other kinds of organization. The application of the principles will have to be tailored to fit the configuration of actors and organizational tasks.

- *Creating new governance structures is not enough.*

The track record of school-based management leading to improvement in school performance is not exemplary. Some studies show that the main positive outcome of SBM has been improvement in the involvement levels of the adult participants in the schools, and that there has been little positive impact on schooling (for example, David, 1990). It is also claimed that the new governance structures (generally councils) have in most cases done little to alter the balance of power between constituencies, and that in many cases only minor increases in school-level authority have occurred.

Explanations of the limited impact of SBM include a focus on the particulars of the council design. They also include a discussion of whether adequate or the right authority has devolved to the school. For example, it has been suggested that unless the principal is selected by the council, true school-based authority cannot exist

(Raywid, 1990). Furthermore, examination of councils has shown that frequently the balance of power within the council reflects the status quo, with principals exercising primary power, either because of the way the council is structured or because of the unequal knowledge bases and hierarchical norms of conduct in the council.

Whatever the reason, the establishment of new governance structures has not led to the ultimate outcomes originally envisioned. This discussion is reminiscent of the literature reviewing the impact of various kinds of participative structures that were introduced into private-sector organizations in the 1970s and 1980s (Ledford, Lawler, and Mohrman, 1988). These approaches were based on similar premises to those underlying the advocacy of SBM: that members of an organizational unit are in the best position to make improvements to the functioning of that unit, and that power needs to be moved out from the distant levels of the hierarchy and closer to the people doing the work and to their clientele. Early results from these efforts were quite disappointing. Despite massive investments in training and time, the creation of such structures proved to be too weak an intervention to alter the status quo of the organization and to introduce meaningful change to the organization (Lawler and Mohrman, 1987).

The early generations of participation groups in the private sector have evolved into a more systemic intervention aimed at changing the operating logic of the organization by redesigning many aspects of how the organization functions (Walton, 1985; Lawler, 1986). SBM interventions will likewise have to be seen as part of a more fundamental change. The focus must be on changes that transcend the more limited spotlight on the governance structures alone. This leads to the next principle of change.

• *School-based management cannot be adopted as an innovation or a program. It is a systemic change that requires a transition to a new way of managing and a new logic of organizing.*

The premise of SBM is that school participants should have authority over the variables required for effective school performance. This very premise raises questions that go well beyond the establishment of governance structures in which to locate such authority. Authority, particularly in a professional organization, relies on much more than formal decision-making power. Legitimacy of authority in a school interacts with professional norms and relies on the ability to establish credibility among a diverse group of constituencies. It stems from knowledge and skills, both in technical and process arenas, and relies on the possession of information.

Bureaucratic organizational school designs have placed organizational authority within the hierarchy, and left a great deal of the day-to-day operating authority in the hands of the classroom teacher. Teachers exercise authority in their classroom and frequently in departments or grade-level groups in making decisions about curriculum implementation. Traditionally, they have exercised little collegial influence on schoolwide issues, and virtually none on central office or school board decisions. The movement to SBM rethinks where various kinds of authority should be placed, and consequently requires that the resources that support such authority be moved to the proper location.

The large-scale transition will include the redesign of organizational systems to ensure that as power is moved, knowledge and skills are developed, and information is shared. As new structures such as councils are designed, the organization will have to determine the roles of these new structures and how they relate to one another and to other existing roles and structures. In addition, because the issue of control is so politically charged (various stakeholders have different preferences for outcomes), there will have to be mechanisms for collectively determining direction and aligning incentives. The reward system will have to be aligned with the valued outcomes of the organization.

Marsh (Chapter Nine) has made the point that the implementation process itself requires the design of approaches to develop skills and knowledge, share information, and align incentives. Setting up a structure and declaring it the seat of power will accomplish little if these other systems needs are not attended to. He recommends a representative, cross-role approach to designing these systems.

If the empowerment of the school site is to truly be a catalyst for improvement in outcomes through changes in the technical core of the school, the knowledge, skill, and information requirements of the participants will go well beyond what is required to make the new governance structures work. School-level participants will have to get broad knowledge and information to enable them to be informed governors. This means that broad knowledge of schooling as well as understanding of organizational issues will be required for the school to redesign itself to be more effective. The new design of the school has to fit with emerging knowledge about the technology of educating.

- *If school-based management is to result in improved school outcomes, it must be implemented in the context of goals for the educational process.*

To date, the major impact of most SBM implementations has been on adults within the system, and there has been little impact on student outcomes (David, 1990). In Chapter Nine, Marsh cites Levine and Eubanks, who caution against confusing teacher satisfaction and student outcomes. Indeed, organizational research has shown no reliable link between employee satisfaction and employee performance (Lawler, 1973). Interventions designed primarily to affect the former can therefore not be expected to necessarily have the latter as a consequence.

Marsh has suggested that one way to ensure that the two are related is to intentionally link the implementation of SBM with the transition toward an educational program that focuses on higher-order thinking, conceptual understanding, and powerful communication for all students. This emphasis on clearly defining the desired organizational outcomes fits with the large-scale change roadmap for self-design presented in Chapter Eight, which prescribes determining values and criteria before redesigning and introducing new organizational features.

The bottom line is that innovations have to have meaning to people if they are to be able to implement them effectively and achieve organizational impact (Fullan, 1991). One part of the shared meaning that must be developed is the goals of the change process—the values that the organization is trying to achieve. Research on team processes in organizations finds that in the absence of a clear organizational strategy and shared goals, work teams are relatively ineffective performers (Mohrman, Cohen, and Mohrman, 1994). In addition, improvement teams, such as task teams, design groups, councils, and quality improvement teams, rely on a clear strategy to help them define the criteria toward which they should be improving the organization. In the absence of performance-related criteria, they will focus on changes that address their own concerns rather than those that achieve an incremental improvement in organizational performance.

The self-design strategy prescribes a multistakeholder process for value clarification. Even within the context of a shareholder-owned business organization, it cannot be assumed that one stakeholder alone can determine the outcomes that drive the behavior of all organizational members. However, a return on shareholder value is an outcome that cannot be compromised without losing the resources required for sustained existence of the firm. In this sense, that outcome serves as a constraint on the goal-setting process. But a focus on shareholder value alone would be insufficient to attract the energies and loyalties of the diverse group of employees and customers whose interests must be addressed for the firm to continue operating. Ownership constitutes only one source of legitimate influence over the purpose of the organization.

Certainly the educational system, with its historical attempts to maintain checks and balances between constituencies, will require that values be determined by multiple stakeholders. In fact, some observers and proponents of SBM see it primarily as a way of restoring balanced influence among multiple constituencies at the school level. The determination of the values and criteria to guide the implementation of SBM and to allow it to be a catalyst for redesign that enables more effective school performance will doubtless be best conducted in a manner that allows for effective influence from many sources. These sources include the various school-level constituencies as well as the bigger organizational system (district) and government constituencies.

- *There is a strong and critical role for the district in the transition to school-based management.*

Marsh has pointed out several studies that have found that effective restructuring requires a strong district role. This is true in part because the relationship between the schools and the district is itself being restructured, a process in which district-level personnel are key stakeholders and therefore must be active. In addition, it has been found that although individual schools can be innovative, they cannot sustain innovation and continuous improvement without the district creating and maintaining the conditions for school-level improvement (Fullan, 1991). One caveat to this principle is that there *is* a district organizational level. We do not yet know whether stand-alone schools, such as charter schools (see Chapter Six), will be able to sustain innovation in isolation.

Transitions to high-involvement management have found that the decentralization of authority is not an all-or-nothing proposition. Rather, it requires conscious design of what tasks and authority should be located at what level of inclusion (for example, corporate or district, business unit or school, department, work team, individual) in the organization. The technology and environmental requirements determine the appropriate locus of decisions. For example, in an organization such as McDonald's, where clientele expect and demand uniform quality and product, decisions about core menu and ingredients are not left to local business units. However, even McDonald's has begun to consider some supplemental menu offerings to appeal to local customers.

At the other extreme, if a corporation contains a number of business units with quite different technologies, products, and markets, the entire design of the organization may be subject to business unit variation. The corporation then manages purely by outcome measures, and units operate within and are held accountable to a broad set of corporate goals. School systems need to determine what value is best added by the district, and what is best added at the school level in order to improve the delivery of educational services that are responsive to the needs of the community population being served.

Schools must ask three design questions to determine what functions and authority should lie at what system level:

1. What, if any, legal or market requirements for uniformity dictate common goals, outcomes, and methods? In the absence of such requirements, local units can be free to evolve different goals and practices and demonstrate their efficacy.
2. What economies of scale dictate the performance of certain functions centrally to avoid wasteful duplication of effort that depletes resources available to maintain and improve the core technology?
3. Do variability of customer requirement and uncertainty of technology dictate local customized product or service delivery and local on-line decision making?

The transition to SBM has been justified largely in terms of the affirmative answer to the third question, and the belief that in determining school activities at the global district level those activities have come to be out of touch with the needs of many constituencies and have been resistant to improvement. On the other hand, it seems probable that a school would not want to perform functions locally if placing them in the school results in inefficiency that achieves local control at a cost that noticeably reduces the total resources available to each school. The areas where value is added by the district level need to be determined. In high-involvement management in the private sector, the most fundamental values added by the corporate level are in the establishment of broad direction (high-level strategy, mission, and measures) and of goals that guide the improvement efforts of local business units in allocating resources across units in a manner consistent with organizational strategy, and in providing the incentives for performance improvement through outcome accountability and rewards. Beyond that, the corporate level may provide shared systems and services to the business units, may audit practices to ensure conformance to the law, and may provide consulting services to help the business units achieve their objectives. Each organization finds its own optimal balance between local and central decision making.

The determination of the roles of the district and the school under school-based management is one of the design challenges in the large-scale change. Another issue is the role of the district vis-à-vis the school in the change process itself. Here the evidence from both Marsh and Mohrman is that the district plays a key but tricky role. Mohrman (Chapter Eight) referred to the tension between the different systems levels in the transition to high-involvement management. This tension arises not only because at issue is how much decentralization will actually occur, but also because of the desire of the schools for autonomy in determining their own change process. Even the existence of broad change objectives within which the units are required to function can be experienced as a violation of the expressed purpose of the transition.

Nevertheless, the district level plays a key role in stimulating, shaping, and motivating the change. In addition, one of the added values of a larger systems level such as the district is the generation of learnings from a number of units to catalyze a learning community.

- *The essence of the transition to school-based management is a learning process that requires the establishment of a learning community.*

Mohrman (Chapter Eight) has stressed that large-scale change requires self-design. There are no off-the-shelf solutions, and each organization has to find its own combination of design features based on its particular environment, valued outcomes, and the technology it employs. Such change is gradual and iterative, and involves unanticipated effects, the generation of new problems that have to be solved, and continual design and redesign. Marsh (Chapter Nine) stressed the need for experience-based learning.

Both Marsh and Mohrman addressed the need to establish learning networks, not only within schools that are redesigning themselves but also across units. Although lateral networks are viewed as the most effective means for cross-site learning to occur, the district can play a role in establishing, encouraging, and enabling these networks. Furthermore, the learning must also occur across system levels, as district-level units and schools learn to deal more effectively with one another and to exercise the mutual influence that Johnson and Boles advocate in Chapter Five. This means that learnings, problems, and successes need to be discussed in networks that span units and levels.

Although recognizing that the change has to be locally designed, both Marsh and Mohrman stressed the need to base designs on knowledge. SBM is being implemented as part of systemic reform that is changing core technology at the same time it is altering the organization. Organizational members need to become familiar with knowledge that has been generated regarding educational processes and organizational design. Training and development, visitation to innovative organizations, and consultation and facilitation are key components of many large-scale transitions. Designs should be based on solid expert knowledge and local learning applied to the agreed-to outcomes.

During the change process, a key aspect of local learning is the learning that occurs as the organization assesses its changes and uses the resulting feedback to refine or redesign the changes and the implementation steps. Marsh cites Fullan and Miles (1992), who stress the need to generate information about implementation problems. This process becomes a means for exchanging views of reality and arriving at a deeper understanding of the change in question.

Clearly the establishment of the learning community requires new behaviors and organizational norms. Surfacing problems, collective multiconstituency planning and designing, and ongoing assessment of the organization (as opposed to assessing the students in the organization) all may represent the establishment of a new school culture.

• *The transition to SBM is a deep change, one that entails changes in attitudes, assumptions, and behaviors.*

As described above, achieving the learning system required to implement SBM and to design the organizational changes required to enhance organizational performance entails creating a collective learning culture. Its essence is similar to the school as an inquiring organization advocated by Gideonse (1990). A number of reform advocates see changes in teacher culture as the key to reform, and propose not altering the formal decision-making structure of the organization until that culture has been changed.

In fact, there is probably a chicken-and-egg phenomenon at work. A case can be made that the current culture in schools does not support either effective SBM behavior or effective large-scale change capabilities. On the other hand, culture exists at a very deep level, and has resulted from the design and operating history of the organization. Many scholars believe that it is impossible to operate directly on culture (for example, Schein, 1985). Rather, culture will gradually change as organizational members relate in new ways as a result of new structures, systems, and events. The new structures and systems pose the necessity for people to try out new behaviors and question old assumptions (Mohrman and Cummings, 1989).

Nevertheless, both Marsh and Mohrman agree that the change

process needs to be conducted in a way that taps into the current reality of participants and helps establish a new culture. For example, the foundation for change (the determination of values, collective learning, and organizational diagnosis) should be built collaboratively, in a manner consistent with the desired culture. The process of laying the foundation for change also lays the foundation for the new cultural values. Fortunately, the learning culture that is required to support large-scale change is relatively consistent with the collaborative, learning-oriented culture that is advocated by those who propose formulating a professional teacher culture to stimulate reform. It can be argued that following the tenets of large-scale change in and of itself will stimulate the development of a professional teaching culture.

• *The role of the community in implementing SBM and stimulating activities to improve school outcomes needs to be carefully designed.*

Although commentators on SBM often stress its role in increasing the school's responsiveness to its local community, little has been written about what this means for the role of the community in making decisions about the school. There has been some discussion about whether its involvement tips the scales toward political control and endangers control by those with professional or expert knowledge. On the other hand, the community includes the clients and the customers of the educational system; in some ultimate sense, the viability of the schools depends on their abilities to meet community requirements.

Clearly, community constituencies are a key stakeholder in the process of generating shared valued outcomes. The role of community members in making personnel, budget, or technical decisions regarding the educational process is more problematical. As was advocated earlier in the chapter with respect to the role of the district office, a challenge in designing SBM is to think through and design the role of the community in these areas.

It is not entirely self-evident that responsiveness to the community is best accomplished through community decision making about technical and management matters. In the private sector, for example, a number of mechanisms have been established to help companies continually stay in touch with and respond to customer concerns, including involving customers in strategy-setting sessions or product-definition clinics, and collecting regular customer satisfaction data. A number of sophisticated techniques have been developed to jointly design the interface of the organization with its customers and clients and to establish a partnership between the organization and its customers. On the other hand, internal organizational decisions regarding personnel, budget, and technology are generally made by the organizational members, taking into account the primary need to meet the expectations of the clients or customers. This outcome is given teeth by including customer satisfaction as an important evaluation criterion for the organization and its members.

This resolution in the private sector is probably not generalizable to public schools, where a tradition of democratic control is highly valued and formal authority is given to the community at the school board level. The line between management and governance is much more blurred in public education. The issue of the appropriate levels and mechanisms of community involvement will require a great deal of thought and learning, as its resolution will critically affect the nature of governance of public schools and the ways they go about improving themselves.

Conclusion

SBM has been offered as one component strategy of school reform. When viewed as large-scale change, it is clear that it is inextricably linked to the other prongs of systemic school reform. The change process requires a clear articulation of valued outcomes, needs to be based on established expert knowledge as well as on local knowledge, and requires the establishment of a teacher culture that supports collective inquiry.

We have proposed that SBM cannot be understood as a single-pronged innovation that is easily adopted. Rather, it implies major change in the design of the school. It is best understood as a change in governance and management whose purpose is to stimulate further organizational change to foster the improvements in educational outcomes and in the ability of the schools to serve the needs of their communities.

This chapter presented a number of principles to guide the change process. It proposed that the change be understood as a systemic change; that SBM be consciously linked to the desired outcomes; that there are important roles for both the district and school levels of the educational system; that the change be understood and managed as a learning process; that because the change is deep, it must be carried out in a manner that enables participants to confront their assumptions and behaviors; and that careful attention be given to defining the appropriate role for the community as participants in school governance.

References

David, J. (1990). Restructuring in progress: Lessons learned from pioneering districts. In R. F. Elmore (Ed.), *Restructuring schools: The next generation of educational reform.* San Francisco: Jossey-Bass.

Elmore, R. F., and Associates. (Eds.). (1990). *Restructuring schools: The next generation of educational reform.* San Francisco: Jossey-Bass.

Fuhrman, S. H. (Ed.). (1993). *Designing coherent education policy: Improving the system.* San Francisco: Jossey-Bass.

Fullan, M. (1991). *The meaning of educational change.* New York: Teachers College Press.

Fullan, M., and Miles, M. (1992). Getting reform right: What works and what doesn't? *Phi Delta Kappan, 73*(10), 745–752.

Gideonse, H. D. (1990). Organizing schools to encourage teacher inquiry. In R. F. Elmore and Associates (Eds.), *Restructuring schools: The next generation of educational reform.* San Francisco: Jossey-Bass.

Lawler, E. E. (1973). *Motivation in work organizations.* Monterey, CA: Brooks/Cole.

Lawler, E. E. (1986). *High-involvement management.* San Francisco: Jossey-Bass.

Lawler, E. E., and Mohrman, S. A. (1987). Quality circles: After the fad. *Harvard Business Review, 63*(1), 64–71.

Ledford, G. E., Lawler, E. E., and Mohrman, S. A. (1988). The quality circle and its variations. In J. P. Campbell, R. J. Campbell, and Associates (Eds.), *Productivity in organizations: New perspectives from industrial and organizational psychology*. San Francisco: Jossey-Bass.

Levine, D., and Eubanks, E. (1989). *Site-based management: Engine for reform or pipe-dream? Problems, pitfalls and prerequisites for success in site-based management*. Manuscript submitted for publication.

Mohrman, S. A., Cohen, S. G., and Mohrman, A. M. (1994). *Designing team-based organizations for knowledge work*. Technical Monograph. Los Angeles: The Center for Effective organizations, The University of Southern California.

Mohrman, S. A., and Cummings, T. G. (1989). *Self-designing organizations: Learning how to create high performance*. Reading, MA: Addison-Wesley.

Raywid, M. A. (1990). Rethinking school governance. In R. F. Elmore and Associates (Eds.), *Restructuring schools: The next generation of educational reform*. San Francisco: Jossey-Bass.

Schein, E. (1985). *Organizational culture and leadership*. San Francisco: Jossey-Bass.

Walton, R. E. (1985). From control to commitment in the workplace. *Harvard Business Review, 63*(2), 76–84.

Chapter Eleven

Conclusion: New Directions for School-Based Management

Priscilla Wohlstetter

Susan Albers Mohrman

School-based management (SBM) has become a popular corner-stone of education reform, with states and school districts across the country adopting polices that decentralize management to improve the performance of educational systems. However, there is scant evidence that SBM enhances organizational performance. The argument underlying this book has been that SBM has not received a fair test because of limitations in the way it has been conceptualized and approached. Viewing SBM solely as a governance change is too constraining a perspective; instead, it needs to be viewed as the redesign of the school organization.

This book uses an analytical perspective that helps focus the direction and nature of organizational redesign toward creating the capacity for high involvement within educational systems. The chapters focus on issues related to organizing for high involvement and high performance. We have argued that SBM schools need to be organized in ways that allow for many modes of involvement, beyond single-site councils. We also argued that through the redesign process, resources need to be put in place to support informed, knowledgeable involvement aimed at achieving school goals. Aside from the focus on the decision-making *process*, we also have advocated redesigning school organizations in ways that couple SBM with ambitious *content* reforms. We have argued that SBM should not be seen as an isolated intervention; rather, it should be part of a more systemic set of changes that include the introduction of new approaches to teaching and learning.

Platitudes of Involvement Versus Deep Questions

An important feature of SBM is high involvement. High involvement helps foster a commitment to the organization and a stake in its performance. Among SBM districts little systematic attention has been given to defining optimal levels and types of stakeholder involvement and ways of encouraging those levels of participation. Instead, many districts appear to embark on SBM full of platitudes: "We believe that by moving decision making to schools, the schools can make decisions that better serve the needs of students"; "We believe that by reducing red tape, teachers will become empowered to make changes that make a difference."

In all types of organizations, platitudes are a common problem in the transition to high involvement. They often reflect wishes rather than theories and generalities and abstractions rather than concrete approaches. Because the move to high-involvement management requires a fundamental rethinking of the logic of the organization and changes in the way its members understand it, platitudes are not enough. They lead to situations where all members attach their own meaning to reform and there is little consensus around what good performance is or the organization's new way of operating.

In order to develop a shared understanding of the new logic under SBM, some very fundamental questions about the school organization must be asked, debated, and answered.

- *In the area of mission/goals:* What is meant by high performance? Is it the same for children of all ability levels? Does the mission drive a uniform set of goals, or can goals be school specific? Where will national academic standards fit in? Who are the legitimate decision makers with respect to goals?

- *In the area of roles and responsibilities:* What is the proper division of responsibility across different levels of the educational system—state, district, building, grade, subject, and classroom? Within school organizations, should governance and management decisions be handled by classroom teachers or should teachers focus on applying their professional skills to developing teaching and learning strategies? What is the role of the principal when the domain of decision making for the school organization is expanded?
- *In the area of accountability:* What is the role of the community in determining whether the school is meeting its needs? More generally, to whom are the school and its teachers accountable? For what? With what consequences?

These are, of course, recurring questions in the field of public education, questions on which society even over time has achieved little consensus. For SBM to be effective, however, there must be at least a dynamic resolution of these issues.

We have observed that different approaches to decentralized management have been taken, surfacing different perspectives on issues related to mission, goals, roles and responsibilities, and accountability. Across SBM districts and even across schools within the same district, the composition of the site council varies. There is little indication, however, that the variation is more than a political manifestation. We have little evidence suggesting, for example, that SBM schools *first* worked with multiple stakeholders to get a shared understanding of fundamental issues—what is the school's mission? what services should the school provide to carry out its mission?—and *then* empowered various stakeholders to effectively contribute to achieving the school mission and delivering responsive, high-quality services. Instead, the initial focus is on who should have power.

Grappling with these fundamental questions helps to define the underlying values of the organization, values that subsequently can be used to guide its design. Through this process, SBM will be integrated into the fabric of the organization rather than constructed as an add-on. Further, the process will help stakeholders develop a more systemic view of how all these pieces of the organization can work together to achieve performance improvement.

Domain of Decision Making

A critical element of organizing for high performance entails expanding the domain of decision making to promote involvement by educators in continuous improvement. We have put forth a research-based argument that the improvement of knowledge work consists of improving decisions that are made about the methods and processes by which work is done, how resources are used, how people organize to do the work, and what the goals for performing the work will be. Such decisions need to be made at a broad level for the organization as a whole, and also within and across work teams for their specific domain related to day-to-day tasks. The strength of a school's decision-making system depends not only on how the school is designed for schoolwide decision making, but also on how it is designed to support decision making that arises in the course of performing the work.

In the field of public education, both levels of decision making are also critical to improving the performance of schools. SBM, however, has concentrated more on who makes the schoolwide decisions and how they are made, rather on the day-to-day decisions related to teaching and learning. The focus has been to move districtwide decisions into the local school, to enable the school to optimize its performance.

In the traditional district structure, we often see instances of organizationwide decision making by local school boards that set priorities for investing in teaching materials and equipment, based on organizationwide data that illustrate which schools are most in need of improvement. Districtwide decisions, even in decentralized SBM districts, continue to be dominant, in part because of concerns for equity pushed by the courts (among others), and partly because of strong centralizing forces—district offices and unions, in particular—that push for districtwide decisions over school-level, department-level, or grade-level matters.

The debate concerning decision making has been over what decisions should move to schools and who should be empowered to make them. SBM schools have not focused much on the other level of decision making, that is, decisions concerning the day-to-day matters of teaching and learning that make up the educational process. At the high school level, for instance, we rarely see a team of teachers making decisions about a course of action for a particular student based on broad data from various departments that give a holistic picture of that student's situation. It may be assumed such decisions happen in individual classrooms, and so information is rarely shared and collective problem solving and decision making almost never occur.

High-involvement approaches include empowering stakeholders to influence organizationwide decisions. Just as important, they build forums for people whose work is interdependent to integrate their efforts and make joint decisions about how they apply their resources, schedule their time, divide up tasks, and deliver services.

This limited focus on schoolwide decision making severely restricts the impact of SBM on teaching and learning, because the school organization has not changed to facilitate improved day-to-day decisions about the educational process. Bolstered by research on teacher professionalism promoting the benefits of collaboration, we are seeing a new view of education emerging, where teams of teachers are being empowered to make educational decisions about teaching and learning and to work together in delivering these services. The models of high-performing schools feature decision-making structures—houses and cadres—focused on day-to-day tasks. These new directions target attention to decision making by performance units within the school organization. In order for them to improve organizational performance, information support, as we have argued elsewhere, will also need to be far more prevalent. Without this, educators will not have data for informed decision making and the impact of SBM will be restrained.

Approaches to Learning and Improvement

The chapters in this book describe the transition to SBM and to new approaches to teaching and learning as an organizational learning process. Contrary to this view, many schools see SBM reform as an end in itself, rather than the start of an improvement process. These schools typically employ a relatively limited set of tools for organizational improvement. Much of the "organizational learning" is conducted by university researchers, who then have to convince schools of what they have learned. The separation of learners from the users of information clearly hampers the school's ability to be empowered as a learning community.

School efforts to expand their approaches to improvement have relied primarily on staff development and skills development through workshops, exposure to new curriculum and pedagogy, and occasionally through national networks. Schools also have used ad hoc committees to get people involved in addressing specific issues or problems. Some, but not many, have employed a total quality management approach and have provided management training to develop a common language and approach to resolving problems and introducing improvements throughout the school.

Compared to the private-sector organizations that have invested heavily in developing a continuous improvement capability, there has been very little systematic analysis in SBM schools of their own process. Introduction of SBM does not generally lead schools to systematically analyze their approaches to teaching and learning—what are the inputs? what processes are being used? what are the outcomes?—and to recommend changes based on data and an assessment of what works. To the extent assessments are done, they are often conducted by university researchers. Within schools, discussion usually centers on the assessment process, rather than the assessment results and how they can be used to improve organizational performance.

Improvement approaches used in schools are further constrained by the status quo. SBM has led to little fundamental reconceptualizing of the processes of education or to profound changes in the way educational services are organized and delivered. Curriculum specialists are critically examining the assumptions underlying what and how schools teach, and advocating more cross-discipline activities and teaching teams and new ways of relating to the community. Reformers also are looking at the social system of schools and recommending breaking down the organization into minischools or houses.

Some schools are employing these techniques effectively. But for the most part, SBM has not led schools to look critically at the way they deliver teaching and learning services and to question the basic methods they employ, including fifty-five-minute periods and self-contained classrooms, having certified teachers responsible for groups of students at all times, and having instruction occur in a building called a school. The seeds for radical reconceptualizations exist in the literature and are being experimented with by a few (design teams for the "new American schools," for example) but the connection to SBM has not been made.

Many insurance companies, health care providers, and other service organizations are making radical changes in their service-delivery processes by reducing steps and combining tasks, eliminating barriers between functions, addressing expanded needs, and creating flexible and user-friendly communications with customers. In most cases, the work redesign is taking place at the corporate or business-unit level, often with representation from different operating units. If schools are going to be the locus of innovation, they will have to develop the analytical tools to reexamine the processes of education, in addition to being empowered to organize quite differently.

A more fundamental question is whether the school is the place for this reconceptualization to occur or whether the learning that is implied occurs best on a more global level, with schools represented in the design process and cast as the units of implementation. The latter approach requires a more centralized vision of where innovation is conceived and a more constrained definition of what schools are being empowered to do. Perhaps this is a more achievable mission for schools, given the time and resource constraints of school-level educators and the political context of public education that includes elected local school boards.

Another issue related to the redesign of organizations and work is the use of technology. The radical changes in service-delivery organizations are in most cases being enabled by computer technology. These organizations have gone through a stage of using the computer as a tool to help them do better what they already have been doing. The current stage is to realize that the computer can extend capabilities and make possible different configurations of service delivery. In some cases, such as the familiar automated teller machine, the machine takes the place of the human service provider. In others, such as the use of automated records in health care, it links together dispersed, highly trained service providers for diagnostic and prescriptive purposes, and enables a much more systematic examination of the factors that go into successful case management. In other cases, it allows service providers to go to the customer rather than having the customer come to the service provider. And in yet other cases, it allows the customer to receive the services without ever leaving home.

These fundamentally different images of how and where work is done are changing the way various service providers, including professionals, do their work and the context in which they operate. In SBM schools, there has been very little experimentation along this dimension; as a result, the use of technology in schools has focused on computer-assisted instruction, with little innovation in staffing pattern, or how educational services are configured and delivered.

Appropriate Roles for Different Organizational Levels

As schools organize for high performance, clarifying the scope of authority at different levels of the organization is critically important. SBM entails decentralizing decision making and creating high-involvement management, but there is no normative model of how much authority in which domains ought to be decentralized and to whom. Consequently, there needs to be very considered deliberation about these issues, taking into account the political context of public education, such as to whom the school is accountable and for what, and its particular organizational constraints. For the educational community to learn to deliver the services that meet the increasingly demanding requirements being placed on schools, knowledge will have to be generated and acted upon at different levels in the educational system.

Fundamental to the issue of organizational redesign is the question of what levels of authority are even needed. SBM schools have operated in traditionally organized districts with the school board at the top of the educational system, a district superintendent and staff to carry out board policy, and building principals and teachers, organized by grade level or department, with responsibility for a specific set of students. Charter schools, however, put into question the appropriateness of the district's regulatory role and, at the extreme, whether in fact a district office is needed at all. Are there other ways to provide the support that districts provide? Are there other ways to audit and hold schools accountable? Concomitant with these issues is the role of the state in a decentralized educational system. Is it feasible for schools to be accountable directly to the state with state authorities overseeing thousands of schools, much like England's Department for Education with grant-maintained schools?

Judging from current trends, there also is the possibility that organizational redesign will lead to the creation of more, rather than fewer, levels of authority. Many large, urban districts have regional or area superintendents who are responsible for clusters of schools (a group of schools positioned geographically close to one another, or a high school and its feeder schools). The district office then is more distant from day-to-day operations at the school level. An even more radical approach to redesign that surfaces every few years, most recently in Los Angeles during the early 1990s, is the option of breaking up the very largest school districts into smaller, autonomous units, based in part on the belief that smaller districts are better because a sense of organization relatedness can more easily be created and sustained.

Within schools, the debate centers on new organizational designs and the appropriate roles for educators within them. Should schools be subdivided into, for example, houses? If so, what is the division of authority between the house and the school? What does this mean for the autonomy of the teacher in the classroom? If providing educational services for students is an interdependent set of activities that have been artificially segmented into classrooms, when the services are reintegrated into houses or other units is the collective group of teachers jointly accountable? To whom and for what?

What Is Management?

Schools of effective managers during times of extensive change show that they exercise both visionary and instrumental leadership. They help the organization envision a different future. They create the conditions for effective performance, including the management systems, and they empower organizational members to perform effectively (Nadler and Tushman, 1989; Tichy and Devanna, 1986).

Managers in settings that are promoting self-management also have a strong role in developing the capabilities for self-management (Manz and Sims, 1989). They play a leadership role in the following areas related to organizational performance: creating a goal-oriented and a value-oriented culture; developing effective management and task processes; efficient resource utilization; appropriate people involvement; and being held accountable and responsive to various organizational stakeholders.

By contrast, in many SBM districts, there is conflict among stakeholders over whether the principal should even be a manager. The tradition has been for the principal to be a school administrator who administers and controls the school organization and the way it operates and delivers the educational services that are dictated by the state and district. As SBM is implemented, debate ensues over whether the principal has the right to veto decisions made by teachers and other stakeholders. Who should run the school?

In some districts, often where SBM was negotiated through a labor contract, teachers push for self-management; some schools are moving to representative executive committees rather than principals. A couple of SBM schools in the United States have taken the radical approach of doing away with the principal position and putting in lead teachers on a rotating basis. Charter schools in England have taken a different approach to local management, adding on more specialized management skills rather than less, as the contributions of local educational authorities disappear.

There are some indications that schools have been undermanaged, not overmanaged. Lack of goal-setting, measurement, and feedback systems is a symptom of that. Alternatively, the rigid educational bureaucracy may be a symptom that schools are over-administered. At least one of the four models of high performing schools (see Chapter Four) stresses the importance of the principal. Implied in the other three is an integrated, systemic model of an effective school that could not happen without skilled leadership, often from a principal who is a skilled manager.

The most advanced high-involvement organizations in the private sector likewise have excellent managers, although fewer of them than traditional organizations. In some cases, management teams are leading organizations rather than one general manager carrying out all leadership roles. In the turbulent world confronting organizations, they find that the quality of their management is critical to their ability to survive, even in organizations such as health care and law firms that are populated by professionals who have traditional norms of autonomy.

These ideas are not necessarily counter to the notion of self-management. In high-involvement organizations, successful managers work with the organization to create conditions where people can self-manage within the overall goals and philosophy of the organization, using methods and approaches that the organization has decided to employ. The key is to define what management roles are played by managers and which are accomplished through self-management and representative management approaches. Those issues must be determined and clarified in a way that promotes a shared understanding among organizational members.

Challenges Confronting Schools

At the core of redesigning school organizations for high performance is the notion of changing fundamental assumptions and rules of operating. Redesign does not mean cutting fat, shuffling boxes, or automating existing ways of doing things. Instead, organizing for high performance requires reexamining assumptions and shedding rules of work that are based on conventional notions about organization and people's roles and responsibilities within the organization.

What we have argued for here is a connection between SBM, organizational redesign, and school improvement. Redesigning schools as high-involvement organizations would require educators to engage in the extensive learning that would lead to the adoption of new approaches to teaching and learning. Further, the design of the organization would have to fit with the requirements of the emerging core technologies of teaching and learning. High-involvement organizations also would require that some managerial functions be integrated with teaching responsibilities, so that educators could become involved and accountable for the continuous improvement of performance. Finally, redesigned school organizations would promote community involvement and be responsive to community needs. To move in these new directions, schools will need to address three key challenges: creating some clarity in the political environment; developing the infrastructure; dedicating resources of time, money, and talent (especially management talent); and building incentives into the organizational design.

Creating Clarity

Educational systems are hierarchically organized and communication patterns are top-down. Policies that govern schools and classrooms largely emanate from the top of the educational system with state authorities, local school boards, and district superintendents. If school organizations are to be redesigned, it first will be necessary to develop a systemic perspective of reform that encompasses all the different levels of organizational authority and that supports the school as the unit of change.

Effective school redesign, therefore, will also alter other parts of the educational system in complimentary ways. As schools take on the task of innovating, district offices (with experience in developing staff capabilities) and state departments of education (with large information networks) can be valuable resources in helping schools to envision new ways of doing things.

There also will be a need to link in key stakeholder groups, who, like other organizational members, will have to reorient themselves away from a centralized system to a decentralized one focused at the school level. Teacher associations, for instance, may need to change from a districtwide teacher collective to one focused on individual school sites.

Developing the Infrastructure

Schools have not developed the organizational infrastructure required for managing performance. They lack the information systems for reporting performance at the school level and for providing process information to enable individual schools to systematically examine factors that contribute to performance and introduce changes to affect outcomes. Goal-setting and accountability systems to monitor and reward progress on outcome performance indicators are not in place. Resources for change, such as specialized positions to help in the transition (facilitators, consultants, master tutors), also are not extensively used. Finally, new ways of delivering development, such as through the Gheens Academy in Louisville, Kentucky (see Chapter Five), are not available in many districts. It remains to be seen whether public school districts will choose to direct resources to the creation of the infrastructure for performance improvement.

Dedicating Resources

A common complaint among people in the field of education is that schools are resource poor. Educators in states that spend over $10,000 per year per student complain they do not have enough money to improve school performance, just as educators in states that spend only slightly more than half that amount. Regardless of resources, the tendency of education reformers is to tinker with the existing system and to invest little in fundamentally new technologies, work structures, and service delivery approaches.

A challenge, therefore, is for districts and schools to learn how to redirect existing resources. This will require that decision makers develop the capability to conduct systematic analyses to make and justify informed decisions about resource tradeoffs. Participative structures and processes will have to be designed and managed so they result in more rather than less efficient use of resources. Choices will have to be made about which decisions are participative and which are truly managerial decisions. How many people need to be involved in which decisions? How can time be freed up to get teachers involved in decisions that will truly enhance the capacity of the school to achieve outcomes?

Rather than set up elaborate participative mechanisms for entire staffs to have input into management decisions or for councils to become the management decision makers, schools may better concentrate on having key representative groups create the policy and directional context; establishing participative work-delivery structures that make teaching and learning decisions; and developing accountability systems so that managerial decisions, whether made by a single principal or by an executive committee, are responsive to the needs of various constituencies. A more clearly defined division of decision-making authority may be a better application of scarce resources.

Building in Incentives

Experience in various organizational settings has found that achieving change in organizational performance capabilities beyond incremental improvement requires fundamental change in technical and organizational approaches and the behavior of employees. Motivation for the demanding and uncomfortable change processes underpinning such transitions almost invariably comes from a sense of crisis: from organizations that know that if they do not improve, their customers will go elsewhere; from individuals who know that if they do not learn how to contribute to the new ways of doing things, they will experience negative consequences.

But successful change is also characterized by positive motivation. Positive motivation comes from the opportunity to participate in creating a more effective organization, and from organizational support for such activities and acknowledgment of accomplishments. It also frequently comes from the opportunity to experience gain personally and organizationally if the organization succeeds, rather than being faced with stagnation and cutbacks. These incentives have not been in place in public education, but there are signs that districts and states are beginning to introduce them.

People will be more likely to be motivated to redesign schools if there is a system of rewards for innovation. Establishing school choice would be one method of inducing educators to be more innovative, since choice would provide important feedback and consequences to schools based on their ability to attract students. Such schools would be very likely to take the initiative to call in consultants to improve their skills and create more responsive services.

Other incentives that result in rewards for school performance will be required, but will have to be carefully thought out to avoid differential impact on student populations. This might be accomplished by approaches such as are mandated by the Kentucky law that provides incentives to schools that achieve improvement targets and provides state intervention and remedial resources to schools that fail to achieve such targets over a multiple-year period. This law also provides ultimately for the identification and replacement of low-performing staff in those low-performing schools.

Educators rightfully argue that the challenge is not theirs alone; neither should the accountability be theirs alone. It is true that the job of educating a community of children requires participation by many stakeholders, not the least of whom are the children themselves and their families. Schools will have to find ways to create positive motivation for them as well. Successful schools are not waiting around for nuclear families to regain their prominence and for kids to come to school less unruly, more compliant, and more interested in being educated. They are taking responsibility for working with their stakeholders to create motivating conditions and incentives for participation. Developing incentives for change takes on a broader meaning in schools than in many other organizations, but is no less important.

Conclusion

We have argued that SBM as a school improvement reform has slim prospects unless its boundaries are expanded beyond the transfer of power to include the design of the organization. To improve school performance, professional and public involvement in our educational systems must be strengthened. The chapters in this book aim at that end by discussing mutually reinforcing strategies that build knowledge and skills, broaden information sharing, and provide rewards for performance among school participants. Applying the notion of high involvement also requires that educational stakeholders develop a shared understanding of the new ways of operating, as well as a shared commitment to continuous improvement of performance.

As educational systems begin to move in these new directions, there will be a move away from the mass production model of education. Individual schools, within parameters set by the district or state, will begin to design their organizations in various ways, based on members' consensus around a particular mission and goals for the school. What will emerge then will be a constellation of different models of schooling, particularly as the educational community learns more about the impact of new approaches on educational outcomes.

To assist schools in this initial phase of the redesign process, research activities in an action research mode could help schools to align the various pieces of their new organization by first working to identify and develop alternative strategies and then assessing the extent to which they are in place and effective. Once a variety of models are operational, research should focus in a more summative way on assessing the kinds of organizational designs that are optimal for different mixes of students.

SBM serves many purposes and thus has widespread appeal, as indicated by the high level of district and state activities now being put in place. However, as we have observed, implementation of school councils is no guarantee that educators will learn about and adopt new approaches to teaching and learning or that school performance will improve. Redesigning schools into high-involvement organizations will be extremely challenging, but the experience of some innovative organizations that have built the infrastructure for high involvement suggests great potential for major gains in school performance and productivity.

References

Manz, C. C., and Sims, H. P. (1989). *Super leadership: Leading others to lead themselves*. New York: Prentice-Hall.

Nadler, D. A., and Tushman, M. L. (1989). Leadership for organizational change. In A. M. Mohrman and Associates (Eds.), *Large-scale organizational change*. San Francisco: Jossey-Bass.

Tichy, N. M., and Devanna, M. A. (1986) *The transformational leader*. New York: Wiley.

Index